The Education Gospel

The Education Gospel

THE ECONOMIC POWER OF SCHOOLING

W. Norton Grubb

Marvin Lazerson

HARVARD UNIVERSITY PRESS

Cambridge, Massachusetts
London, England

First Harvard University Press paperback edition, 2007

Library of Congress Cataloging-in-Publication Data
Grubb, W. Norton.
  The education gospel : the economic power of schooling /
W. Norton Grubb, Marvin Lazerson.
      p.   cm.
  Includes bibliographical references and index.
  ISBN-13: 978-0-674-01537-1 (cloth : alk. paper)
  ISBN-10: 0-674-01537-1 (cloth : alk. paper)
  ISBN-13: 978-0-674-02545-5 (pbk.)
  ISBN-10: 0-674-02545-8 (pbk.)
    1. Education—Economic aspects—United States.   2. Vocational
education—United States.   3. Education—Effect of technological innovations
on.   I. Lazerson, Marvin.   II. Title.
LC66.G78   2004
38.4'737–dc23   2004052298

Contents

Preface

In many ways we began writing this book more than thirty years ago, when we collaborated on a history of vocational education in high schools. We coined the term *vocationalism* to signify that the changes associated with that movement were much larger than the introduction of a specific curriculum. They transformed the basic purposes of K–12 schools, and of postsecondary education as well, and they have continued to influence new forms of education and training such as community colleges, comprehensive universities, short-term job training, and proprietary schools and universities. Indeed, the evolution of economic purposes for schooling was the single most important educational development of the twentieth century, and it affected many other—we're tempted to say most other—changes, including the enormous expansion of formal schooling in the United States, well before all other countries; the battles over equity and access; many curricular debates; and the central ways of getting ahead and fulfilling the American dream. But while many observers both in the United States and elsewhere adopted our vocabulary of vocationalism, most of them continued to focus on relatively specific forms of vocational and professional education. This book, then, is our attempt to examine the larger phenomenon and its many consequences, at least in the American version of vocationalism.

Over the past thirty years, of course, much has changed. The specific details of educational institutions have changed substantially, and the kinds of jobs for which schools and universities prepare students have changed as well. The economic and political context has been immeasurably altered. The decade of the 1960s, which shaped both of us in so many ways and solidified our commitment to education, is now ancient history to most Americans, particularly young Americans. The hopefulness of that period—the active politics; the commitment to equity; the movements for civil rights, women's rights, and environmental quality; the high levels of economic growth with some promise that the benefits would be publicly committed and widely distributed—has been replaced by a kind of circus democracy driven by big money, by higher levels of inequality and a waning commitment to equity, by unequal growth in which the benefits are privately appropriated. In some ways this book, particularly its last two chapters, is our effort to right the balance of public responsibilities and private gains.

Over the past thirty years the rhetoric we call the Education Gospel—the notion that the Knowledge Revolution (or the information society) is changing the nature of work and enhancing the "higher-order" skills learned in schools and universities—has become increasingly insistent, even though some version has been around for a century. The expansion of schooling that began in the 1960s has continued, and along the way has transformed every older educational institution, and several new ones. The debates over equity are increasingly debates over schooling, particularly as the welfare state has waned under the concerted attacks of conservative ideologues and free-market advocates. So, at the beginning of the twenty-first century, it is all the more necessary to understand the economic roles of formal education in order to understand the possibilities both for schooling and for a broader array of social policies.

Along the way we have incurred debts to many people and several institutions. Norton Grubb was part of the National Center for Research in Vocational Education (NCRVE) at the University of California, Berkeley, during the period 1988 to 2000, funded by the U.S. Department of Education. Among many colleagues there, he is particularly indebted to the late Charles Benson, the first director; David Stern, the second director; Tom Bailey, Gary Hoachlander, Alan Phelps, and Cathy Stasz. His work on community colleges has recently been part of the Community College Research Center (CCRC) at

Teachers College, Columbia University, where Tom Bailey, Jim Jacobs, and Vanessa Morest have been particularly helpful; CCRC also provided a supportive home during a leave in the fall of 1999. The many high school and community college instructors who participated in workshops, sponsored first by NCRVE and then by the Community College Cooperative at UC Berkeley under the direction of Norena Badway, have been enormously valuable in helping bridge the gulf between research and practice. The participants in the Center for Research on Education and Work (CREW) at UC Berkeley, supported by the Pew Charitable Trusts, were helpful colleagues, particularly Stuart Tannock. The David Gardner Chair in Higher Education, which Grubb has held since 1998, has provided funding for research assistance and collaboration. Finally, a sabbatical in the spring of 2003 at the Organization for Economic Cooperation and Development in Paris, facilitated by Abrar Hasan, enabled both of us to concentrate on the completion of the manuscript, and also provided further information on the international dimensions of vocationalism.

At the University of Pennsylvania, Kathleen Hall Jamieson, former dean of the Annenberg School for Communications and director of the Annenberg Center for Public Policy, offered Marvin Lazerson the opportunity to pursue the issues raised in this book as a senior fellow at the center. Susan Fuhrman, dean of the Graduate School of Education, shared her unparalleled knowledge of education at all levels, co-taught with Lazerson for the past five years, and continues to collaborate with him on the relationship of public schooling to democratic citizenship. The Howard P. and Judith R. Berkowitz Endowed Professorship of Education, named for two Penn alumni, gave Lazerson the time to write, and to study and think about the Education Gospel outside the United States. Andrea King aided us in countless ways.

Patricia Albjerg Graham was, as always, gracious and rigorous in her review of the manuscript. Dan Perlstein was consistently helpful on historical references. Other colleagues and friends who offered help and comments include Matt Hartley, Judith Warren Little, Julie Reuben, Mike Rose, David Stern, and J. Douglas Toma. The *Journal of Higher Education* published a version of Chapter 2 in a special issue edited by Steve Brint, who provided valuable comments and also shared his data on professional majors.

A number of students and research assistants have contributed to the development of this manuscript. Julia Menard-Warwick unearthed a great deal of the research on the mismatches between school skills and work skills reported in Chapter 7. Analiese Richard reviewed the historical and anthropological literature on apprenticeships; Miguel Fuentes examined the economic growth literature; Jane Robbins reviewed the developments in several professional areas, incorporated into Chapter 2. Ann Tiao helped us figure out the relationships between education and democratic aspirations. And Shereen Madjd-Sadjadi did a terrific job of finding materials to document these developments over more than a century.

As always, our beloved wives provided help in more ways than we can name. Ursula Wagener kept asking the right questions, even if we could not come up with the right answers. Erica Grubb edited the penultimate version of the manuscript, and served as a willing sounding board and voice of moderation for her book-obsessed spouse.

The Education Gospel

↶ Introduction:
Believers and Dissenters

𝒜MERICANS have developed a standard litany of complaints about schooling. We call this ritual of critique and reaffirmation the Education Gospel because it has become an article of faith, rather than inviting questions about its empirical assumptions. Starting from damnation of current schooling, it also brings glad tidings about the potential, in this case the possibility that education reform can lead to economic and social and individual salvation.[1] Like a gospel, it has been accepted by an extraordinary range of report writers, policy makers, reformers, many (but not all) educators, and much of the public. It has also been the subject of constant proselytizing, particularly through its celebratory texts: *A Nation at Risk* (NCEE, 1983), other national commission reports, the state and local groups following national reports, the writings of prominent academics, and the manifestos of international agencies. Like disciples of religious and secular gospels, its true believers have acted on its rhetoric: they have promoted the practices we call vocationalism—the emphasis of formal schooling on preparation for vocations—that transformed education throughout the past century.

While the Education Gospel has a number of variants, its essential vision goes like this: The Knowledge Revolution (or the information society, or the high-tech revolution) is changing the nature of work, shifting away from occupations rooted in industrial production to oc-

1

cupations associated with knowledge and information. This transformation has both increased the skills required for new occupations and updated the three R's, enhancing the importance of "higher-order" skills, including communications skills, problem solving, and reasoning. Obtaining these skills normally requires formal schooling past the high school level, so that some college—though not necessarily a baccalaureate degree—will be necessary for the jobs of the future, a conclusion that leads to the belief in "College for All." Currently, 87 percent of Americans agree that a college diploma has become as important as a high school diploma used to be, and 77 percent say that getting a college education is more important than it was even ten years ago.[2] As the National Commission on the High School Senior Year (2001) summarized the new "common sense": "In the agricultural age, post-secondary education was a pipe dream for most Americans. In the industrial age it was the birthright of only a few. By the space age it became common for many. Today, it is just common sense for all."

Another strand of the Education Gospel maintains that individuals are more likely to find their skills becoming obsolete because of the pace of technological change. To keep up with advances in technology, and to change employment as firms innovate, workers must engage in lifelong learning. New forms of work organization—especially contingent labor, when employers hire temporary rather than permanent workers to increase the flexibility of hiring as technologies and products change—have exacerbated job changing, reinforcing the need for lifelong learning. Other forms of work reorganization—including lean production, the elimination of multiple layers of responsibility—require frontline workers to have a greater variety of skills, including personal skills (sometimes called "soft" skills) like independence and initiative. International competition has also increased, and because no developed country wants to fall into the ranks of underdeveloped countries relying on an economy of raw materials and unskilled labor, the need for greater levels of education over the lifespan is even more compelling. Countries may have to work harder just to maintain their standards of living, and individuals need more schooling just to maintain their own earnings. But the good news is that an expanded and reformed education system can meet all these challenges. The Education Gospel therefore includes both a conception of economic and social change and a vision of how to respond to that change through education and training.

While much of the Gospel's rhetoric emphasizes national needs, it also incorporates the individual goal of "getting ahead." Broad access to education, including college for all, is necessary so that each individual has the opportunity to compete for economic position. The Education Gospel thus balances the public purposes of an expansive education system with the private intentions of using education for personal ends. The two are best combined, and the public goal noblest, in the effort to make schooling more inclusive and equitable. As the founder of Project GRAD, a reform designed to improve urban schools, described his motives: "Saving inner-city children from academic failure is one of the most critical issues now facing our state and our nation. I got involved because I believe inner-city education has to be solved for the good of all of us. The cost of failure is too high—a devastating waste of human potential and severe economic costs to our country. To remain competitive as a nation, we must reverse the dropout rate and insure our graduates have the skills to compete in an increasingly high-tech world."[3] In some versions, then—though certainly not all[4]—the Education Gospel implies a degree of equity, one justified by economic rhetoric and fears of competition as well as the moral consequences of inequality.

The Education Gospel contains both a critique of current schooling—the "rising tide of mediocrity," as *A Nation at Risk* described it—and an assertion of its importance. While the Gospel itself is largely rhetoric, it assumes and reinforces a set of educational *practices* that we and others call vocationalism: an educational system whose purposes are dominated by preparation for economic roles, one where there is sufficient access so that many individuals might have reasonable hope of more schooling, and one that is responsive to external demands—in this case, to demands for the "essential skills employers want" (Carnevale, 1990) and the "skills of the twenty-first century." Vocationalism is an awkward but useful term referring primarily not to traditional vocational education but to preparation for *vocations*. By vocations we mean occupations as careers rather than mere jobs, employment that provides personal meaning, economic benefits, continued development over the course of a life, social status, and connections to the greater society.[5] Our vocationalized system of education emerged in fits and starts, beginning with changes in high schools and the establishment of university-based professional schools at the end of the nineteenth century. It accelerated over the course of the twentieth century—the century of vocationalism, the century of professionalization, or (as economists might say) the century of human capital (Goldin, undated). It has been, we argue, the most substantial transformation in American schooling over the past century, opening the door to enormous growth in enrollments as well as to many other changes in the purposes of education, the curricula, the meaning schooling has in our society, the mechanisms of upward mobility, the patterns of inequality, conceptions of equity, and a new version of the American dream. It has taken somewhat different forms at different levels of the system—in high schools, four-year colleges and universities, community colleges, job training programs, and adult education—though with enough common features so that we can describe, particularly in Chapter 5, a distinctly American variety of vocationalism. Understanding the nature of schooling and its potential future therefore requires us to examine the origins of vocationalism and its many consequences.

We can understand the Education Gospel and different forms of vocationalism by examining some of their sacred texts. *A Nation at Risk* (1983), surely the most influential report of recent decades, opened by lamenting that "our once unchallenged preeminence in commerce, industry, science, and technological innovation is being overtaken by competitors throughout the world." It went on to blame the schools: "The educational foundations of our society are presently eroded by a rising tide of mediocrity that threatens our very future as a Nation and a people." Its remedy emphasized the "New Basics"—really the old basics (English, math, science, and social studies) plus computers—and reaffirmed the role of schooling in turning back the economic threats to our nation. It did not mention overtly occupational subjects, like business or medicine or automotive repair, but preparation for economic roles was clearly paramount.

Other reports soon followed, for universities as well as K–12 education (Peterson, 1983), and they hewed to a similar argument: the United States was threatened by its economic competitors, and improvement of schooling at all levels was crucial to turning the tide. To be sure, both *A Nation at Risk* and *Higher Education and the American Resurgence* (Newman, 1985) quoted Thomas Jefferson approvingly, about the civic goals of education: "I know of no safe depository of the ultimate power of the society but the people themselves; and if we think them not ready enough to exercise their control with a wholesome discretion, the remedy is not to take it from them but to inform their discretion." But they quickly blew by this reference to political purposes, returning to international comparisons and complaints about the economic effects of illiteracy. The glancing references in these documents to civic and intellectual development are more rhetorical than substantive, as if to placate the few dissenters who still embrace older conceptions of education. The apparently new conception, the one that will work in the twenty-first century, emphasizes preparation for employment.

Less than ten years later, another influential report elaborated a slightly different form of the argument. The Secretary of Labor's Commission on Achieving Necessary Skills (or SCANS) reaffirmed the challenges of international competition and the weakness of conventional learning, and it added the need to develop an augmented list of "necessary skills" for high-performance work. These "foundation skills" encompassed traditional basic skills (the three R's plus speaking and listening), thinking skills (creativity, decision making, problem solving, conceptualization, reasoning, knowing how to learn), and personal qualities like individual responsibility, sociability, and self-management. The SCANS report used its interpretation of work requirements to load yet more responsibility onto schools. It called for the teaching of five new competencies: the ability to allocate resources; interpersonal skills, such as negotiation, the ability to work in teams, and collaboration with culturally diverse people; interpreting and organizing information; understanding social, organizational, and technological systems; and using technology. No longer were standard school subjects and conventional teaching adequate, since problem solving and systems thinking might not be taught in orthodox English and math classes. Instead, schools were to follow the practice that "the most effective way of teaching skills is 'in context.' Placing learning objectives within real environments is better than insisting that students first learn in the abstract what they will then be expected to apply." The SCANS report differed from *A Nation at Risk* in its specific remedies, but its diagnosis of the problem was similar, and reshaping formal schooling was still the obvious solution (SCANS, 1991, 19–20).

Other reports followed, with essentially the same message. One summarized the argument succinctly in its title, complete with exclamation point: *America's Choice: High Skills or Low Wages!* The U.S. Department of Commerce, not usually involved in education, weighed in with *21st Century Skills for 21st Century Jobs* (1999), claiming that "America's competitiveness and the prosperity of our people in a changing economy depend increasingly on high-wage, high-skilled jobs. Realizing our potential will require investing in education and learning for all of our people throughout their lifetimes." Academics added their voices, like Robert Reich (1991), professor and secretary of labor in the Clinton administration, with his identification of "symbolic analysts" among the crucial occupations of the future, replacing "routine producers," and Richard Murnane and Frank Levy (1996) with their promotion of the "new basic skills"—"hard skills" like math, reading, and problem solving; "soft skills" like the ability to work in groups; the use of personal computers; and conventional behavioral traits like reliability, hard work, and positive attitudes.

With global competition, many other countries have struggled with the relation between economic well-being and their educational system, and have come up with similar conclusions: Great Britain searching for "key" or "core" skills, Germany trying to develop *Schlusselqualificationem* (key qualifications), the European Union promoting the Europe of Knowledge, the Organization for Economic Cooperation and Development (OECD) (2001a) emphasizing the implications of the Knowledge Revolution, Korea calling for an Edutopia, Australia promoting reports like *Sleepers, Wake!* (Jones, 1984), an effort by its prime minister to dispel Australians' complacency and to develop a "clever country." All over the globe, countries have discovered the importance of the Knowledge Revolution's "core" skills, "skills for the twenty-first century"—higher levels and new forms of human capital for competing in the new millennium. And all are struggling to make their education systems more "relevant" to the apparent trends in job requirements and global competition—that is, to make their education more vocational.

Believers, Then and Now

The dominant critique in the Education Gospel is that formal schooling remains overly academic and has failed to respond to the needs of the twenty-first century, and its believers want first and foremost to correct such flaws. This position is at least a century old, however, at least in the United States. Near the end of the nineteenth century most schooling was "academic," both in the sense that it concentrated on the conventional academic subjects developed during the nineteenth century, and in the pejorative sense that it was relatively distant from concerns of the everyday world. To be sure, there were glimmers of occupational elements—secretarial programs in some high schools, the land-grant colleges with their charge to provide "a liberal *and* practical education." But high schools were dominated by core academic subjects that gave little thought to the workplace, and colleges and universities were still dominated by the liberal arts, with professional education still marginal.

Around 1900 a version of the Education Gospel was developed to justify new forms of schooling that were emerging. Then as now, social commentators worried about transformations in the economy, about the technological changes that required new competencies and new occupations, about the "communications revolution" caused by the expansion of newspapers and magazines, letters and post offices, telegraph lines, book printing and books, and about international competition (Bledstein, 1978, ch. 2). Then as now, the inequality of earnings was growing, and it reached new highs just before World War I. Real annual earnings were falling among the working poor, and poverty was increasing (Williamson and Lindert, 1980, figs. 4.3 and 4.4); immigration added to poverty, the sense of instability, and the challenges to schools. The pace of change was a subject of great concern, and the expansion of opportunities—new kinds of work in the factories and the offices of expanding corporations, white-collar jobs opening up for women as well as men—presented a bewildering picture. Charles Eliot, president of Harvard, noted in 1908 that "one hundred years ago there did not exist the great variety of complicated occupations based on applied science, with which we are now confronted." One of the earliest proponents of vocational guidance in the schools argued that "real help may be given, where help is now wanting, to thousands of perplexed youth groping through the complex conditions and demands of the twentieth century" (Bloomfield, 1915, vi). The 1917 Cardinal Principles of Secondary Education, one of the most influential educational documents of the time, began with a section on the "Changes in Society," proclaiming that "as a worker he must adjust himself to a more complex economic order (NEA, 1918, 11).

Then as now, levels of schooling were considered too low, at least by believers. School reformers complained about the high numbers of students dropping out of high school, and worried about the "wasted years" between age fourteen, when large numbers of youths left school, and age sixteen, when individuals might gain access to serious employment. One report argued that "sixty-eight percent of the children who commence work between fourteen and sixteen are subjected to the evil influences of these unskilled industries or are in the mills. They have wasted the years as far as industrial development is concerned."[6] The educators around 1900 who worried about high school dropouts promoted policies that would help all students to complete high school, including vocational education, extracurricular activities, and child labor laws. We might call the pressure to reduce dropouts "high school for all," an earlier version of college for all. The authors of *Learning to Earn*, a title that has captured the fancy of many subsequent authors, argued for some kind of formal education extending at least to age eighteen (Lapp and Mote, 1915). At a time when only 13 percent of each cohort graduated from high school, they called for universal high school education for the "great mass of people and not merely the fortunate few," and introduced an early version of lifelong learning: "Plans for universal education will take account of the fact also that education is not confined to a few years in school, but extends through life."

The problem was not only the level of schooling but also the kind of education necessary. President Theodore Roosevelt, in his 1907 message to Congress, declared, "Our school system is gravely defective insofar as it puts a premium upon mere literacy training and tends therefore to train the boy away from the farm and workshop" (Krug, 1969, 225). The country needed skilled workers with "industrial intelligence," an early version of higher-order skills and a capacity poorly taught in the public schools. As the Massachusetts Commission on Industrial and Technical Education noted in 1906 (Lazerson and Grubb, 1974, doc. 4):

> The Commission was told at every hearing that in many industries the processes of manufacture and construction are made more difficult and more expensive by a lack of skilled workmen. This lack is not chiefly a want of manual dexterity, . . . but a want of what

may be called *industrial intelligence*. By this is meant mental power to see beyond the task which occupies the hands for the moment to the operations which have preceded and to those which will follow it—power to take in the whole process, knowledge of materials, ideas of cost, ideas of organizations, business sense, and a conscience which recognizes obligations.

In a precursor of recent calls for higher-order skills, reformers called for changes in the subjects taught; as the Massachusetts commission argued: "The opinion was expressed by many speakers that the schools are too exclusively literary in their spirit, scope, and methods . . . The State needs a wider diffusion of industrial intelligence as a foundation for the highest technical success, and this can only be acquired with the general system of education into which it should enter as an integral part from the beginning." Similarly, Paul Douglas (later an influential U.S. senator) noted that only 27.7 percent of workers were highly skilled, and argued that workers needed both more schooling and a different type of schooling (Douglas, 1921, 21): "The worker and more especially the juvenile worker needs perhaps more education than he ever did before; but its nature is far different from that which the old apprenticeship boy required. The education which the worker needs today is at once broader and narrower: broader in that it should include more training in industrial life, in hygiene, civics, and so forth; narrower in that trade training in the specific trade processes need not be so prolonged." And John Dewey, who opposed narrow forms of vocational training, noted that the pace of change required a broader education (Dewey, 1916a, 119):

Industry at the present time undergoes rapid and abrupt changes through the evolution of new inventions. New industries spring up, and old ones are revolutionized. Consequently an attempt to train for too specific a mode of efficiency defeats its own purpose. When the occupation changes its methods, such individuals are left behind with even less ability to readjust themselves than if they had a less definite training.

The movement for more relevant forms of schooling extended to older occupations too, not just to the new occupations in industry and

offices. The editor of *Wallace's Farmer* criticized the "cut and dried for-
mula of a period when a man was 'educated' only when he knew Greek
and Latin," and recommended greater attention to the materials of
the farm, including seeds, honeycombs, milk testers, and animals. The
Farmers' Union, organized in 1902, was committed to "educate the agricultural class in scientific farming" (Cremin 1961, 44–46). So too the
advances of science transformed the routine tasks of homemaking into
"domestic science," bringing home economics into the movement for
vocational education. Science and efficiency had transformed all walks
of life, and schools needed to incorporate these changes even for the
students going into the most traditional jobs—just as the Education
Gospel now promotes the skills of the twenty-first century and college
for all, whether or not students are bound for the high-tech jobs of the
Knowledge Revolution.

In the early twentieth century and again at the beginning of the
twenty-first, the emphasis on preparing individuals for occupational
roles has given business and labor markets enormous influence over educational reform, with the dominant theme of making schools more responsive to the new economic order. A century ago this meant adapting
schooling to the demands of an industrial economy, increasingly a national economy rather than a set of regional economics, and one dominated by large corporations. As the National Education Association
argued, "Industry, as a controlling factor in social progress, has for
education a fundamental and permanent significance" (Lazerson and
Grubb, 1974, doc. 6). The statement in the Cardinal Principles that the
worker "must adjust himself to a more complex economic order" implied changing schools to accommodate occupational shifts and organizational changes. Reforming the economic order was not an option:
education should help individuals mold themselves to the economic order rather than the other way around. Nor was it sufficient for mere
educators to determine the content of schools, based on old-fashioned
ideals of mental discipline and moral progress; outside forces, including technology, business interests, and employment trends, would gov-
ern the curriculum. Today, this means adapting schools and students to
the requirements of the Knowledge Revolution in a globally competitive environment, a world dominated by a global economy rather than
national economies. The language of the NEA and the Cardinal Principles could with only minor editing be applied to current develop-

ments: the search for "the essential skills employers want" (Carnevale, 1990) echoes earlier language about the "fundamental and permanent significance" of industry. The logic of markets, individual gain, and consumer choice has come to dominate much of formal schooling, reinforcing marketlike mechanisms even in educational institutions originating from nonmarket ideals.[7] And this deeply rooted strain of thought indicates that schools should be reformed but that employment and labor policies are off limits in public discussion.

Then as now, fears of international competition were rampant. Germany was a major competitor around 1900, and school reformers cast an envious eye on the German system of work-based apprenticeship, misinterpreting it to justify school-based vocational education. As the National Association of Manufacturers noted in "Why Germany's Competition Is to Be Feared," "The German technical and trade schools are at once the admiration and fear of all countries. In the world's race for industrial supremacy we must copy and improve upon the German method of education."[8] In rhetoric worthy of *A Nation at Risk*, the Commission on National Aid to Vocational Education (1914) declared that "the battles of the future between nations will be fought in the markets of the world. That nation will triumph . . . which is able to put the greatest amount of skill and brains into what it produces." The commission went on to cite Germany, France, England, "and even far-off Japan" as concerns because of their superior systems of vocational education (Lazerson and Grubb, 1974, doc. 10).

The believers in education around 1900 were also concerned with inequality and the social unrest that could arise from poverty. Even as some educators questioned the need for the "children of the plain people" to attend school so long, others argued that extending vocational schooling to working-class students would be more egalitarian. Then as now, educators and reformers stressed equality of educational opportunity as the appropriate conception of equity. Indeed, as schooling became more important as a path to occupations, educational opportunity became more important to equity than it had been in the nineteenth century. As the 1914 Commission on National Aid to Vocational Education claimed: "The social and educational need for vocational training is equally urgent. Widespread vocational training will democratize the education of the country: (1) by recognizing different tastes and abilities and by giving an equal opportunity to all to prepare for their life work; (2) by extending education through part-time and evening instruction to those who are at work in the shop or on the farm."

In the rhetoric of the Education Gospel around 1900, and in the changes in high schools, colleges, and universities since then, a distinctive group of believers in vocationalism emerged—a group we call the Education Coalition. (We might call them the Gospel choir, but we fear pressing the metaphor too far.) They have included economic reformers concerned about international competition and economic growth, parents and their children seeking to use schooling to get ahead, social reformers interested in reducing poverty and urban decay, educators promoting the centrality of schooling, and business interests happy to socialize the costs of training. With the rise of schooling as the dominant path to employment, the vast number of Americans who believe in the American dream—"If you work hard and play by the rules you should be given a chance to go as far as your God-given ability will take you," in Bill Clinton's version—now look to formal schooling as the way to realize this dream (Hochschild and Scovronick, 2003). The Education Coalition has emerged time and again to support vocationalism, each member with somewhat different interests, each working in slightly different ways. Vocationalism has triumphed in part because of this political support, against which the dissenters described in the next section have been relatively few and unorganized.

Since 1900 technology has changed, work has changed, social conditions have changed, and the details of the Education Gospel have changed with them. The technological shifts of the late nineteenth century were associated with electricity, complex machinery, scientific agriculture, and the maturation of the Industrial Revolution, not with computers and the Knowledge Revolution. The reorganization of work then depended on the assembly line and the division of labor, not on contingent work and new conceptions of flexible labor. The immigrants flooding into cities and into schools were eastern Europeans and African Americans from the rural South, not Latinos and Asians. The rhetoric around 1900 was much more explicitly moral in its tone than our language is today: advocates worried about the "evil influence of the unskilled industries" and extolled the dignity and sacredness of hand labor ("in all true work there is something divine"). The earlier claims were also more obsessed with efficiency—individual efficiency, social efficiency, the efficiency of matching workers to jobs, the efficiency of liberation from dead traditions (Veysey, 1965, 116–118). But the essential elements of the Education Gospel have been in place for a century, changing in their specifics but remaining remarkably stable in their broad descriptions of economic change and educational response.

Along with the obvious changes in technology, employment, and social conditions, our system of formal schooling has changed too, pushed along by the rhetoric of the Education Gospel and the pressures of the Education Coalition. Virtually all educational institutions from the high school on up have become more explicitly vocational, concerned first and foremost with preparation for employment.[9] New institutions and programs have developed, especially comprehensive public universities, community colleges, and (for a while) short-term job training. The process of change continues still, in ways we explore throughout this volume, and we argue in Chapter 5 that it has become self-reinforcing. In the course of these developments much of education has improved as well. While the dissenters may lament the "world we have lost" and its apparent intellectual rigor, that world was often one of circumscribed educational opportunities, of inequitable access based on social class, race, gender, immigrant status, and other ascribed characteristics. It was a world of rigid and stultifying teaching that now seems impossibly ineffectual, of "academic" education in the worst sense of the term. The greater breadth of subjects now taught, the development of more flexible and "relevant" forms of schooling and pedagogy, the greater access for working-class youth, women, minorities, and immigrants are all distinctive advances of twentieth-century schooling. These are gains few Americans would protest.

In the process, every level of education, from elementary and secondary schools through colleges and universities and postgraduate programs, has ballooned. In 1900 only 6.3 percent of each cohort completed high school. This proportion increased to a high of 79.1 percent in 1969 before dropping back to 70.6 percent in 2000—not quite high school for all, but close. In 1900 only 2.3 percent of those age eighteen to twenty-four attended college; by the close of the century, 58 percent of this group attended college—again short of college for all, but still a majority. In 1940, on the eve of World War II, only 14 percent of the entire population had completed high school, and 4.5 percent had completed four years of college; by 1999 83.4 percent had completed high school, and college completion had increased to 25.2 percent by the end of the century.[10] As we will see, the coming of vocational purposes triggered the expansion of schooling, since enrollment increases took place only after vocational practices were instituted.

The Education Gospel has given new purposes to older educational institutions that predate the century of vocationalism. It has created new institutions, new conceptions of how to get ahead in life, new visions of equality of opportunity, new ideas of why education counts, and new agendas for policy makers seeking responses to old problems. While other visions of education persist, the Education Gospel has created a powerful and well-recognized narrative that has justified public support for education, including enormous increases in K–12 spending as well as an expansion of public postsecondary funding that was inconceivable a century ago. In battles over the limited public purse, the narrative of economic and technological development and of education's role in preparing people for these changes has been crucial in keeping schooling a *public* commodity.[11] Since *A Nation at Risk*, every presidential candidate has wanted to be the "education president," governors have prided themselves on their education records, and the expansion and improvement of schooling have been constants on both national and state agendas. Those committed to public education owe the Education Gospel a great deal.

Dissenters and the Limits of Vocationalism

The process of changing education is almost never complete, however, as older practices and norms persist. Academics and curmudgeons and dissenters supporting older ideals have protested vocational and professional transformations as well as economic and market arguments, and older practices associated with civic education and intellectual discipline have persisted in academic subjects and in liberal or general education. There have always been partisans of the "school of hard knocks" who have distrusted formal schooling, and work experience still remains one of the important ways to enter the labor market, with work-based forms of learning—cooperative education, internships, and periodic efforts to emulate German-style apprenticeship—a persistent dream. The transformation of schooling by vocationalism is therefore a checkered story, with both believers and dissenters, with new possibilities (if imperfectly realized) to be reckoned against older practices lost or weakened.

The dissenters in this process have come from many different points of view, sometimes overlapping and sometimes incompatible. One familiar form of dissent has come from those who fear that vocationalism will undermine the public purposes of education, especially its civic roles. While much of the rhetoric of the Education Gospel has, now and in the past, stressed public purposes including economic growth and stability—"our very future as a Nation and a people"—vocationalism has simultaneously promoted private gain. The rhetoric of college for all advocates college education not as a way of developing moral leadership for religious and secular society, as in the eighteenth and nineteenth centuries, but as a way to increase individual status and income. The role of students and their parents in the Education Coalition has been largely to promote schooling to get themselves ahead, not schooling for "other people's children." In contrast, defenders of civic education hark back to the nineteenth century and the common school's emphasis on the knowledge and behavior necessary for a democracy. They include many academics and educators who argue that civic responsibility has declined—as in the influential *Bowling Alone* (Putnam, 2000), in which bowling individually rather than in clubs is a metaphor for the decline of community—and that democratic education must be revitalized (Goodlad and McMannon, 1997). Others have noted that the expansion of marketlike mechanisms such as vouchers and credentials—partly a result, as we argue in Chapters 6, of the dominance of private goals over public purposes—threatens to erode public responsibilities (Levin, 1980). So the balance of public and private purposes remains a subject of contention, at least among those who believe that the common good can and should be articulated.

Another school of dissenters, sometimes out of concern for democratic citizenship, has worried more about what vocationalism does to academic standards and rigor. These partisans have been the defenders of the academic tradition of the nineteenth century, of intellectual discipline as the aim of education, and of liberal and general education in the college and university. Their views have persisted in the frequent calls to revitalize the humanities and in popular lists of "what every American needs to know" (e.g., Hirsch, 1987)—antidotes to the narrowing and specialization that occurs under vocationalism. For this group, vocationalism has brought low-status vocational education for the "manually minded" into the high school, has led to enormous growth in academically suspect professional majors in the university (like apparel and accessories marketing, or recreation management), and has weakened the academic transfer function and the collegiate aspirations of the community college. At the same time, vocationalism has undermined liberal or general education in all its forms, substituting a utilitarian question—Why do I need to know this?—for an earlier faith in the power of intellectual breadth and rigor. These dissenters are often educators and academics, and they are easily caricatured as curmudgeons trying to hold back progress. But they also express a view that, while less popular among students and business representatives, is widely supported by the public at large and widely considered necessary for maintaining educational traditions, including conceptions of what a "real college" should be.

Another strand of skepticism about vocationalism has come from those who do not trust schools to prepare workers. As we will see, the proposals to develop land-grant universities in the mid-nineteenth century to train farmers and engineers led to jeers from those who rejected "fancy farmers" and "fancy mechanics" and extolled the "school of experience" or the "school of hard knocks." The Horatio Alger stories of the late nineteenth century describe boys succeeding through pluck, luck, and determination, not through formal schooling. Even after professionalism began to require college as the source of specialized knowledge, there was considerable doubt that educational institutions could do the job well—or that the job needed to be done at all. That skepticism has continued as educational attainments have continued to increase, and as negative conceptions of credentialism—the notion that students attend schools simply for the paper diploma, not for the competencies that schools convey—have spread (Collins, 1979). And since the capacities that really matter at work are often best learned on the job and not in school, the match between "school skills" and "work skills" is necessarily imperfect, as we will argue at greater length in Chapter 7.

Still another group of dissenters has feared that vocationalism would create new forms of inequality, driven by the inequalities and the hierarchies in labor markets. Education was unequal before vocationalism transformed it, of course. Despite nearly universal access to grammar schooling (grades 1–8) in the nineteenth century, high schools and especially colleges served a tiny elite and a small number of the aspiring middle class, largely from families with higher earnings and higher-status occupations. But vocationalism created new dimensions of inequality based on the curriculum track students followed in high school, the type of college they attended, or the major they pursued. In postsecondary education especially, the fragmentation of colleges and universities, following a differentiated occupational structure, created new types of educational divisions among classes and among races. The early dissenters therefore included proponents of equity and many unionists, who feared that vocationalism would create a second-class education for working-class students. In criticizing the "evil forces" that proposed to incorporate vocational education into the Chicago schools, John Dewey declared: "Those who believe in the continued separate existence of what they are pleased to call the 'lower classes' or the 'laboring classes' would naturally rejoice to have schools in which these 'classes' would be separated . . . All others should be united against every proposition, in whatever form advanced, to separate training of employees from training for citizenship, training of intelligence and character from training for narrow industrial efficiency." Along the same lines, a famous debate between Booker T. Washington and W. E. B. Du Bois turned on whether vocational education would teach honesty, persistence, and industriousness "to the downtrodden child of ignorance, shiftlessness, and moral weakness," as Washington declaimed, or would instead prevent black students from learning the professional skills necessary for economic success in an advanced industrial economy, as Du Bois feared.[12] Ever since, various forms of vocational and professional fragmentation—the differentiation of the high school, the development of the community college, the endless differences among universities—have stirred charges of tracking, segregation, and "cooling out."

A different kind of dissent, as evident in the early twentieth century as in the twenty-first, has noted that change never takes place as swiftly as advocates of the Education Gospel claim. This form of disagreement depends on careful empirical analysis, something that the faith-based belief in the Education Gospel discourages. In 1921, even as he promoted more schooling in broader forms, Paul Douglas also commented that "leaders in the vocational education movement had hitherto been reluctant to face the facts of modern large-scale production with its specialization of labor." Partly because of the introduction of machinery tended by semiskilled labor, there weren't real shortages of skilled labor after 1900, except in some specialty areas like machine repair. When spot shortages developed, employers imported foreign skilled workers or created their own training programs, so shortages were generally temporary and limited to a few geographic areas. Currently, the same pattern holds: while there were certainly shortages of computer workers during the boom of 1995 to 2000, employers imported foreign workers and made do with individuals who had not yet finished their educational programs. Shortages did not affect the vast number of occupations—and certainly did not when the economy turned down after 2000.

The pace of change has indeed been exaggerated by the current rhetoric of the Education Gospel. There have been substantial transformations over the past century, of course. Agricultural workers have diminished from 19 percent of the workforce in 1900 to 2.6 percent in 1999; craftsmen and operatives, the backbone of the Industrial Revolution, have decreased from 25.2 percent to 20.6 percent. Professionals, managers, and technicians, groups relying on formal schooling for the foundation of their specialized knowledge, have increased from 10 percent to 33.6 percent; sales and clerical workers have increased from 8.2 percent to 25.9 percent, representing the inflation of administrative operations; and nonhousehold service workers have increased from 6.7 percent to 12.8 percent. These shifts are roughly consistent with the major claims of the Education Gospel, but they have taken place over a century. Over shorter periods of time changes have been comparatively small, as Levin and Rumberger (1987) noted fifteen years ago. In 2000 only 28.8 percent of jobs were filled by individuals with education beyond the high school diploma, as Table I.1 reveals. While this proportion is expected to continue growing, it is still forecast to be only 30.5 percent by 2010, a rate of growth slow enough for existing postsecondary institutions to accommodate easily. Similarly, only 34.7 percent of the current labor force needs work-related or on-the-job training longer than a month, and this fraction will actually *decline* slightly, to 33.3 percent by 2010. In terms of job openings during these ten years—the openings that matter most to students now going through schooling—only 30.2 percent of new jobs will require more than a high school degree, and only 27.1 percent will require more than a trivial amount of on-the-job training. To be sure the growth *rates* are highest for those occupations requiring associate degrees, followed by doctoral degrees and master's degrees; and anyone who wants access to professional and managerial employment, or to the best jobs created by the high-tech revolution, must enroll in college or postgraduate school. But the notion of an overwhelming surge in education requirements for jobs is absurd, and the promotion of college for all is in some ways dishonest.

In addition, the contribution of technological change is often oversold. Many renditions of the Education Gospel emphasize the Knowledge Revolution and changes in computer-based technology. But unless we engage in massive relabeling, calling secretaries and schoolteachers "knowledge workers," or exaggerate the transformation of old skills by new technologies—substituting personal computers for typewriters, or computerized tracking systems for paper records—then the transformations of the knowledge economy have been much more limited thus far. For example, Brint (2001) estimates that the scientific and professional knowledge (SPK) sector accounted for about 36 percent of all employment in the years 1973 to 1996 and 37 percent of the gross domestic product in 1994, up from 27.2 percent in 1959. But these figures include government, whose contribution to GDP is difficult to measure, as well as all legal services (with the highest proportion of educated workers), all elementary and secondary school personnel, all religious organizations, dentists' offices, and many other sectors in which highly educated workers carry out quite traditional jobs. When we restrict employment in the knowledge economy to computer-related work, less than 1 percent of nongovernment employment—0.92 percent—is part of this segment. Adding in other arguably high-tech sectors—pharmaceuticals, engineering services, industrial chemicals, plastics and synthetics, commercial research, optical and health equipment—increases this number only to 2.75 percent of employment.[13] Even with exaggerated estimates, then, the vast majority of goods and services are produced in sectors that cannot be considered part of the knowledge economy. While aspects of the computer revolution have touched many types of work, all but a small percentage of jobs are in long-standing occupations rather than in "revolutionized" work.

Perhaps the only plausible way to understand the believers in the

Table I.1. Employment and total job openings, 2000 and 2010, by education or training category (in thousands of jobs)

Most significant source of education or training	Number of jobs		% distribution		Job openings due to growth and net replacements, 2000–2010		
	2000	2010	2000	2010	% change	Number of jobs	% distribution
Total all occupations	145,594	187,754	100.0%	100.0%	15.2%	57,982	100.0%
Bachelor's or higher degree	30,072	36,556	20.7	21.8	21.6	12,130	20.9
First professional degree	2,034	2,404	1.4	1.4	18.2	691	1.2
Doctoral degree	1,492	1,845	1.1	1.1	23.7	760	1.3
Master's degree	1,426	1,759	1.0	1.0	23.4	634	1.1
Bachelor's or higher, plus work experience	7,319	8,741	5.0	5.2	19.4	2,741	4.7
Bachelor's degree	17,801	21,807	12.2	13.0	22.5	7,304	12.6
Sub-baccalaureate awards	11,761	14,600	8.1	8.7	24.1	5,383	9.3
Associate degree	5,083	6,710	3.5	4.0	32.0	2,608	4.5
Postsecondary vocational award	6,678	7,891	4.6	4.7	18.2	2,775	4.8
Work-related training	103,760	116,597	71.3	69.5	12.4	40,419	69.8
Work experience in a related occupation	10,456	11,559	7.2	6.9	10.5	3,180	5.5
Long-term on-the-job training	12,435	13,373	8.5	8.0	7.5	3,737	6.5
Moderate-term on-the-job training	27,871	30,794	19.0	18.4	11.3	8,767	15.1
Short-term on-the-job training	53,198	60,871	36.5	36.3	14.4	24,735	42.7

Source: Hecker (2001), table 6.

Education Gospel and the Knowledge Revolution is to interpret their view as forecasting *what might happen over the next century* if current trends continue, not describing what is true now. Given this interpretation, the believers are wrestling with the possibilities over the next long wave of development, over a century rather than over the next decade. This, too, replicates earlier patterns; past generations worried about the long-run transformations of the Industrial Revolution, agonized about the pace of change, and around 1900, worried about the long-term consequences of new developments, from the telegraph, the telephone, and the cell phone to the automobile and the airplane, from electrical power to nuclear and solar power, from corporate consolidation to multinational and transnational corporations.[14]

In addition, the emphasis on technological change today (as in 1900) often fails to recognize causes of instability that have little to do with technology, and that influence individuals at all levels of the occupational structure. These include the reorganization of work, as with the rise of contingent labor, the development of "lean production" and its increased responsibility for frontline workers, the instability of employment stemming from corporate takeovers and exporting jobs to low-wage countries, and mobility within the country (from the Rustbelt to the Sunbelt, for example). If instead of attributing change to technology we had to confront organizational changes as responsible, then various governments might have to intervene more directly into labor markets and corporate practices. This happened a century ago with antitrust legislation and the regulation of hours and working conditions, and it has surfaced recently in efforts to stem the growth of contingent work and the loss of jobs overseas.

A final strand of dissent is, to us, one of the most consequential as well as one of the most difficult for educators. The rhetoric underlying vocationalism has promised that it could resolve a host of economic and social problems. These have included poverty and inequality, the transition problems of immigrants, social conditions in cities, the unemployment caused by the Great Depression and then by technological change after 1960, the shifts in employment caused by the communications revolution and now the Knowledge Revolution, and many other problems large and small. We can therefore interpret the Education Gospel as another in a long line of arguments looking to education as a panacea (Perkinson, 1991). It further assumes—if only because believers in the Gospel are usually silent about other reforms—that improvements in schooling can *by themselves* cure a range of social problems, and it provides a rhetorical justification for keeping government out of broader economic and employment policies. The Education Gospel by its very nature provides little incentive to examine the organization of work, the nature of labor markets, or the economic consequences of globalism, since—apparently—more and better education can solve whatever problems exist.

Sometimes the claims on behalf of education take on truly fantastic dimensions. Michael Bloomberg, the mayor of New York, claimed that if schools were improved then "a lot of what Dr. [Martin Luther] King wanted to accomplish in our society will take care of itself" (Rothstein, 2002b). But this is a vast exaggeration, since King argued eloquently for eliminating the "manacles of segregation," the "chains of discrimination," the limitations on "the Negro's basic mobility from a smaller ghetto to a larger one." These are dimensions of our society that are unlikely to change just through educational improvements, because they require more basic efforts to alleviate housing segregation, employment discrimination, urban blight, and the large and small manifestations of racism. Similarly, the No Child Left Behind Act (NCLB) passed in 2001 has offered a straightforward solution to achievement differences among different racial and ethnic groups: "Attack the soft bigotry of low expectations and demand that the schools close the achievement gap." But how schools can accomplish this on their own when bigotry persists in other aspects of American life, and when so many other aspects of policy contribute to the gap, including inequalities in access to health care, to housing, and to basic income, seems not to have occurred to the bipartisan coalition responsible for NCLB.

The efforts to improve various social and economic and racial problems through schooling are humane, but they're also impossible—humane because they try to improve social and economic conditions for future generations, but impossible because the ability of schooling to undo inequality is limited, particularly when conventional interest-group politics undermines any effort to introduce radical equalization through schooling.[15] This element of the Education Gospel has displaced attention from other policies that might have more powerful effects on economic opportunities, on stable employment, on housing and health care, and on the life of urban communities; it presents education and training as *substitutes* for other forms of social and economic policy, rather than as *complements* or parallel efforts. In the process, vocationalism and the Education Gospel have put educators in an impossible bind. On the one hand, vocational practices have created a mass education system with new responsibilities, and educators cannot readily oppose these roles—indeed, they have usually embraced expanded responsibilities, for reasons ranging from deep principle to responsibility for students to self-aggrandizement. On the other hand, the Education Gospel, with its stress on improvement through education and equal opportunity through schooling, places too great a burden on educators—though saying so appears to be a weak excuse for not trying hard enough, particularly during periods (like the present) when educators are under attack. Educators have therefore accepted responsibility for most claims of the Education Gospel, attempting to eliminate inequities—like closing the achievement gap between rich and poor students, or between white and minority students—even when there are valid reasons to think that other social and economic policies are also necessary. In the process, our understanding of what schools can do and what other policies must accomplish has gotten seriously out of balance (Rothstein, 2002a).

In response to this dilemma, some dissenters have dismissed the possibilities of educational reform and have instead advocated more radical changes in society. When George Counts (1932) asked the bold question, *Dare the Schools Build a New Social Order?* he went on to tackle what he called the most profound social issue—the "control of the machine," the requirement of public ownership of capital in a democracy. Some reformers, implicitly following his lead, reject any form of school reform as a solution, opting instead for socialism or massive redistribution. But we might instead remember the words of John Dewey, who consistently reminded us that debates framed in polar opposites—civic purposes versus occupational goals, academic versus vocational education, behaviorist versus constructivist pedagogies, educational solutions versus economic reforms—often reflect false dichotomies. In his introduction to *Experience and Education* (1938) he wrote: "Mankind likes to think in terms of extreme opposites. It is given to formulating its beliefs in terms of Either-Ors, between which it recognizes no intermediate possibilities" (17). In discussing traditional and progressive pedagogies, for example, he lamented that "the problems are not even recognized, to say nothing of being solved, when it is assumed that it suffices to reject the ideas and practices of the old education and then go to the opposite extreme" (22). A better solution to the dilemma of whether to reform schools or to reform social and economic conditions affecting schools might be a "both-and" rather than an "either-or" position. For example, Harold Howe, commissioner of education under Lyndon Johnson, suggested that rather than concentrating on fixing the schools *or* directly attacking poverty, "the only possible response to this question is that both policies must be followed at the same time" (Howe, 1993, 31). Bowles and Gintis (1975), among the most prominent critics of U.S. public education, called in their last chapter for a distinctive American socialism as well as a different educational system. And so, when we confront this dilemma in subsequent chapters, we will use Dewey's warning to avoid false dichotomies, and instead emphasize "both-and" positions. We will outline our concept for the Foundational State, a government whose practices provide the foundations for a dynamic economy, a vibrant democracy, and a broad version of the Education Gospel—a conception of government that provides a crucial role for reformed versions of schooling *as well as* other supportive social and economic policies.

At the start of the new millennium a central question is, Where we are likely to go from here? If the twentieth century was the century of vocationalism and professionalism, what will the twenty-first century bring for American schooling? In addition to understanding the transformation of schooling under vocational pressures, another ambition for this book is to explore the possibilities for the new century. We hope to disentangle the progressive and admirable features of twentieth-century developments from those that are less wonderful, to understand the power of the Education Gospel as well as its limits, to see which elements should continue into the twenty-first century. Our aim is certainly not to turn back the clock, to eliminate the relationship between education and occupations, or to denounce occupational goals as entirely false. Even if we had the power to take such action against the political clout of the Education Coalition, too much of value has come from the extension of schooling over the past century, and it is too late in the development of schooling to undo vocational changes. But if we as a country are to make good on the central promises of schooling, then we need to understand the ways in which vocationalism and the rhetoric of the Education Gospel have also limited our vision and our policies. Only then will it be possible to develop a conception of vocationalism worthy of our highest hopes for both schooling and for work.

The Plan of This Book

The first section of this book examines the ways that the major education and training institutions in this country have developed vocational purposes. The institutions we look at in Chapters 1 to 3—the high school, the college and university, and the community college—have been remarkably similar in some ways, including their drift from academic to occupational purposes. Each has expanded only after occupational goals were added to earlier academic goals; each has become a comprehensive institution incorporating a diversity of purposes and an increasing variety of students.

But we also stress the different roles they have played in the overall process of vocationalism. The changes in high school were most obviously responses to the decline of apprenticeships, and they reveal a great deal about the advantages of school-based preparation over work-based learning. Much of the rhetoric of vocationalism was crafted for the high school, and—paradoxically—the high school continues to be a vocational institution as well as a route into college, even though it offers very little overtly vocational training anymore. The transformation of colleges and universities has been interwoven with conceptions of professionalism, an idea that specifically promotes formal schooling as the basis of stature and privilege. Professionalism is the wealthy cousin of vocationalism, justifying high-level occupational preparation even though it suffers from many of the same dilemmas. The increasingly occupational purposes of community colleges, which are relatively new institutions, have followed the trajectories of older forms of schooling, though "the people's college" has differed in its inclusiveness and its heterogeneity. But this in turn has created challenges—particularly providing the noneducational policies, including income support and family support, necessary to keep "nontraditional" students in school— that highlight the inadequacy of education alone in achieving equity.

We examine short-term job training programs and adult education in Chapter 4, both "second-chance" opportunities for individuals trying to change careers or reenter the job market. Usually such programs are examined in isolation from education, but we interpret job training and its many failures as the result of an effort to devise an alternative to school-based preparation for work, and therefore as a part of vocationalism more generally. Job training and adult education can help us understand some of the positive elements of the Education Gospel, at the same time that their weaknesses provide a series of warnings.

In Chapter 5 we summarize the distinctively American approach to vocationalism. Many countries have focused their educational systems on occupational preparation, to be sure, but the particular histories and institutions involved have meant that vocationalism differs from country to country.[16] In the United States, occupational preparation has taken place largely in comprehensive rather than specialized institutions, with relatively weak mechanisms linking the education system to employment. Compared with other developed countries, American vocationalism is embedded in an impotent welfare state. In many different ways vocationalism has been incomplete—not only because dissenters have held on to older civic and intellectual purposes, but also because there exist many different conceptions of what vocational and professional education mean. Nonetheless, once the process of vocationalizing schools and colleges started in this country, it became self-reinforcing—and we can be sure that the process will continue in the twenty-first century, here and elsewhere.

We next examine the consequences of locating occupational preparation in schools and colleges. Chapter 6 discusses one of the basic promises of vocationalism and the Education Gospel—that more schooling will enhance employment, earnings, and status for individuals, as well as enhance economic growth and stability for society as a whole. Contrary to the attempt to balance private and public interests in the Education Gospel, we find that private benefits have dominated public benefits.

In Chapter 7 we look at another enduring promise of vocationalism: that vocational education will prepare individuals for work better than preparation at work itself would. From the simple observation that vocationalism separates preparation for work from employment, we examine the disjunction between "work skills," those competencies necessary in employment, and "school skills," the competencies readily taught in schools. While there are ways of bringing the two together, differences are both unavoidable and desirable, because we want different outcomes from our educational institutions and our institutions of production.

In Chapter 8, we consider how vocationalism has transformed the inequities that have always been present in schools and colleges. Vocationalism has moved the question of access to employment from the realm of private decisions—in families, apprenticeships, and informal networks—into the arena of public policy, *potentially* creating levers for greater equity. At the same time schools and colleges, in preparing their students for employment, have replicated the endless divisions of the labor market, recreating older educational inequalities in new forms. We also explain why educational reforms have to occur simultaneously with complementary social and economic policies, within a Foundational State that creates the conditions for a more equitable version of vocationalism. While this may seem a tall order, the alternative is a version of vocationalism that will never live up to its promises because noneducational policies are entirely too limited.

In Chapter 9 we address possible directions for the twenty-first century. Having examined both the positive and the negative developments over the century of American vocationalism, we first clarify what seems right and wrong with the Education Gospel. We then summarize what's right and what's wrong with the American version of vocationalism, to clarify that while broad and equitable versions of vocationalism could exist, so too could a narrow and inegalitarian version—a world we caricature as HyperVoc. We conclude by outlining a broader approach to vocationalism and a reasonable version of the Education Gospel, supported by the expanded policies of the Foundational State. Throughout, we try to heed John Dewey's warnings against either-or proposals, and specifically against the dualisms that have arisen under the American version of vocationalism—academic versus vocational education, school-based preparation versus work-based learning, theory versus practice, management versus execution. Instead, we identify a variety of integrative strategies that would balance the academic and the vocational, school-based learning with work experience, the theoretical and the applied.

The integrative strategies in education we propose, combined with a commitment to the Foundational State, contrast sharply with the narrowness of the Education Gospel and its exclusive emphasis on the occupational purposes of education. It would require only a slight expansion of that Gospel to incorporate multiple purposes of schooling and a richer view of how educational institutions prepare their students for the future. After all, society is becoming more complex in many more ways than just the proliferation of new occupations and new skills. Analytic abilities are increasingly necessary for the exercise of international understanding and citizenship; immigration and the globalization of trade and policy and culture require greater sensitivity to multiple cultures, and—in a post–September 11 world—the interconnections among peoples and policies have become painfully obvious. A broader version of the Education Gospel would stress the complexity of political and cultural life, both in this country and abroad, *in addition to* the complexity of occupational alternatives. A larger framing could undo the damage of the last century, when vocational and professional practices—many of them positive—were nonetheless justified by rhetoric that neglected the civic, moral, and intellectual purposes of education. If we could integrate the nineteenth-century vision of education with the occupational emphasis of the twentieth century, a noble version of the Education Gospel might be within our grasp.

1

∽ Transforming the High School

$\mathcal{T}$HE PROMISE of the American high school once seemed unbounded. From a small and unimportant institution—in 1900, less than 10 percent of the fourteen- to seventeen-year-old cohort was enrolled—high school became nearly universal during the twentieth century. Yet despite its great hopes, the high school is now a blighted institution, its academic purposes reduced to preparing some students for vocational study in college and its direct vocational role eliminated by the collapse of the youth labor market. The irony is that both the high school's promise and its tragedy are rooted in the same phenomenon: the vocationalizing of American education.

A century ago the high school was primarily an academic institution—in the sense that its curriculum was dominated by academic subjects, and in the more disparaging sense that formal schooling was distant from the political, community, and economic life outside its doors. Academic dominance gave way under the pressure to vocationalize the curriculum, to prepare students directly for entry-level jobs that traditionally did not require secondary schooling. The vocational education movement changed the high school, as trade and industrial training, secretarial and clerical preparation, home economics, and agricultural education became staples of the curriculum. But the broader significance of vocational education lay in its role in transforming the conception of schooling to one of getting *all* students better jobs, not just those in voc ed. Since that change, even the efforts to make high school more academic, like the recent accountability mechanisms focused on basic English and math and the pressure of College for All, have also had to show that they would improve students' future opportunities, either directly or through their access to college. The transformation of the high school has been crucial to revising our basic concept of its purpose.

Schools had always prepared youth for work, but they typically did so by embedding basic competencies—reading, writing, and arithmetic—in shared moral values like hard work, individual responsibility, and commitment to family, church, and community. In the last half of the nineteenth century, however, changes in the American economy increased the pressure on the schools to modify their approach to job preparation. The long decline in apprenticeships became apparent. The growth of large-scale industrial corporations, the complexities of technology, and the increasing need for office workers led employers to shift away from hiring adolescents and toward hiring less transient adults, often immigrants and rural migrants newly arrived in America's booming cities. As the youth labor market deteriorated, concerns for social stability mounted because of the large numbers of young people now unemployed or drifting from one dead-end job to another.

These shifts encouraged the vocational education movement. Initially, the goal was to integrate traditional learning—with its emphasis on moral and mental discipline—with occupational instruction. But the bridge between older purposes of schooling and job preparation was unstable, and an Education Coalition composed of the business community, unions, social reformers, philanthropists, educators, and federal and state policy makers formed to establish vocational education in America's high schools.

The success of this Education Coalition changed the structure of secondary schooling. During the twentieth century, high school for all became a reasonable goal, as secondary education expanded to include most fourteen- to seventeen-year-olds. Vocational tracking, followed by other forms of stratification like IQ testing and the "general" curriculum track, differentiated the comprehensive high school internally, so that while all students went to a common school, they were treated in different ways. Vocational education opened the way for a curricular explosion and widespread student choice. It also created a new conception of equity rooted in equality of educational opportunity.

In the early twenty-first century, with high school now seemingly the most intractable problem in American education, the consequences of vocationalism are less attractive than they were a century ago. Out of concerns ranging from "a rising tide of mediocrity" to violence in the schools, secondary schools have become the center of reform efforts. Policy makers focus on imposing higher academic standards, while large numbers of students regard high school as a necessary evil—necessary for individual advancement but intrinsically dreary. In the absence of a serious job market for their graduates, high schools primarily function as a transmission belt to college or simply as a warehouse for keeping young people off the streets until they leave school. Many flaws in the high school can be traced to its ambiguous occupational roles, to its provision of academic learning in the service of long-run vocational purposes, and to the explosion of curricular choices that both divide the student body and minimize the expectations of learning—all part of the process that transformed secondary education in the century of vocationalism.

There are many ways out of the high school's current dilemmas. As we argue in the last section of this chapter, these alternatives require confronting the dualisms that the movement for vocational education created—between the academic and the vocational, between school and work as locations for learning, between the serious business of growing up and the trivial demands on high school students. Only by overcoming these dualisms will it be possible to construct an institution worthy of high school for all.

The Decline of Work-Based Education

Learning at work—either informally or in formal apprenticeships— was traditionally the way youths made the transition to adulthood. For young men, apprenticeships moved them from family to work and independence; for young women, learning adult roles usually occurred within their own household rather than in the household of a relative or trusted friend. In its idealized form, apprenticeship seems a marvelous way to learn. A skilled and respected adult models the desired competencies, and then supervises practice by the apprentice. A broad range of knowledge may be gained in this way: manual abilities; literacy, numeracy, visual and oral skills; knowledge of the informal culture of a workplace and the ethics of a craft or profession; how to balance individual responsibility and cooperation; trade secrets that give experts their special reputations. When the process works well, the apprentice sees the final product—crops grown, books printed, food preserved, a patient cured, a computer program online—and understands the relationship of all subtasks to the outcome. This is a model that many Americans hold dear, "the way we learn most naturally." Various individuals have tried to resurrect it both as a model for academic learning—sometimes called "cognitive apprenticeship" (Collins, Brown, and Newman, 1989)—and as an ideal of work-based learning, attempted most recently in the School-to-Work Opportunities Act of 1994 (Berryman, 1995).

As attractive as work-based learning seems, in practice it has never achieved substantial importance in America, and the reasons for this help us understand the growing emphasis on formal schooling for vocational preparation.[1] Colonial Americans tried to import European apprenticeship models, but without a system of highly regulated craft guilds or a legal system to enforce apprenticeship contracts, both masters and apprentices routinely violated their agreements. Apprentices often walked away from their contracts when masters did not live up to the terms of agreement. Ben Franklin, abused by his master and unpaid, was the most famous of these runaways; he sailed from Boston to Philadelphia, where he set up his own printing shop. Masters often kept their apprentices at repetitive and menial tasks, emphasizing production and neglecting the educational side of apprenticeship. Employers often "poached" those already trained from competitors, or hired partly trained apprentices as they needed them, so that they did not have to pay for training. The fledgling unions of the early nineteenth century tried various strategies to overcome the flaws of apprenticeships—preventing the overemployment of apprentices to control periodic glut, regulating the duration of apprenticeship to forestall inadequate training, and increasing the wages of apprentices and journeymen—but they did not have much influence.[2]

The economic fluctuations of a market economy played further havoc with apprenticeships. In recessions, apprentices were simply let go; in robust economic times, young men easily found jobs on their own. Technological changes undermined traditional skills, and craftwork declined as it was replaced by labor-saving machinery tended by semiskilled workers. And without the stability of long-term relationships, the role of the master standing in loco parentis, overseeing the moral development of the young apprentice, essentially collapsed in the decades after 1800. Under these conditions it made more economic sense to hire workers who concentrated exclusively on production, train them in narrow ways to do specific jobs, pay them what the labor market required, and leave the noneconomic aspects of apprenticeship—education in a broad sense and moral supervision—to someone else. By the early twentieth century, it became an article of faith that apprenticeships no longer functioned well. The authors of *Learning to Earn* summed up the prevailing wisdom (Lapp and Mote, 1915, 67): "Apprenticeship had its origins and served its purpose in an industrial era altogether different from that prevailing. Apprenticeship does not meet the present needs of industry. As a scheme of education it is altogether inadequate."

In its place, other modes of work-based education developed. These included private trade schools sponsored by employers and philanthropists; schools run by corporations to train their own workers; public continuation schools, inspired by those in Germany, where adolescents could attend school part-time while they worked; and cooperative education combining school-based and work-based learning. But none of these efforts served large numbers, and many of them did not endure. They foundered on the problems apprenticeships had suffered—particularly on the costs to employers and the inability to prevent poaching, as well as on the unwillingness of students to enter a training system in the absence of enforceable standards and widely recognized credentials.

The weakness of work-based learning, both in apprenticeships and in other experiments around 1900, illustrates why it has been so difficult to resurrect this apparently "natural" form of learning. To succeed, apprenticeship requires regulation to enforce the terms of contract, a balance of education and production, some mechanism to prevent employers from avoiding training by poaching, stable employment and economic conditions, and a personal and paternal relationship between master and apprentice that is quite at odds with the impersonal authority structure of the modern workplace. And without strict regulation, apprenticeship has no way of enhancing equity, of moderating the inevitable variation among families in their ability to find apprenticeships for their sons or to promote nontraditional opportunities for their daughters. So Americans have periodically embraced work-based learning as both "natural" and ideal, but in the main they have placed their faith in formal schooling as the vehicle for occupational preparation.

From Moral and Civic Purposes to Vocational Goals

From the start, American schools embodied both religious and moral purposes.[3] Colonial and nineteenth-century Americans did not separate moral behavior from religion. This unity was first articulated in the Massachusetts Bay Colony's school law of 1647: "It being one chief project of that old Deluder Satan, to keep men from knowledge of the Scriptures . . . It is therefore ordered that every township [shall] appoint one within their town to teach all such children as shall resort to him to read and write." The nineteenth-century expectation that the Scriptures and the Golden Rule would be taught also reflected the belief that schooling was a moral enterprise based in religion, specifically Protestantism. In the most popular textbooks of the nineteenth century, the McGuffey Readers, children learned to read through stories about the rewards of virtuous behavior, the risks of vice, the family as the center of moral life, the necessity of schooling, the virtue of work, and the centrality of community and citizenship. Literacy, the most fundamental task of formal schooling, was not just a skill to be applied in multiple contexts but was a way to learn the precepts necessary for life in a moral community (Gorn, 1998).

The moral purposes of schooling were critical to the expansion of public education. Calling for public support of education early in the nineteenth century, the New York Free School Society found the city's poor children "reared up by parents who . . . are either indifferent to the best interests of their offspring, or, through intemperate lives, are rendered unable to defray the expense of their education," a situation that led to "ignorance and vice, and all those manifold evils resulting from every species of immorality" (Kaestle, 1973, ch. 4). Public schools could compensate by instructing such children in the moral values and behavior they could not learn from their parents—a theme that would resonate into the twenty-first century.

The moral purposes of education flowed naturally into civic purposes. The American Revolution and the establishment of the new nation gave education a broad political goal: citizens of the democratic republic needed to be literate as well as moral. Unless individuals were educated to be democrats, steeped in a morality tied to the common good, the nation would be torn apart by individualism and selfish "interests." The common schools thus had to be institutions where *all* children might learn the common core of knowledge, abilities, and values necessary for the nation. In practice, of course, there were all sorts of restrictions on who attended common schools. "Republican motherhood" meant teaching women to be sufficiently literate only to educate their children in appropriate values. Slavery meant that African Americans were formally denied citizenship, thus limiting their schooling; Native Americans and Mexicans suffered the same exclusion. But the consensus that schooling had civic and moral purposes was rarely contested. The earliest version of the Education Gospel that propelled the expansion of public education was dedicated to public goals, the strengthening of the nation through the moral, civic, and social responsibilities of individuals.

Economic development was also part of the early Education Gospel. Advocates argued that education increased the nation's material riches as well as individuals' chances of economic success. Horace Mann, the champion of public education, proclaimed in the 1830s that the common school would be "the most prolific parent of material riches" whereby "even the poorest may pass on to the realization of cherished hopes." The increase in material riches was contingent on moral and civic education, not primarily on "skills"; literacy and numeracy furthered individual economic success but only when married to such character traits as working hard, restraining one's self, supporting republican government, and respecting private property. (The phrase that George W. Bush invoked during the Enron scandal—"No capitalism without conscience, no wealth without character"—could have come from the nineteenth century, with its emphasis on moral character as a precondition for wealth.) Similarly, the introduction of such "relevant" subjects as mathematics and the sciences in high schools was simultaneously a way of deepening one's intellectual and moral powers and a source of knowledge that would be useful in a surging commercial and industrial economy. The influence of schooling on economic success was thus indirect; learning the technical skills of a particular occupation still occurred on the job, not in the classroom.

The public purposes of schooling continued as ideals through the twentieth century. But the balance that made economic goals an outgrowth of moral and civic learning changed to an emphasis on direct vocational preparation. The fate of the manual training movement in the late nineteenth century illustrates the process. Advocates of woodworking and other handwork assumed that students learned more effectively through direct (or hands-on) experiences, not through "the sameness and monotony" of traditional recitation and book learning. While the skills learned in industrial drawing or woodworking would be useful when students became employed, manual training's primary purpose was moral: to teach the value of hard work through the discipline of manual exercises—"training the head through training the hand." Manual learning promoted an integration of "head" and "hand" that had not been part of the common schools; as the cover of Calvin Woodward's 1887 manifesto proclaimed:

> Hail to the skillful, cunning hand!
>   Hail to the cultured mind!
> Contending for the World's command,
>   Here let them be combined.

The manual training movement served as an important bridge between the past and the future by encompassing multiple messages. It simultaneously looked to the past to recreate a preindustrial world of autonomous artisans and to the future dominated by industrial work. It reinforced the values of the common school by insisting that all students—girls as well as boys, and students of all classes and races—could benefit from direct experience, while also suggesting that manual training was especially appropriate for poor and minority students needing special forms of education.

These multiple purposes were contradictory and deeply unstable, and the combination of moral goals, hands-on learning, and occupational training quickly came apart. By the first decades of the twentieth century, manual training was replaced by efforts to teach explicitly vocational skills directly applicable to jobs. The Massachusetts Commission on Industrial and Technical Education in 1906 criticized manual training as "a cultural subject mainly useful as a stimulus to other forms of intellectual effort—a sort of mustard relish, an appetizer . . . severed from real life as completely as have [been] other school activities." Charles Prosser, prominent in the movement for vocational education, argued in 1912 that "manual training is not the sort of education which [students] need to fit them for their life-work"—and by life work Prosser meant vocations (Kliebard, 1999, 26).

The movement for an explicitly vocational education attracted a broad group of supporters, including manufacturers, unions, social reformers, philanthropists, public officials, and educators. Between 1880 and 1917, when the Smith-Hughes Act began providing federal funds for vocational education, this version of the Education Coalition included the most prominent believers in vocational training.[4] But they were believers with quite different perspectives on why school-based vocational preparation was necessary.

Manufacturing associations, worried about the growing labor movement and competition with Germany, hoped to use vocational education to overcome a perceived shortage of skilled labor—carpenters, plumbers, metal pattern and tool makers, machinists and mechanics, and electricians—and to limit union influence over access to those jobs.[5] They saw school-based vocational preparation as a way to avoid the expense of elaborate skill training on the job.

Organized labor, primarily represented by the American Federation of Labor (AFL), was more ambivalent about school-based vocational training. To the AFL, vocational education had the potential to keep working-class students in school longer, preventing them from flooding the labor market as cheap workers, and it promised greater skills and higher earnings for working-class children. But the labor movement and other reformers feared the erosion of broad preparation and "industrial intelligence"—the "mental power to see beyond the task which occupies the hands for the moment." They worried, too, that vocational education was a second-class education leading to second-class jobs, a way of diverting working-class students away from academic education. Ultimately labor joined the Education Coalition, partly to prevent it from being dominated by business and to avoid the worst forms of narrow vocational education. As one unionist admitted, "We cannot stop the trend in the direction of this kind of education in the school; but we can, if we cooperate with the educators, have it come our way" (Lazerson and Grubb, 1974, doc. 8). Organized labor and organized capital therefore compromised; neither wanted the other to control access to occupational preparation, and moving it into the public schools was one way to retain a modicum of control and avoid domination by the enemy.

A third group to join the Education Coalition included settlement-house workers, urban reformers, philanthropists, and public officials concerned with the well-being of poor and immigrant children. Their arguments tended to be both economic and moral: vocational education would prepare children of the poor for better jobs than the unskilled work currently available to them, and the combination of work skills and work values would help eliminate the social problems of poverty—overcrowding, disease, crime, vagrancy, abandonment of families.

The coalition was rounded out by educators who wanted to make schooling more important. Most early twentieth-century educators were committed to the traditional purposes of preparing moral and literate citizens based on a traditional curriculum. But they were also coping with a flood of new responsibilities—immigrant children, labor market changes, the health and social development of students, concern about the Sturm und Drang of adolescence, special classes for students with special needs, and an emerging extracurriculum of clubs and athletics. In this maelstrom, multiple arguments on behalf of vocational education proved persuasive. One was especially attractive: that vocational programs would keep students in school longer, since educators had come to believe that young people left school as much because of the irrelevant curriculum as for economic reasons. Vocational education would introduce a curriculum and pedagogy that were more relevant and more conducive to "active learning" than the traditional memorization and recitation. The primary dropout problem involved boys, and advocates especially hoped that vocational training would provide young males with a relevant and active curriculum, keeping them out of unskilled labor markets and avoiding the "the wasted years" syndrome, the period of time after leaving high school that many spent moving from one unskilled job to another (Kantor, 1988; Kliebard, 1999).

For girls, the growth and feminization of office work created a quiet revolution in their occupational preparation. To be sure, the notion of preparing women for jobs outside the home was still troubling; the vocational program of choice was home economics, designed to prepare young women to be mothers and homemakers. But the numbers of women engaged in manufacturing, mechanical, and clerical jobs increased threefold from 1890 to 1920. Fueled by the need for office workers, the clerical labor market for women helped make commercial education the success story of vocational education. The percentage of high school students enrolled in commercial courses rose from 21.7 percent in 1900 to 57.7 percent in 1934 (Powers, 1992). In fact, surveys in the first three decades of the twentieth century often found office work as the top occupational choice of young girls, even ahead of teaching—especially for working-class girls.[6]

The growing emphasis on a vocationally oriented curriculum was strengthened by an emerging belief in educational opportunity based on differentiated learning. The nineteenth-century common school had stressed the same education for all students. Even if children possessed different capacities to learn, the school's goal was to teach common values through a shared curriculum. The early high schools also emphasized a homogeneous curriculum; as the Committee of Ten, a group of educators convened to bring coherence to the curriculum, declared in 1894, "Every subject which is taught at all in a secondary school should be taught in the same way and to the same extent to every pupil so long as he pursues it, no matter what the probable destination of the pupil may be, or at what point his education is to cease." At the end of the nineteenth century, however, such views were declining in favor of a revised vision emphasizing different learning for different students. This was especially true for those "children of the plain people," as the president of the National Education Association referred to the children of immigrant, working-class, and minority parents, who by the seventh grade had "demonstrated their unfitness for what might be called a professional career." A uniform curriculum was now considered inegalitarian, and the new conception of equal opportunity emphasized differences among students as the basis for reorganizing schools: "Instead of affording equality of educational opportunity to all, the elementary school by offering but one course of instruction . . . neglects in a measure the taste, capacity, and educational destination of all others . . . In a word, what was intended to be a school for the masses and afford equality of educational opportunity to all . . . serves well the interests of but the few" (Elson and Bachman, 1910, 361).

The new conception of equality of educational opportunity achieved enormous support because it seemed appropriately democratic. As the Commission on National Aid to Vocational Education put it in 1914, "Widespread vocational training will democratize the education of the country . . . by recognizing different tastes and abilities and by giving an equal opportunity to all to prepare for their life work." This ideal provided separate but supposedly equal opportunities depending on students' "evident and probable destinies," as Harvard's president Charles Eliot described the process: the academic track for middle-class students bound for college and professional or managerial work (for boys, and for a few girls going into teaching and nursing); industrial education for working-class boys bound for factories; commercial education for working-class girls heading for clerical positions; and home economics for future homemakers (Lazerson and Grubb, 1974, 116–132). The explicit tracking of students generated some sharp protest—from figures like John Dewey, opposed to vocational education as a form of low-level "trade training" and class division, and from W. E. B. Du Bois, who worried that it would be used to teach black youth "the techniques of a rapidly disappearing era of hand work"— and it seems impossibly inegalitarian to us now. But at the time it represented a commitment of public schools to greater access, and it helped propel educators into the ranks of those supporting vocational education.[7]

As the twentieth century progressed, vocational education in the sense of explicit preparation for working-class jobs became widely accepted. Federal legislation expanded the Smith-Hughes Act of 1917 in 1929, 1934, and 1936. Building on the support that World War II generated for vocational education, legislation in 1946 again increased federal funding and introduced some flexibility in the use of funds. But vocational education came in for its share of criticism too, as dissenters objected to the quality of training provided and to the diminution of academic learning. Some of this dissent was implicit—for example, when the Roosevelt administration in the 1930s established job training programs outside the schools, and again in the 1960s when manpower programs independent of schools were created, partly because of the perceived inadequacy of vocational education. Some dissent was more explicit: a 1937 report by a Roosevelt advisory committee criticized educators for promoting narrow conceptions of vocational education, preparing students for a limited range of occupations, neglecting low-income students, and creating a two-track education system. But the report still reaffirmed the importance of school-based voc ed, repeating arguments from the early twentieth-century version of the Education Gospel.

A different development took place during the late 1940s and early 1950s, one that revealed a grand flaw in the vocationalized high school. Once the expanded high school was designed to prepare students for their occupational roles, then clearly one group needed academic education for college and the professions and a second group needed vocational education for skilled labor. But this left behind a third group of students, those bound for the vast numbers of unskilled jobs and thus for whom the role of the high school was unclear. The most common solution, already apparent in the 1920s and 1930s, was to create a third "general" track, neither academic nor vocational, with academic and occupational content degraded into "general" English, math and science for everyday living, and watered-down versions of other courses for students who would never need an understanding of those subjects in their employment. This triple-track "solution" developed its clearest justification in the Life Adjustment movement that arose after World War II. As Charles Prosser made the case (Kliebard, 1999, 204):

> The vocational school as a community will be able better to prepare 20 percent of the youth of secondary school age for entrance upon desirable skilled occupations; and that the high school will continue to prepare another 20 percent for entrance to college. We do not believe that the remaining 60 percent of our youth of secondary school age will receive the life adjustment training they need and to which they are entitled as American citizens—unless and until the administrators of public education with the assistance of the vocational education leaders formulate a similar program for this group.

The program for Life Adjustment education included "functional experiences in the areas of practical arts, home and family life, health and physical fitness, and civic competence," as well as work experience programs, all aimed at the bottom 60 percent of students.

Life Adjustment education and other versions of general education —including the general track, career education in the 1970s, and many job training and welfare-to-work programs emphasizing "life skills"—have come under withering attack for abandoning any legitimate purpose, whether civic, vocational, or intellectual.[8] But in an economy where a large number of jobs are relatively unskilled—where, as we noted in the Introduction, only 29 percent of jobs in 2000 required education beyond the high school diploma—it is difficult to know what vocationalized high schools ought to be doing for the great mass of students bound for unskilled work. The consistent response—whether overt, as in Life Adjustment, or covert, as in the varying quality of the "shopping mall high school" (Powell, Farrar, and Cohen, 1985)—has been to provide low-quality electives and simplified versions of core courses that at least continue the appearance of education.

Other rounds of critique and reaffirmation took place after 1960. A national commission named by President Kennedy in 1963 criticized voc ed for its insensitivity to the labor market and to the needs of many students, especially minority students and women; it tried to broaden the scope of vocational preparation and to focus on low-income students. Findings of another critical advisory committee in 1968 led to increased funding while again promoting more general forms of vocational education and affirming its role for disadvantaged students. Subsequent federal developments continued to stress the importance of serving "special populations" and of program improvement, while round after round of national assessments concluded that congressional intent had not been satisfied. Vocational education continued to be relatively narrow, skill-specific, and confined to entry-level jobs associated with an earlier era: agriculture, clerical work, retail positions, industrial-era craftwork, and the inevitable home economics.

Not until the end of the twentieth century did a consensus develop that traditional vocational education was failing. Both vocational education and the general track, the remnant of Life Adjustment, were overtaken by other agendas. Since the 1980s, the emphasis on improved academic learning and academic graduation requirements has led to declines in vocational enrollment—though not without objections from traditional vocational educators (National Commission on Secondary Vocational Education, 1985). The pressure for college for all also affected enrollments in vocational courses, since traditional vocational education always defined itself as a "terminal" program leading to employment rather than to college. When states began to develop accountability mechanisms, they included only academic courses—mostly English and math—which further discouraged vocational courses. While a few high schools and area schools (often in the South) still have serious vocational curricula, most have just a smattering of offerings: a keyboarding course here, a home economics course there, some business education for clerks and retail workers, but very few sustained *programs* that allow students to develop greater skills than those required in entry-level positions.[9] The real vocational preparation is now academic—the preparation of youth for college, where occupational (or professional) education begins. Those not heading for college are simply biding their time.

Why It Matters

The movement for vocational education may seem like ancient history, irrelevant to the schools of the twenty-first century. The reformers who introduced mechanical drawing and carpentry for boys, and dressmaking and domestic science for girls, seem no different from countless other educational reformers who promoted their little solutions only to see them wane—an American phenomenon that David Tyack and Larry Cuban (1995) call "reforming again and again and again." And yet the vocational education movement mattered, for it created the comprehensive high school, substantially widened access to secondary schooling, and shifted the goals of secondary education to vocational purposes. As formal schooling including the university became increasingly necessary for employment, particularly for high-status careers, it also became the linchpin of the American dream—advancement through individual effort regardless of one's background.

A central outcome of the movement for vocational education was a rationale for more youths to stay in school for longer periods. In the first half of the twentieth century, the comprehensive high school found a definitive role for everybody: It prepared large numbers of students (both boys and girls) directly for the labor market, a smaller number of students for college and professional careers, and some middle-class girls for scientific domesticity. The president of the Muncie, Indiana, school board confirmed the dominance of vocational purposes in the mid-1920s: "For a long time all boys were trained to be President. Then for a while we trained them all to be professional men.

Now we are training boys to get jobs" (Lynd and Lynd, 1929, 194–198).

The vocational education movement also fostered a curriculum explosion of highly differentiated coursework. In California during the 1920s, shops, kitchens, and commercial classes became common in schools; Los Angeles high schools in 1930 offered 129 courses in industrial arts, 47 courses in home economics, and 42 commercial courses, as well as substantial numbers of courses in conventional academic subjects. The same pattern was repeated across the country, forming the curricular basis for what would become the shopping mall high school (Kantor, 1988; Angus and Mirel, 1999; Lynd and Lynd, 1929).

After vocational tracking became prominent, ability grouping followed, justified by a rationale similar to that for vocational differentiation. Lewis Terman, usually regarded as the father of IQ testing, complained about poorly performing students who "clog the educational machinery" and argued that tests could be used to segregate them in special classrooms so they would not detract from the education of others. Linking issues of mental ability to vocation, he noted that these "backward students" were "a good argument for the introduction of manual training and domestic science" (Terman, 1922, ch. 1). The differentiation of courses by ability levels created both a "horizontal curriculum," with an incredible array of electives, and a "vertical curriculum" that offered different versions of required subjects for students of different ability levels—algebra, general math, and math for daily living, for example, or advanced-placement (AP) chemistry alongside science in everyday life (Powell, Farrar, and Cohen, 1985). The creation of the general education track and the Life Adjustment movement added their own roster of general courses and "life skills," many of which have persisted despite the ire of educational conservatives.

Curriculum differentiation spawned further segregation of students by social class, race, and gender within comprehensive high schools, and gaps widened as working-class youth—both male and female—tended to be overrepresented in commercial and industrial education courses. Black and Latino students were relegated to home economics, agricultural, and industrial education, while middle-class white students remained in academic programs. As Angus and Mirel (1999) have noted, the democratic high school "equalized the opportunity to *attend* high school by providing curricular programs that were profoundly *unequal* in the adult roles for which students prepared." The lower tracks put up with the worst teachers, provided a lackadaisical curriculum (either vocational or general) without much pressure for students to learn,[10] and offered vocational courses that led only to low-level jobs rather than to the new occupations of the knowledge economy. Vocational tracks and the general track became known as dumping grounds for those unable to succeed in the college prep curriculum. Creating separate but equal programs, always difficult in an unequal society, proved impossible.

While the high school of the early twenty-first century has largely returned to academic education, it has been thoroughly transformed by vocationalism. It has become a mass rather than an elite institution. It is highly differentiated, in a way that gives much more choice to students but also leads to curricular incoherence and inequity. Many students understand the point of high school to be vocational, particularly since high school dropouts stand little chance of making a decent living. When John Goodlad questioned students in the early 1980s, the greatest number—31 percent—responded that the purpose of high school was vocational, with smaller proportions citing personal development (25.6 percent), intellectual development (27.3 percent), and social activity (15.9 percent). For better and for worse, the high school has become irreversibly vocational.

The Degradation of Secondary Education

The years just after World War II were the heyday of the American high school. The rapid expansion of suburbia, with its dependence on the federal highway system, inexpensive houses, and manicured lawns, was also predicated on good schools, and Americans built them at almost every opportunity. The public comprehensive high school became the citadel of American democracy (Hampel, 1986), defending the American way of life and expressing the triumph of education. It connected students to their future working lives, either through direct training for the labor market or through preparation for college, but it also incorporated civics, history, and other expressions of democratic learning. Extracurricular activities also taught the personal attributes— leadership, the responsibilities of group membership, loyalty, initiative—that led to success as community and family members, citizens and wage earners. Athletics, drama, band, and social clubs connected schools to their communities. High schools became teenage social centers where friendship, competition, and the sexual mores of the era could be explored under the watchful eyes of adults. By 1950, 68 percent of the cohort aged fourteen to seventeen were enrolled in high school, in contrast to 8.5 percent in 1900. While critics complained about declining academic standards in the face of international competition and about racial discrimination in education, the combination of open access, comprehensiveness, and curricular differentiation made the high school an enormously popular institution.

By the end of the twentieth century, however, the high school had lost its luster. During the 1970s, critics lamented the isolation of the high school from the world of adults and the world of work. In the 1980s, led by the report *A Nation at Risk* (1983), the low level of academic learning came under withering attack. Other critics noted the shapelessness of the high school, the lack of any central purpose, the fragmentation inherent in the shopping mall curriculum.[11] The high school remained crucial, certainly for students wanting to go on to college, and the costs of dropping out increased as the differences in employment opportunities between dropouts and graduates widened over the 1980s and 1990s. But what had once been viewed as the strongest part of the education system had become its weakest link—and, with the crucial role of college, a weak link at a particularly decisive juncture.

While there are many reasons for the decline of the high school, a number relate directly to vocationalism. Perhaps the most consequential is that the high school has ceased to be a place for any serious endeavor, except for those few students—perhaps 5 to 10 percent—who aspire to highly selective colleges.[12] For the rest, the academic curriculum is something to be endured, since even the pretensions to intellectual mastery have vanished, replaced by the goal of accumulating the credits and grades necessary to get into college. The vocational curriculum itself is not serious, as it is usually fragmented, and even at its best it focuses on low-level jobs without any real benefits in employment; most students drift through the undemanding programs with low aspirations.[13] And certainly the general track, with its "life skills" and courses designed for those bound for unskilled jobs, has never offered serious options, and critics have been right to poke fun at its courses.

Vocational education has failed at its most important goal, connecting schooling to work. An explicitly occupational school might have established close relationships with employers outside the school, breaking down the isolation of the nineteenth-century academic high school. Instead the pattern has been to establish separate vocational programs within comprehensive high schools, very few of which have work-based components. When a round of criticism during the 1970s lambasted high schools for being too isolated from life outside, some experimentation with work experience took place, but most of those efforts were of low quality—many, for example, provided credit for "youth jobs" at fast-food restaurants and gas stations. They were never institutionalized, and they were blown away by the rush to academic education in the 1980s. Similarly, the School-to-Work Opportunities Act of 1994—justified by concerns straight out of the Education Gospel, especially fears about falling productivity and increases in education-related inequality—created federal funding for work experiences in high schools and "connecting activities" between school and work-based components. In practice, however, this led to the minor expansion of conventional activities like counseling, and it expired after five years without much of a trace.[14] Opening up the high school to outside influences has proved difficult, despite its vocational drift and despite the evidence that students value work placements more than other career development activities (Hershey et al., 1998; Stern et al. 1995; Ryken, 2001). Vocational education has failed on its own terms, by its distance from any serious skilled work.

Vocationalism has undermined the academic program as well. Except for the few students vying for places at the top colleges, grades don't make much difference. The second-tier four-year colleges are not especially competitive, since they accept 80 to 90 percent of applicants. For those whose grades and test scores deny them access to state and regional colleges, the community college is available without any entrance requirements—further undermining any incentive to work hard. (Counselors report that students think performance in high school doesn't matter since "we can always make it up in community college.") The irony is that the shift toward college for all, one of the promising features of America's enthusiasm for schooling, has further undermined the motivation for doing well in high school.

A further problem is the disjunction between student perceptions and the reality of the high school. While students acknowledge the importance of high school for vocational reasons (Goodlad, 1984, ch. 2), the school itself is no longer overtly vocational. Explicitly vocational courses have all but vanished from the curriculum. The academic courses do not seem related to future employment, and the vocationalist question—"Why do I have to learn this?"—rarely has a good answer. Textbook chapters often start off with a "real-world" application, but this is usually a thin veneer on a curriculum of conventional drills with decontextualized skills. Little career-oriented guidance and counseling occurs in most high schools—too little to make students think in any serious way about the alternative futures they face, or about the relationship between occupations they might want and the educational decisions they make during high school. Most counselors preach college for all, partly because they fear being charged with tracking students. The majority of teachers do the same, although a few vocational teachers are willing to be realistic with students (Krei and Rosenbaum, 2001; Rosenbaum, 2001). All too often, students drift through high school with no clear ideas about the future. They have high ambitions bred by the glistening attractions of American culture, but no clear plans that might help them realize their ambitions. These students are, as Schneider and Stevenson (1999) have described them, "ambitious but directionless," and for them high school is not a serious place to prepare for future options.

The other traditional purposes of education—moral and civic purposes, the preparation of a new citizenry—have been undermined by vocational goals and by the dreariness of such subjects as history and social studies, now the least-favorite subjects. A few students do find real meaning in civic issues, by participating in student government and in trips to statehouses and Washington, D.C.; an occasional social studies program can breathe new life into the curriculum, and various organizations have urged substantial revision of the social studies curriculum.[15] But no one looks to the high school as a place to revitalize democratic participation, and the periodic mocking of student ignorance about history and geography clarifies the ineffectiveness of high school as a place of civic learning.

A powerful consequence of these trends is that many students have simply become disengaged from learning of any sort. This point has been documented by Laurence Steinberg's (1996, 75) study of 20,000 high school students: "Do students believe in the benefits of schooling?

Yes and no. Students believe in the benefits associated with getting a diploma or a degree, but they are skeptical about the benefits associated with either learning or doing well in class . . . they do not associate later success either with *doing well* in school . . . or with *learning* what schools have to teach. In students' eyes, then, what matters is only whether one graduates—not how well one does or what one learns along the way." John Bishop (1989) has made the same point: what counts in the labor market is the quantity of education an individual has completed, not the quality of learning, and so every student has an incentive to continue as long as possible without expending more than the minimum amount of effort to pass. This leads to overeducation, or more accurately overschooling, in which students get more schooling than they need for the jobs they are likely to get, a theme we develop more fully in Chapter 7. Since academic achievement has become virtually irrelevant for most students, the high school has become a warehouse with a variety of controls designed to hold students until they are ready to move on to college and begin serious preparation for life's goals.

The inequities of the high school also undermine its legitimacy as a place of serious learning. The movement for vocational education promised to provide a place for every student, just as the common school had—if not in the college track, then in one of the vocational tracks or the general track. But the differences among these tracks, including the class, race, and gender inequities that mirror those of the labor force, have made it increasingly difficult to accept the multitracked high school as an expression of equal opportunity. Even after the detracking movement of the 1980s and 1990s eliminated a great deal of formal tracking, informal tracking persists (Lucas, 1999). It reflects deeper issues than ways of grouping students, including differences in academic preparation inherited from middle schools, the structure of course prerequisites, variation in the availability of college-track and AP courses, and variation in the motivation of students from different backgrounds in large, impersonal institutions (National Research Council, 2003). Among high school graduates, some have passed four or five AP courses and are ready to jump to their sophomore year in an elite college, while others read at the sixth-grade level and face years of remediation if they do manage to enroll in community colleges. In this world of extremes, it's no wonder that *A Nation at Risk* and other expressions of the Education Gospel have chastised the schools for producing "a rising tide of mediocrity" of students at the bottom, or that international comparisons find our students on the average lagging behind those of other countries. If the high school has become largely a warehouse, there's no reason for most students to make much academic or vocational effort.

The most obvious evidence of the degradation of the high school is the high rate at which students drop out before graduation. While Americans were rightly proud of the movement toward high school for all that took place over most of the twentieth century, this vision has been marred by dropout rates between 25 and 30 percent.[16] Recently dropout rates have increased, from about 19 percent in 1993 to about 25 percent of each cohort. These figures are much worse in urban districts and for minority students. For example, Green (2001) found a national graduation rate of 74 percent in 1998, but only 52 percent in New York City, with the black graduation rate 42 percent and the Latino rate 45 percent, compared with 80 percent among whites. A century after educators articulated the goal of high school for all, and well after we have established a new goal of college for all, an extraordinary number of students still do not graduate from high school.

Unfortunately, current "solutions" for the high school are unlikely to improve matters, and may make them worse. In increasing exasperation, legislators turned first to expanding high school graduation requirements, expressed in conventional academic coursework, and then to accountability measures based on standardized tests in English and math, and now to exit exams requiring basic academic competence before graduating. Expecting more from high schools and from students is not the problem; indeed, that is part of the solution to making the high school a place of serious endeavor. But schools have been subjected to accountability requirements without the additional resources to meet these new goals, especially in urban areas. The simple-minded accountability measures are usually different from the standards that states have established for subjects; and the competencies tested—basic English and math, for the most part—are hardly the complex "skills of the twenty-first century" that the Education Gospel has promoted. Some tests—particularly exit exams—are likely to exacerbate the dropout rate, increasing the numbers of students with dire prospects in the labor market. The accountability movement is just "more of the

same"—more of the academic content that seems pointless in a vocationalized high school.

Finding Ways Out

Given the crisis of the high school, particularly the lack of serious
learning and the rampant inequities, what are the ways out? First, it is
imperative that high schools be reconstituted as communities with a
clear sense of purpose, and with something serious to accomplish.[17]
What constitutes a serious endeavor should vary, of course, since not
all students are drawn to the same goals. For some, it might be explor-
ing literature, or the humanities more generally, even by returning to
the morally tinged curriculum of the nineteenth century or to Great
Books programs, while others would explore a greater range of literature by women, by racial minorities, by non-Western authors, in what
have become standard courses in the high school curriculum. For other
students, a serious high school might examine political issues, perhaps
using city, state, and federal politics as "texts," developing political
projects in the community, establishing a political community within
the high school (Power, 1985), or engaging in service learning. Others
might take up environmental concerns, studying the underlying science, politics, and economics while engaging in restoration and conservation projects. Many magnet schools now have themes that combine some curricular choice with focused study: science and technology
schools, performing arts schools, health magnet schools, the Aviation
High School in New York, an agriculture magnet school in Chicago.

The most appealing theme-based schools focus on a broad occupational area—what we have labeled "education through occupations,"
recalling John Dewey's (1916b, ch. 23) argument that "education
through occupations consequently combines within itself more of the
factors conducive to learning than any other method." These programs
typically emphasize an array of related occupations rather than the narrow occupations of traditional vocational education—health occupations, rather than nurse assistants; industrial production, rather than
welding. Such a broad occupational focus is elastic enough to encompass a variety of learning, including standard academic subjects, and
allows for the integration of academic and occupational education.

These programs have generally restructured the high school in several
ways, creating schools within schools, or clusters, that reduce the scale
and anonymity of high school, focus the curricular clutter, and often
incorporate work-based learning. In almost every way, programs of
"education through occupations" provide a distinct alternative to traditional vocational education *and* conventional academic education. As
Stern (1999) has emphasized in calling this approach "college and careers," the programs prepare students both for college and further
learning (as traditional voc ed did not), or for employment and future
work responsibilities, or for the combination of further education and
employment that has become so common. Broadly defined occupational themes also have some advantages over other themes: they help
eliminate the disjunction between the students' occupational goals and
the academic focus of the high school, and they help students focus on
their future options and on the connections to schooling. The prelimi-
nary evidence indicates that these reforms can, when properly implemented, enhance the motivation and engagement of high school students, reduce dropout rates, and increase the number of students who
go on to college.[18]

Second, creating serious activities in high schools, particularly
around themes of some inherent interest and connection to the world
outside the high school, would become much easier if high schools
were smaller, or if schools within schools were created to promote
more coherent communities of learning. The large high school dates
from the period around 1900, when the drive for efficiency dictated
large schools to realize economies of scale. In the 1950s, James Conant
called for the consolidation of small high schools, since he was concerned that only large schools could provide the extensive array of
courses, including laboratories and advanced academic curricula, that
he believed the most talented students required. In retrospect, it has
become clear that large schools with more facilities and more courses
miss the essential nature of learning communities. The fragmented
curriculum of most shopping mall high schools undermines their capacity to provide any common purpose that might strengthen the desire to learn. In contrast, schools within schools, theme-based schools,
charter schools, magnet schools, and schools where teachers stay with
their students as they progress hold out some hope that common purposes built on a community of learners can be used to restore coher-

ence, engagement, and motivation, closer relationships with peers and teachers, and more focused attention to subjects that matter.[19]

Third, high schools would be dramatically strengthened by connecting academic learning and school experiences with life outside of school. Increasingly, social studies teaching has turned to student projects to create connections between school and what takes place in political life. Similarly, service learning has emerged as a serious alternative, providing placements out of school and internships that develop a sense of community and responsibility, always part of civic education. For some theme-based high schools, out-of-school activities are obvious: environmental academies can engage in environmental protection and reconstruction, and a school-within-a-school focused on the economic and cultural life of cities can map local cities (Rosenstock and Steinberg, 1995a, 1995b; Steinberg 1998). For "education through occupations," work-based internships and co-op placements—*if* they are carefully constructed and supervised—provide other kinds of learning, other teachers (supervisors), and peers (coworkers), along with complementary perspectives to learning within school. Creating a greater array of related activities outside schools would redress one of the great ironies of vocational education: its belief that the best way to prepare youth for work was to keep them in school, disconnected from the workplace. Creating new forms of learning outside schools is not a simple or short-term activity. The struggle of service learning to establish itself, and the demise of work-based learning both in the 1970s and again in the 1990s, indicate that considerable funding will be necessary over substantial periods of development, and that out-of-school activities must be aligned with in-school instruction. But the alternative is to continue the high school as an institution cloistered from political, economic, and community life, to the detriment of students looking for something real to do.

Fourth, secondary schools need to do a better job of clarifying students' future options and their relationship to both secondary and postsecondary education. Almost as soon as educators began developing vocational alternatives a century ago, some understood that students should be prepared to make educational and occupational choices, and the field of career guidance emerged (Parsons, 1909). Over the years, however, career guidance has been steadily displaced, first by personal counseling related to students' psychological issues, then by academic counseling to help students get through required courses and apply to college, and more recently by mounds and mounds of paperwork. The result is that very few students gain access to any systematic career guidance. What little exists either preaches college for all or follows trait-and-factor approaches, determining student interests and matching them to occupations, sometimes belittled as "test 'em and tell 'em." When counselors do provide career information, it is often in the form of an "information dump," quite useless for unsophisticated students (Grubb, 2002b; Grubb and Watson, 2002). So while resources in counseling are clearly inadequate, it wouldn't do much good simply to increase the numbers of conventional counselors. The more promising approaches are embedded in the curriculum, including career guidance as part of "education through occupations." Another model is the Puente program in California, which supports counselors who work actively with teachers as well as students and parents, and who serve many different roles in helping students think about their educational and occupational futures. The National School Counselor Training Initiative envisions counselors who diagnose problems and work with teachers and students to develop systematic solutions to school issues, rather than engaging simply in one-on-one counseling. Yet another approach is for every adult in a high school to be assigned to a small group of students that they stay with as long as the students are at the school; they maintain regular contact with students and their families to develop a broad view of the students' needs and ensure their access to counseling and other forms of support.[20] But without serious improvement in the practice of career counseling, too many students will continue to drift through high school clueless about why they are there.

Finally, and most difficult of all, the high school will never emerge from its vale of criticism unless it becomes more equitable. We have already mentioned some approaches to equity. Theme-based schools, smaller learning communities, out-of-school activities including internships and service learning, and revamping career guidance are in part efforts to help the least motivated students find their places in the high school. The problem is that too many other school practices contribute to inequality, including the lack of well-qualified teachers in many urban schools; the mobility of students themselves (often caused by housing problems) as well as the instability of teachers, principals, and superintendents; the chaotic politics of urban school districts; the lack of adequate resources, documented in new rounds of court cases; inadequate access among low-income students to health care, mental health services, and other support services.[21] The equity agenda requires reshaping the high school's relationship to both academic and occupational education, but its origins are deeper than the conflicts over vocationalism, and its solutions must be similarly comprehensive. We will address these solutions more fully in Chapters 5 and 8, including health and mental health policies, housing polices to reduce student instability in living conditions, and better approaches to shoring up the incomes of both the working and the nonworking poor. While high schools can reform the practices associated with their own missions, they can solve their most difficult problems only with an equity agenda that extends outside the schools.

In the end, reconstructing the high school requires giving it some meaning of its own. If the curriculum is important only in instrumental ways, as preparation for college or later employment, then it is simply something to endure while waiting for something else. If high school is merely a locus for socializing, then it is again dispensable, since social life can take place in other places, outside of school hours. If the curriculum has no intrinsic value, calls to learn will continue to fall by the wayside, and the threats to enforce learning through high-stakes tests are likely to do little good. The real challenge is to tie educational standards to the world around us, recasting academic disciplines *and* vocational applications, connecting private and personal goals to intellectual, civic, and moral values. Only then will young people better understand that world, and be equipped to explore its richness and to start formulating roles in it for themselves. Only then will the high school reach its potential as the citadel of American democracy and the safeguard of the American dream.

2

～ Professionalism in Higher Education

$\mathcal{I}$N MANY WAYS the fullest expression of vocationalism has taken place in America's colleges and universities. As higher education became a mass institution by exalting its public purposes—its benefits to the nation's economy, the protection of national defense, the creation of new knowledge, and the promise of equal educational opportunity—its private benefits in helping individuals gain access to professional status and earnings became its dominant rationale. Despite occasional sound bites extolling the entrepreneurial college dropout—like Ray Kroc of McDonald's and Bill Gates of Microsoft—higher education is now the clearest embodiment of the American dream of getting ahead through one's own labor.

The process of vocationalizing colleges and universities proceeded in a series of steps that allowed for steady expansion. The growth has been extraordinary. In 1870 about 563 institutions were identified as four-year colleges and universities. By 1900 that number had almost doubled to 977. In 1970 there were 1,639 four-year colleges and universities, and the number now stands at 2,450. In 1900 only 2.3 percent of those aged eighteen to twenty-four went to college; in 2000, 36 percent of this group attended college. In 1940, only 4.5 percent of the entire population had completed four years of college; by the end of the century it was 25.2 percent. About 63 percent of high school graduates

56

now continue on to some form of postsecondary schooling. Americans have overwhelmingly supported this expansion, expecting governments to subsidize postsecondary education through state universities and community colleges as well as tax-free college savings plans, tax credits, and grants and loans. College for all, a ridiculous idea a hundred years ago, seems within our grasp at the beginning of the new century.[1]

At the same time, the nature of the college degree has changed as the number of those entering vocational (or professional) fields has expanded from very few in the 1880s, before most professional schools were established, to about two-thirds of graduating students in 2000. Particularly with the creation of second-tier comprehensive public universities—the less-selective institutions ranked below flagship universities, such as the California State University system—higher education has both expanded and become substantially vocational (or professional) in its purposes. For individuals, the expansion of higher education makes sense because it now enjoys a virtual monopoly over access to professional status and the highest earnings. Higher education is now inescapably vocational. As just about every high school counselor tells students: Without a college degree, don't count on being economically successful or entering a profession.

But the vocationalizing of higher education has brought dissent from those dubious about the creation of a mass system. The critiques have taken many forms, but they often reflect concern that vocational purposes have overwhelmed traditional moral, civic, and intellectual goals, fragmenting the collegiate curriculum and corrupting the very idea of what is an educated person. Other critics worry that the focus on preparing students for their occupational futures has created a structure of educational inequality, even as it has increased access to postsecondary schooling. Still others contend that advanced schooling is not an especially good way to prepare people for work because it distances them from the workplace, where genuine job training occurs. And yet, despite the chorus of doubts, there appears to be no serious counter to the view that higher education is necessary to meet the needs of a technologically complex economy and to prepare individuals for professional and managerial vocations. The Education Gospel and the knowledge economy point in the same direction—toward more postsecondary education within a vocationalized system.

From Moral to Vocational Purposes

America's colleges did not begin as vocational institutions, at least not in the way we currently use the term. Instead early Americans believed that the classic liberal arts were essential to prepare moral, civic, and intellectual leaders, and that one's vocation (often as a minister) emerged out of a broad preparation for leadership. The goal of higher education was therefore to hone character and discipline the intellect. As President Dunster of Harvard declared in the late seventeenth century (Rudolph, 1962, 6): "You shall take care to advance in all learning, divine and humane, each and every student who is or will be entrusted to your tutelage, according to their several abilities; and especially to take care that their conduct and manners be honorable and without blame." College was not meant for everybody, since by design it was intended to prepare only the few leaders of society's institutions.

During the nineteenth century the synthesis of moral, civic, and intellectual purposes in higher education eroded, eventually giving way to professional goals. The first glimmers of more utilitarian goals came with the establishment of West Point in 1802, of Rensselaer Polytechnic in 1824, and of agricultural colleges in the 1850s. Advocates for usefulness, in favor of including science rather than the humanities and modern languages rather than ancient ones like Greek and Latin, grew in number. The concept of useful knowledge—rooted in practice and experience, and expanded through the application of scientific methods—began to spread.

When the Morrill Act was passed in 1862, providing federal land to the states to establish land-grant universities, the U.S. Congress formally recognized the role of higher education in preparing people for vocations. The Morrill Act required each state to establish at least one institution "to teach such branches of learning as are related to agriculture and the mechanic arts . . . in order to promote the liberal and practical education of the industrial classes in the several pursuits and professions in life." The emphasis on the liberal *and* the practical suggested that the traditional values of intellectual, moral, and civic learning should coexist with the newer expectation that learning be practical and vocational. Like the manual training movement in high schools, the land-grant colleges provided a bridge between older ideals of liberal education and newer conceptions of occupational education. Senator Morrill called himself "a liberal educator for the industrial classes." The dean of the School of Engineering at the University of Wisconsin noted that "scientific agriculture, mining, manufacturing, and commerce will in the future form the material foundation of all high and noble living" (Veysey, 1965, 79).

Passage of the Morrill Act had been contentious, and not just because of federal participation. Many expressed doubt that going to college was a good way to prepare for employment; college-based preparation for work was viewed as "academic," irrelevant, even sissified. Leading figures, like the industrialist and self-made man Andrew Carnegie, dismissed school-based learning in favor of the school of experience: "While the college student has been learning a little about the barbarous and petty squabbles of a far-distant past, or trying to master languages that are dead . . . the future captain of industry is hotly engaged in the school of experience, obtaining the very knowledge required for his triumphs." Even those advocating better training for agricultural and industrial occupations, like Jonathan Turner of Illinois, argued that it was absurd "attempting to educate the man of work in unknown tongues, abstract problems and theories, and metaphysical figments, and quibbles." Others simply said, "We want no fancy farmers; we want no fancy mechanics."[2]

The growth of the land-grant institutions was initially slow, and then it accelerated around 1900. In 1896, 57 land-grant institutions enrolled 14,000 students, amounting to about 6 percent of the country's 977 collegiate institutions and 238,000 students. A little more than a decade later, in 1910, the land-grant colleges enrolled 20 percent of all college students (Eddy, 1957, ch. 4). The land-grant school leaders saw their institutions' future less as technical training institutions and more as universities with broad public responsibilities. State universities came to symbolize the view that practical knowledge and liberal education could be combined with occupational preparation, offering students a wide range of subject matter from which to choose. The president of the University of Wisconsin, Charles Van Hise, articulated in 1903 the fundamental rationale that ultimately shaped American higher education: "Be the choice of the sons and daughters of the state, language, literature, history, political economy, pure science, agriculture, engineering, architecture, sculpture, painting or music, they should find at the state university ample opportunity for the pursuit of the chosen subject . . . Nothing short of such opportunity is just, for each has an equal right to find at the state university the advanced intellectual life adapted to his need."[3] During the nineteenth century some other institutions had already adopted this view. A number of small colleges had diversified their liberal arts curricula to attract more students, introducing vocationally oriented courses to increase their students' job opportunities and serve the communities in which they were located. Often these multipurpose colleges established separate departments of science, engineering, and agriculture, instituted short courses for commercial occupations, and prepared women for teaching (Geiger, 2000a).

The shift in higher education toward more explicitly vocational purposes was initially connected to moral and civic goals. Higher education had treated knowledge and moral values—the combination of intellect and character—as a unified whole. At many colleges the final year included a required course in moral philosophy that sought to reconcile moral and secular values. Even as new subjects, including the sciences, entered the curriculum, knowledge still had to serve a moral purpose. But the integration of the moral and the secular weakened considerably during the first decades of the twentieth century, especially at the research universities that were reshaping higher education. The new view treated the search for scientific truth as removed from ethical concerns. The methodologies and language of scholarly experts required advanced training, a professional credential (the PhD), and specialized expertise at the expense of any moral or civic purposes, which were deemed irrelevant to the conduct of science (Reuben, 1996).

While the separation of science and research from moral and civic values came to dominate the research tradition, it has always been controversial. Dissent emerges periodically in demands that universities be moral institutions resisting investmenting in immoral corporations (like those operating in apartheid South Africa) or opposing immoral research (like weapons development or corporate-sponsored research). Dissent exists in efforts to expand racial and class diversity as an expression of equity and to adopt moral positions about what a society should look like. It persists in the assertion of the liberal arts and general education as values-based learning, and it has recently appeared in "service learning" that engages students in political and social activities. Some colleges have retained religious affiliations and seek as institutions to speak in moral terms. The ethos of a moral and civic purpose to higher education has never disappeared, but it has become a minority view in the world of scholarly research and in the vocational preparation of students.

The Rise of the Professions

The growth of professional schools after 1880 redefined the relation of higher education to the labor market. The idea of the professional became someone who possessed expert knowledge and a specialized vocabulary, best learned in college or graduate school rather than on the job. Between 1880 and the 1930s, the appearance of schools of business, engineering, education, social work, nursing, and dentistry, and the growth of law and medical schools, led to a dramatic shift in the way individuals entered the professions. The proportion of undergraduates enrolled in professional majors rather than academic subjects grew from almost none in the 1880s to about 60 percent in the 1930s and 1940s—jumping to a majority of students in just fifty years.[4]

One reason for the explosion in postsecondary professional preparation was the development of a clear educational trajectory, from high school to college to professional employment, in place of a simultaneous process of schooling and working. Through the end of the nineteenth century, no profession—not even medicine, law, or engineering—required a college degree to practice. Professional preparation took place on the job, sometimes under apprenticeship arrangements but often on one's own; one started to work in an occupation and moved in and out of formal schooling as necessary. Lawyers might attend lectures, but they also trained through apprenticeship methods, by clerking in law offices; many physicians acquired degrees from medical schools after they began to practice, and some never received any degree. The basic pattern was to go to school as one found it necessary or useful, but the lack of schooling did not stand in the way of practicing (Kett, 1994; Douglas, 1921, ch. 1).

This pattern reflected a relatively dim view of school-based preparation, as well as the absence of clear differentiation among educational institutions. In the nineteenth century, colleges, academies, and high schools were often interchangeable, and a high school diploma was rarely required for enrollment in college. Most institutions labeled "colleges" were really secondary schools. To improve their status, a number of colleges and universities established admissions agreements with local high schools, certifying their graduates for college enrollment if they met certain academic standards. In the early twentieth century, this sequence from high school to college was reinforced with the founding of the College Entrance Examination Board, which developed standardized tests for admission to college, ultimately leading to today's SAT (Johanek, 2001). These changes meant that working professionals could no longer simply enroll for a few courses in a local college, since a high school education was a prerequisite.

The movement of occupational preparation into colleges and universities—always called *professional* education to distinguish it from lower-level *vocational* education in high schools—was closely tied to the growing authority of science. Every profession created a liturgy about the importance of specialized knowledge—biology and chemistry for doctors, legal procedure and precedent for lawyers, applied science for engineers—and it was scientific knowledge that enabled professionals to serve their clients better and to benefit society. These claims seem self-serving in retrospect, but they also had considerable merit. The requirements of structural engineering in building the modern city went beyond what could be learned on the job. Better understanding of disease required more sophisticated knowledge than day-to-day practice could teach. Those responsible for directing and assessing enormous corporations needed to understand economic principles and the techniques of accounting.

Since professional expertise required greater scientific understanding, school-based knowledge came to be more highly prized than work-based knowledge. Useful knowledge evolved from a concept rooted in the workshop and experience, augmented by scientific study —epitomized by Ben Franklin, carrying out his humble experiments with kites in thunderstorms—to one rooted in the university laboratory and scientific procedure. In an example that has widespread parallels, Cornell University's engineering school began with a "shop" orientation but changed after 1885 to an academic model with higher admission standards and two years of required coursework. The conception of the professional, dependent on specialized knowledge learned in school rather than practical knowledge, now separated him or her from the production worker.[5] A professional needed a deep conceptual understanding in order to penetrate "beyond the rich confusion of ordinary experience as he isolated and controlled the factors, hidden to the untrained eye, which made an elaborate system workable or impractical, successful or unattainable" (Bledstein, 1978)—not merely the "ordinary experience" of a production worker.

As formal schooling displaced experience and apprenticeship methods, higher education standardized the necessary expertise by using easily recognized criteria to certify professional knowledge—entrance examinations, formal courses of study, degree requirements, and (in conjunction with national and state oversight boards) licensing examinations. Doctors and lawyers now had to become licensed before they practiced; between 1870 and 1918 the proportion of engineers graduating from engineering schools grew from 11 percent to 50 percent. America's traditional faith in self-education, or education on the job, was transformed into a belief that going to school—and especially learning a curriculum connected to professional requirements—was crucial.

The history of every profession reveals the same story: determined efforts to shift preparation away from apprenticeship methods and work experience toward graduation from specialized university programs including, in many cases, graduate school. Medicine, law, and engineering were the most obvious examples, but the pattern even included occupations like business, education, social work, and nursing, which had lower status, weaker control over the conditions of entry, and greater proportions of women.[6] The process continued throughout the twentieth century and it continues still, reaching lower and lower in the hierarchy of occupational status and earnings in what we describe in Chapter 5 as the self-reinforcing nature of vocationalism. To be sure, such developments have always been resisted by an old guard, and the effectiveness of professional education continues to be controversial, as we examine later in this chapter. But continuing disagreements over precisely what a professional education should include has not slowed its growth as the central characteristic of American higher education.

The occupational role of higher education was not widely recognized before World War II. As late as 1940, only 9 percent of the country's eighteen- to twenty-four-year-olds were enrolled in college, and many people viewed college primarily as a social experience. But by the

1930s, college attendance was tied to what David Levine (1986) has called "the culture of aspiration." In cities, the children of working-class parents and immigrants flooded into low-cost public colleges, often as part-time students in evening classes, to gain access to the professions and middle-class status. As more students sought entry into higher-status colleges, selective admissions emerged, along with quotas to keep out those who might not "fit in." The growing public universities expanded their curricula, adding more occupational programs to attract students. When enrollments expanded during the 1920s and 1930s, they did so within institutions that had already established professional schools and majors. And with expansion came increases in the proportion of students in those professional programs: from 25 and 30 percent in the years between 1910 and 1920, when only 3 percent of the relevant cohort was enrolled, to about 35 percent in the 1920s, when 6 to 7 percent of the cohort was in college, to between 50 and 60 percent in the 1930s and 1940s, when 7.5 to 9 percent of the relevant age group was enrolled (Brint et al., 2002).

By the mid-twentieth century, the current structure of higher education was in place, with large numbers of colleges emphasizing professional preparation to attract enrollments and a majority of students in professional rather than academic programs. Increasing high school graduation rates, combined with the monopoly that higher education claimed over entry into the professions, gave higher education new status. When America's soldiers returned from World War II, the GI Bill provided them with federal money to attend college. The chance to get ahead through schooling was irresistible.

The System Vocationalized

After World War II, the Education Coalition that had earlier sought universal high school attendance used its power to expand higher education. During the cold war, colleges and universities became crucial to providing technological training for the nation's defense and for economic competition with the Soviet Union. The Education Coalition united behind the expansion of postsecondary education: students trying to get ahead, backed by their parents; educational institutions seeking to expand; policy makers responding to these pressures; and social reformers seeking access for nontraditional students. States created more low-tuition public universities and community colleges, and as a result students in public institutions climbed from 49 percent of enrollments in 1947 to 76 percent by the end of the century, including 35 percent in community colleges and perhaps another 25 percent in second-tier public universities.[7]

While the post–World War II expansion drew on a rhetoric of public purposes, students attended college because of the possibilities for individual gain. One measure of advancing vocationalism was the attitude of students, reflected in an annual survey of freshmen. In the late 1960s, developing a meaningful philosophy of life was the most important goal of freshmen, rated "essential" or "very important" by 80 percent of respondents, while fewer than 45 percent thought it important to be well-off financially. At the end of the century these two values had traded places: developing a meaningful philosophy was most important for only 42 percent of freshmen, while 74 percent cited being well-off financially (Astin, 1998).

Another measure of vocationalism was the continued expansion of course and program offerings; colleges did everything possible to attract more students. The typical undergraduate at a university in the 1990s chose from a catalog that offered 3,000 to 5,000 courses. Even at much smaller colleges, the number of courses ranged from 800 to 1,500, revealing the triumph of the shopping mall college, parallel to the shopping mall high school. Such expansion brought the familiar problems of curricular chaos, lack of focus, student uncertainty, competition for students, grade inflation, and the relentless vocational questions: "How is this relevant?" and, in response to general education requirements, "Why should I have to take this?"

Probably the clearest measure of professional purpose is the continued drift toward explicitly occupational majors. While the 1960s with their idealism and economic expansion saw a slight fall in occupational majors, from 62 percent in 1959–60 to 58 percent in 1970–71, the proportion went back up to about 65 percent in 1987–88 and then declined slightly during the expansionary period of the 1990s. These figures are probably underestimates; at the beginning of the twenty-first century, it's safe to say, two-thirds to three-fourths of undergraduates are in fields with overtly vocational goals. Virtually every field of study that has seen growth in the past few decades has been occupational, including business, health professions and biology, computer systems, and various recreation studies. No liberal arts fields have grown relative to other fields except for psychology and the life sciences, both closely linked to health occupations, and two small fields labeled liberal/general studies and interdisciplinary studies. The result has been a substantial shift in higher education (Brint et al., 2002): "During a period in which the system grew by 50 percent, almost every field which constituted the old liberal arts core of the undergraduate college was in absolute decline."

The late twentieth-century expansion also reflected the egalitarian commitment of American society to those "nontraditional" students who might not otherwise go to college—those whose parents had not been educated past high school, lower-income and minority students, immigrants who might get ahead through schooling and avoid the menial work their parents had done. Once equality of educational opportunity became a widespread ideal after 1900, and once higher education became the route to the professions, it was impossible to prevent the system from expanding for all students, not just an elite preparing to be leaders. The federal government contributed grants and loans for low-income students; the states subsidized their systems of higher education and created a variety of outreach programs for nontraditional students. Colleges and universities adopted various forms of affirmative action, providing increasing opportunities for minorities, sometimes low-income students, and women (especially in nontraditional fields) to jump the admissions queue, justified once again by both social goals—the promise of a better-integrated society—and individual incentives (Bowen and Bok, 1998).

In addition, a number of institutional transformations have helped the development of more vocational forms of higher education. One has been the shopping mall college, with its increasing amounts of student choice, in place of the nineteenth-century college's prescribed curriculum. To be sure, faculty still seek to exert control over what is taught, and professional organizations impose requirements on occupational majors. But the student choices *among* institutions, and the choices of majors *within* institutions, determine most of the curriculum. If humanities departments have declined and business schools increased, if general education seems to be a sideshow compared with specialized majors, if the balance of "the liberal and practical" threatens to come apart, the combination of access to the professions and student choice is to blame. Currently it seems quaint to envision a college with a single curriculum, and those that try—St. John's College with its Great Books program, Columbia with its prescribed freshman courses —have not been widely emulated. Indeed, the expansion of student choice is consistent with the bewildering array of occupations needing specialized preparation, as well as the general preference for choice in a liberal society. But the dark side of student choice is the power it has given to professional aspirations and to the ethos of getting ahead in shaping the contemporary college and university.

The most dramatic expressions of vocationalism appear in the two largest and fastest growing sectors of postsecondary education: community colleges, which we examine in Chapter 3, and the second-tier, comprehensive public universities. Both institutions respond to regional and local labor market demands, but the comprehensive universities have especially welcomed those occupations trying to gain professional status by embedding themselves in universities. Most second-tier comprehensives evolved from teacher-training colleges or technical and agricultural colleges, and therefore originated as explicitly occupational institutions; others emerged from multipurpose colleges, or from junior colleges to which two more years of study were added. While they provide a vast array of academic and professional offerings, they are overwhelming occupational, enrolling 80 percent or more of their students in professional fields; almost none of them has recreated the old liberal arts colleges (except Evergreen State College in Washington and St. Mary's College in Maryland). They are much less selective than the first-tier universities and often accept 80 to 90 percent of students who apply. Perhaps reflecting this fact, their graduation rates are often low, mostly in the range of 40 to 55 percent but with a distressing number graduating only 25 to 40 percent.[8] Every state has established such institutions: they are the California State Universities, as opposed to the University of California system; the state colleges in Texas rather than the universities; the Universities of Western and Northern Illinois rather than the University of Illinois at Urbana-Champaign.[9] These second-tier institutions now account for about 57 percent of public university enrollments and about 37 percent of all postsecondary enrollments. They are now the most common institutions of higher education, even if the ideal continues to be the private liberal arts colleges like Swarthmore and Oberlin, or the large research universities like Harvard and Berkeley. So the enrollment growth of the post–World War II era has taken place in the creation and expansion of highly professionalized institutions—more evidence of how expansion and vocationalism have gone hand in hand.

Even private liberal arts colleges have turned into vocational institutions, a phenomenon that was already apparent in the 1950s (McGrath and Russell, 1958). When David Breneman (1994) went searching for liberal arts colleges, most of them had become "small professional schools with a liberal arts tradition, but little of the reality of a traditional liberal college." Defining liberal arts colleges as residential institutions that award most degrees in academic subjects, he concluded that only 212 of the 540 colleges so labeled deserved the distinction. In the less selective ones, the proportion of professional degrees increased from 41 percent in 1972 to 64 percent in 1988. Breneman concluded that "we are indeed losing many of our liberal arts colleges, not through closures but through steady change into a different type of institution"—driven by the combination of student choice and vocational pressure.

Of course, some genuine liberal arts colleges persist, the Swarthmores, Reeds, and Wellesleys—all private, all expensive, and all selective. But they too have seen a subtle transformation, since a high proportion of their students continue on to graduate school, where their real vocational preparation takes place. Like the academic track in high school that prepares students to enter college, the academic curriculum of the selective liberal arts college also serves an indirect vocational purpose, even though the college itself offers a respite from immediate vocational pressures. Thus the liberal arts college, too, has become vocationalized.

America's greatest educational success story has been the creation of a mass system of higher education inextricably linked to occupational purposes. Students come to get ahead, to become credentialed and licensed in the labor market. By now many believe, rightly, that they have no choice. The deterioration of the labor market for high school graduates, who have to settle for low-skill, low-paid, and insecure work, has meant that going to college is a much better bet than finding a job right after high school. The pressure to go beyond college for graduate professional training furthers vocationalism, in a self-reinforcing process. Along the way, older conceptions of character and intellect have given way to newer ideals of professional skill, and the institutions comprising the postsecondary landscape have changed irreversibly.

Dilemmas of the Professionalized University

The development of higher education, over the past fifty years in particular, has had a number of triumphs: expanding enrollments, greater funding, a central role in the economy, and greater access for nontraditional students. Colleges and universities are treasured places, refuges from the outside world, where dissent and free speech are valued and where culture and intellect can thrive in many forms. The country's research universities are revered for their national and international contributions; comprehensive state universities are important to their regional communities in similar ways; and many community colleges are the focus of their community. The benefits of an expansive higher education system are extraordinary.

And yet criticism abounds, captured by such book titles as *The Fall of the American University, Illiberal Education, Dry Rot in the Ivory Tower, The Moral Collapse of the University, ProfScam, The Hollow Men* (a reference to faculty, of course), and *The Closing of the American Mind*. Some criticize the faculty, some the students, and others contrast the older image of college with the more utilitarian reality of a vocationalized university (Lazerson, 1998). The irony is that vocationalism, which has allowed postsecondary education to expand, has created many of these controversies, particularly the complaints about the decline of liberal education and the pressures for equity. And the professional drift of colleges and universities has propelled them into the arena of public debate over the adequacy of professional preparation. While vocationalism has elevated higher education from its marginal status of a century ago, it has also brought more intense conflict.

The Fragility of Liberal Education

Critics of rampant vocationalism have often concentrated on making the curriculum serve intellectual and civic purposes, particularly through general education, the re-creation of the humanities, and restatements of public goals.[10] They invariably have battled against overwhelming trends: the rise in professional majors; the large number of professionally dominated institutions, like the second-tier universities, with weak traditions of liberal education; and the conversion of many liberal arts colleges into comprehensive institutions. Faculties are themselves divided about what higher education means. Business and medical faculties vote along with philosophers and English professors. In many institutions, the occupational faculty outweighs the academic faculty, in both numbers and status. Without faculty consensus, it is unclear where the defense of liberal education can come from—not from students with their increasingly utilitarian goals, not from policymakers with their concern about benefits and costs, and certainly not from the community of employers with its emphasis on the bottom line. The Education Coalition tends to fall apart around liberal or general education. The liberal arts have not been eliminated, of course, but professional domination means that older justifications of the curriculum's civic, intellectual, and moral purposes are not what most faculty or students think higher education is about.

The weakening of *liberal* education has been hastened by its conversion to *general* education. The nineteenth-century curriculum was almost wholly prescribed by the college, to cultivate intellect and piety. The early twentieth-century versions, like the Great Books program at the University of Chicago or the Contemporary Civilization curriculum at Columbia University, continued the tradition of compulsory courses. But the notion of a required liberal education gave way in the last half of the twentieth century. The efforts at Harvard after World War II illustrate how difficult it was to make the case for required moral and civic education. *General Education in a Free Society* (1947), the most famous of the modern general education proposals, called for one course in Great Texts of Literature and another in Western Thought and Institutions. But the Harvard faculty could not limit itself to a core curriculum and added multiple options, so that the general education program became a set of unrelated courses from which students could chose. Since then most colleges and universities have justified general education as a way of preparing well-rounded individuals, but it has entailed multiple and disconnected electives—like the rest of the shopping mall curriculum. While faculties regularly debate gen-ed requirements, they have abandoned the effort to determine what knowledge would create the best citizens. As a committee of the Stanford University faculty put it in 1968, "The University cannot in any event impress upon its students the total content of present knowledge, and it is impossible to choose what exactly it is that every student should know without imposing arbitrary constraints on the range of free inquiry." Instead, professors teach their specialties and students have the freedom "to discover new interests . . . and to explore the many fields and endeavors" available (Levine, 1996, ch. 3).

Other aspects of student choice have further weakened coherent programs of liberal education. Both traditional-age students and older students have shifted toward a pattern sometimes referred to as "swirling," taking courses at a variety of institutions and accumulating degrees credit by credit. Often the result is a patchwork of courses without any coherence, a potpourri lacking the consistency that might emerge at a single institution (Smith, 1993).

Finally, even the courses included in general education requirements have been redirected toward the ubiquitous "skills of the twenty-first century." George Mason University requires students to take courses in oral communications, written communications, quantitative reasoning, information technology, and global understanding as well as more conventional breadth requirements. James Madison University has defined Cluster One of its general education program as "Skills for the 21st Century" including "effective oral and written communication, critical thinking, and technology used for interpersonal communication and information retrieval." The California State University campuses require oral communication, written communication, and critical thinking as well as what Chico State calls "lifelong learning," which includes "life skills" like child development, human sexuality, basic nutrition, and leisure pursuits. Southwest Texas State requires a physical fitness and wellness course as part of gen ed, something that can be fulfilled with a varsity sport, the marching band, or Strutters (a drill team). It is easy to get on the Web and find examples of general education run amuck—all well-intentioned, all related to some worthy purpose, but far from the intellectual discipline and moral intention of the liberal arts ideal.

The decline of liberal education is an example of "death by a thousand cuts," particularly the transformation of student and faculty goals and the exaltation of student choice as part of vocationalism. The intellectual and moral traditions associated with liberal education are most vibrant in institutions where occupational pressures are postponed, in the elite private and public colleges where most students will go on to graduate school for their occupational preparation. The defenders of intellectual and civic traditions continue to fight, but with limited success.

Equity Effects of Postsecondary Vocationalism

One of the most obvious consequences of vocationalism has been the differentiation of the *system* of higher education along largely vocational lines. At the bottom level are the community colleges, whose open access allows a second chance for students who did poorly in high school, who made mistakes in their earlier plans, or who have immigrated to this country and need to start anew. With relatively low rates of completion, community colleges prepare students for the middle-level labor force—and some students take the option of transferring up to the next institutional level. The second-tier public comprehensive universities and similar less-selective private universities, for students with a little more money and a somewhat better high school record, have minimal admissions standards and offer a great variety of occupational majors leading to middle-level managerial positions and the less prestigious, lower-paid professions (like teaching and social work); like community colleges, they have low graduation rates. The public universities and flagship campuses stand above them, and the elite research universities rise triumphant at the apex, preparing their students for professional and graduate schools and access to well-paid, high-status professions. Thus equity and meritocracy can coexist: the system has simultaneously opened up college for millions of Americans—a version of college for all—and has allowed a variety of elite institutions to thrive.

The state systems of higher education after World War II have reflected this duality of expansive opportunity and inegalitarian differentiation. California provides the most successful and formalized example: the state's 1960 Master Plan designated the University of California system for professional education and PhD's, and reserved them for the top 12.5 percent of graduating high school students. The state colleges admitted the top 33 percent of the high school graduates and provided baccalaureate degrees and a few master's degrees, but no

PhD's. The community colleges were accessible to all, virtually without cost, and offered both occupational preparation and academic transfer to four-year institutions. By design, the students in each segment vary in the quality of their high school preparation. Because of the strong link between school achievement and family background, they vary as well in their socioeconomic status, with community college students most likely to come from low-income families without a history of going to college, or black, Latino, or immigrant families. The differences in institutional status show up in sharp differences in spending: the research universities spent $16,293 per student for instructional purposes in 2000–2001, the state colleges spent $10,787, and the community colleges—the level with the greatest variety of students and the greatest teaching challenges—spent $4,606 per student.[11] Other states have more or less emulated California, though the boundaries between their elite and second-tier universities are sometimes less precise. Nationally, spending per full-time-equivalent student varies from $32,512 in research universities to $17,780 in public doctoral institutions to $11,345 in public universities granting master's degrees to $7,665 in community colleges (NCES 2002, table 342). States thus provide equality of educational opportunity, but only in the sense of access to *some* form of postsecondary education. Equality of opportunity does not apply to the amount of resources invested in different types of students, nor to the likelihood of their completing a degree, nor to the kinds of occupations for which they are being prepared.

One consequence is that debates about access to different types of institutions and to funding are pandemic. The most obvious point of conflict is affirmative action, which pits conceptions of meritocracy against equity, and clarifies our ambivalence about a mass system of higher education. On the one hand, nineteenth-century conceptions of elite higher education and early twentieth-century notions of meritocratic access through grades and test scores are hostile to any form of affirmative action. On the other hand, equality of educational opportunity and the ethic of college for all argue for a greater inclusiveness in postsecondary education. Equally vitriolic debates have taken place over outreach programs, the standardized testing used in admissions (especially the SAT), the extent of public funding and the costs of tuition, and federal funding for grants and loans. The funding issues are where the gap is clearest between older conceptions of college, as a privilege for those who can afford it, and newer conceptions that treat college as an entitlement like K–12 schooling. From the latter perspective, even the modest tuitions of public colleges seem excessive and set off incendiary headlines about the high cost of college.

On the equity issues public policy takes the clearest stand on who will win and who will lose—on who will have access to which colleges and to which degrees, with the status and employment benefits that depend on these decisions. Vocationalism has shaped these battles and given them much of their significance: if higher education were not the gateway to professional occupations, levels of public funding or affirmative action would not have the political and emotional intensity they currently possess. The role of higher education in providing access to the American dream is simultaneously its foundation and its burden, and conflict is the price it has to pay.

Problems of Professional Preparation

Many complaints of the Education Gospel have critiqued K–12 schooling for its inadequate preparation of the "workforce of the twenty-first century." We might expect schooling and employment to be most congruent at the level of professional preparation, partly because professionalism has been founded on specialized knowledge available through formal schooling. However, the content of professional education has itself been a source of unending complaint, and amazingly identical attacks have appeared in one profession after another. While almost everyone believes that the professions require extended formal schooling, almost no one is satisfied with the preparation that is provided.

Most obviously, critics have regularly faulted professional schools for providing the wrong kinds of skills. The critics of medical education have cited a bloated curriculum, emphasis on rote memory, and inattention to patients as people (Ludmerer, 1999; Association of American Medical Colleges, 1984). Reformers of nursing education have listed "twenty-one competencies for the twenty-first century," advocating greater attention to higher order and interpersonal skills: "critical thinking, reflection, and problem-solving skills"; the use of "communication and information technology effectively and appropriately"; the ability to work in interdisciplinary teams; and the capacity to recognize "the multiple determinants of health in clinical care" (O'Neil and Pew Health Professions Commission, 1998). The American Bar Association (ABA) regularly complains about the lack of attention paid in law school to written and oral expression, problem solving and legal analysis, communication, counseling, and negotiation (Dutile, 1981; Mac-Crate, 1992). Business educators have been urged to improve "creative analytical power," including imaginative thinking, interpersonal abilities, communication skills, and willingness to take responsibility (Porter and McKibbin, 1988; Commission on Admission, 1990). The criticisms of education schools have pushed for intellectually more demanding preparation and professionally relevant standards of entry (Holmes Group, 1986).

While one strand of the Education Gospel has criticized professional education for neglecting the "competencies for the twenty-first century," a second strand has persistently attacked professional schools for elevating research and academic knowledge over practice and on-the-job learning. The American Bar Association criticized law professors for failing to provide a "practitioner role model"; ten years later an ABA report complained that new lawyers could not draft contracts or complete forms routinely required by courts, and had been taught by professors who had never practiced law (MacCrate, 1992). In teacher education, complaints about overly academic teaching—teaching theory with few classroom applications, with the result that new teachers are poorly prepared to manage their classrooms—has been common. The National League of Nursing has called for more collaboration between nursing programs and practice. In engineering education, the Olin Foundation was so disgusted with the separation of education from practice that it set up a new engineering school—Olin College—rather than attempting to reform existing schools (Marcus, 2002). The antidotes in these examples include recruiting more practitioners to teach, incorporating more practice-oriented coursework, and introducing more intensive internships.

Still other efforts to overcome the separation of professional education from practice have included calls to incorporate social and ethical dimensions, as in the demand that doctors and nurses treat the "whole person" and respect patient and familial desires, rather than emphasizing the technical dimensions of care. Lawyers have been criticized for not considering the personal costs and ethical questions that affect their clients. In the wake of Enron and WorldCom scandals, business professionals are now told to make ethics central to their practice. And other professionals, especially in teaching and social work, are exhorted to recognize the economic, social, and cultural conditions in which their clients live, to be more sensitive to low-income and minority clients and to linguistic differences. These are in effect calls for conceiving of professional competence in context, instead of emphasizing the individual and technical conceptions of skills that have dominated professional education.

The responses to these critiques have also been quite similar across the vast array of professions, reflecting the ways educational institutions are structured. The dominant change has been curricular reform—adding ethics courses, updating courses with new developments, paying greater attention to multicultural environments—while leaving the basic structure of professional preparation relatively unchanged. Professional education continues to rely on classroom-based learning rather than practice, emphasizes cognitive abilities rather than interpersonal skills, and accords greater prestige to research than to practice. Despite several decades of similar criticisms, the distance between educational institutions and the conditions of practice remains substantial.

Reformers have tended to blame university faculty—the "hollow men," the entrenched scammers with tenure, more in love with their research and potty ideas than teaching, out of touch with the real world outside the academy. But other institutional factors are also to blame: the unwillingness of many employers to participate actively with colleges; the system of funding, which supports enrollments within classes but not learning outside the academy; the incentives of the university that reinforce research over teaching. And what appears as conservatism and entrenchment is often allegiance to prevocational ideals of the university—to learning for its own sake, to student development beyond mere employability, to public values rather than individual gain, to the value of the university as a haven from the acquisitiveness of commerce. The basic conflicts over professional preparation within the academy stem from the inherent difficulty of lodging occupational preparation in educational institutions, with values, rhythms, and goals that are different from students' desires for vocations and employers' demands for job-ready hires.

The similarities in the various critiques of professional education are stunning, and they reflect the same criticisms that the Education Gospel has leveled at K–12 schooling. Even at the professional level, where the links between education and employment are the most consistent and where the need for school-based learning has been best established, the mismatch between school-based learning and job requirements remains pervasive—a theme we will pursue in Chapter 7. Even as vocationalism has given the university new goals and greater stature, it has brought to it new and greater conflicts.

Renegotiating Higher Education

There's been no lack of recommendations for reforming higher education. One school of thought has focused on resurrecting general education and de-vocationalizing the university as the way to define an educated person. But general or liberal education has been undermined in many different ways, and insufficient consensus exists at most colleges and universities to require a genuine liberal education. Looming above that fray is the reality of student choice, well accepted in all aspects of the shopping mall college. Returning to the liberal arts in any simple way is an unlikely possibility, attractive as it may be to academics like ourselves. Vocationalism has become too powerful.

A somewhat different move to improve higher education includes recent efforts to improve the quality of teaching and learning. In the wake of blistering criticisms during the 1980s and 1990s that professors had abandoned teaching and that students were underprepared, states began to call for more rigorous assessment of student learning. The National Governors' Association's Task Force on College Quality (1986) concluded that colleges and universities had an obligation to "demonstrate that student learning is occurring," and most states instituted some kind of assessment process. The assessment movement spread rapidly, but little more than a decade later it has lost much of its steam. In a state-by-state "report card" on higher education, the National Center for Public Policy and Higher Education (2002) declared itself "astonished and disturbed" by the lack of state information about students' knowledge and skills and gave every state an incomplete grade on assessment. In retrospect, it is clear there was never any possibility that an assessment movement could succeed. The private col-

leges and universities that usually set the tone for higher education are
virtually immune from assessment, and most assessments require little
more than another set of forms to be filled out (Lazerson, Wagener,
and Shumanis, 2000). The abilities "to think critically, communicate
effectively, and solve problems" mean such different things in a Berkeley physics program, a teacher training program at Chico State, and an
automotive program at Solano Community College that the notion of
developing comprehensive state assessment measures is ludicrous.

Another approach might be the higher-education equivalent of
whole-school reform: creating new institutions that avoid the dilemmas of the vocationalized university. The establishment of Hampshire
College in the 1960s and the creation of Olin College are examples, as
are private institutions like the University of Phoenix and National
University that fill specialized niches for older working students. But as
a general strategy, creating new institutions can't possibly work: it's un-
thinkable to create that many new institutions, the status rankings of
existing universities are too stable for new ones to break into the front
ranks (Kerr, 1991), and enrollments in institutions like the University
of Phoenix are too small (about 3 percent of total enrollments in higher
education, according to Gilpin, 2002) and too specialized to have more
than a trivial influence. When new public institutions emerge, they almost always follow the standard model of a comprehensive university.
In the California system, for example, the effort to establish UC Santa
Cruz as a liberal arts institution with unconventional instructional
practices (smaller colleges and no grades) has given way to a conventional structure, and there's been no clamor for the new University of
California at Merced to be experimental. Too many pressures, from too
many members of the Education Coalition, keep public universities
from too much reform.

Still another possible direction would be to eliminate the conception
of a *system* of higher education and replace it with a multitude of segments that don't interact with one another. For example, there would
be a segment of elite private colleges, one of national research universities, one of enormous second-tier comprehensive universities, one of
low-quality private universities for students unable to get in anywhere
else, long-distance education for home-bound mothers and students
unable to get out of bed in the morning, and proprietary trade schools
oriented to immediate job placement (Kerr, 2002). Most colleges and

universities would be intensely vocational, with no commitment to general education, while a few would remain liberal arts colleges that prepare students for graduate school. Markets and choice would take over completely, and most universities would become high-level trade schools—and probably unsuccessful ones, because professional preparation would continue to be separated from employment. This would be vocationalism in extremis, a world we describe as HyperVoc in Chapter 9, and it is an unappealing vision.

A more progressive approach needs to start, in our view, with acknowledging the professional orientation of higher education. It is too late to reverse the developments of the past century, and failing to understand the occupational goals of most students can lead only to old, stale debates. Instead we must recognize the professional trends of the past century and—following John Dewey's warnings against false dichotomies and "either-ors"—integrate these not-so-new realities with the nonvocational ideals we still hold. We deplore the tendency toward narrow vocationalism both because it undermines the kind of occupational preparation necessary for the twenty-first century and because it impoverishes the intellectual and civic roles that colleges and universities can play. But professionalism broadly understood provides its own avenues back to liberal education. Ethical issues, central to every profession, provide a hook for the deeper study of philosophical issues. An understanding of the development of specific professions, and of professionalism in general, can provide an approach to history, to the conflicts over technological and social change, to the responsibilities of different groups (including professional groups) within society, to conceptions of work and occupation relative to other spheres of life. And a frank introduction to the professional's civic responsibilities can provide a logical entry to many elements of liberal education, one that can be exploited through interdisciplinary and general education courses for professional students.

At the same time it is important to recognize the complexity of work preparation. The attacks from professional associations indicate some ways in which professional education needs to be reshaped. A first step would be to make sure that students have a broad understanding of underlying theories and concepts in ways that allow professionals to organize and understand "the rich confusion of ordinary experience." The constant complaint that university-based preparation drifts too far

from the world of practice suggests a second necessary step, obvious in
outline if difficult in execution: integrating practice more thoroughly
into the professionalized university through internships, cooperative
education, service learning, and other forms of work-based experience
that could provide an antidote to the excessively "academic" elements
of professional preparation.

In many fields there are also ways of redirecting research so that it is
less divorced from practice. In our own field of education, for example,
teacher-research and principal-research—teachers examining their
own practices and principals analyzing problems in their own schools
—have become increasingly common (Cochran-Smith and Lytle,
1999; Zeichner and Nofke, 2001; Viadero, 2002; Grubb, Tredway, and
Furco, 2003). More generally, Ernest Boyer (1990) has articulated conceptions of research that move beyond the scholarship of discovery,
which dominates the research university, to the scholarship of integration, including synthetic and multidisciplinary work; the scholarship
of application, including service to communities of practice; and the
scholarship of teaching, in which professors carry out research on their
own teaching. If the concept of what constitutes research were broad-
ened, then the gulf between research and practice, the "academic" and
the "vocational," might be more readily bridged.

Pedagogical differences among occupational areas should also be
acknowledged. The vocationalized system of higher education gives
surprisingly little attention to occupational instruction; the model of
teaching remains pretty much the same no matter what the subject.
Postsecondary education has neglected the challenges of incorporating
nonstandard competencies into professional curricula—visual competency for architects and graphic designers, interpersonal skills for the
helping professions, diagnostic abilities for engineers and computer
scientists, problem-solving abilities for those in policy-oriented fields
and many scientific areas, and nonstandard applications of reading,
writing, and mathematics in many professional areas. There has been
little attention given to the preparation of instructors in professional
fields, and therefore no clear way to improve the quality of instruction
except through trial and error. Taking the nature of professional teaching more seriously, as a subject in its own right, would help diminish
the distance between the academy and practice.[12]

One way to make teaching and learning more prominent is through communities of learning, which were ideals of the nineteenth-century college. While most universities and colleges are now too big to emulate the small residential college, higher education has repeatedly experimented with small programs to bring professors and students together intellectually. In recent years these efforts have accelerated, much as high schools are experimenting with more intimate learning environments. Almost every large institution is experimenting with special freshman-year learning experiences, colleges within colleges, intellectual activities within residential settings, more seminars and tutorials, and learning centers for commuting and nontraditional students. These are all ways to break impersonal and anomic environments into vital, smaller-scale learning communities. Community colleges, which celebrate their small classes, are now creating learning communities and linking courses across disciplines. Doing this is more expensive, of course, since it does not allow for packing 500 freshmen and sophomores into large lecture courses, and it is more difficult in commuter institutions like comprehensive universities and community colleges. But there are good reasons to think that smaller learning communities enhance retention and progress toward the degree, and that students value the support and the intellectual exchange they make possible.[13] If colleges and universities can think of themselves as places of learning as well as professional preparation—and not simply as enrollment mills—then the benefits of smaller communities should outweigh the additional costs involved.

By refocusing their attention on learning within the context of professional preparation, many colleges and universities can escape the burden of searching for prestige. For substantial numbers of faculty awaiting the call from prestigious universities, and for countless administrators and trustees hoping to emulate their more famous peers, the Holy Grail is to mimic selective research universities by ratcheting up admissions standards, creating honors programs, dropping remedial programs, adding doctoral degrees, and expanding research. While it may be too late to undo this kind of institutional competition, a clear alternative is for institutions to be as good as they can be *in their own terms*—thus creating multiple conceptions of excellence.[14] This would allow regional institutions and second-tier universities to focus on what they do well instead of trying to emulate the elite, to emphasize how best to serve their region, to expand conceptions of applied research and useful knowledge, to see how well they can prepare the middle-level students they have rather than the elite students they would like to have, and to develop faculties that are enthusiastic about teaching and public service rather than feeling like wannabe researchers. Then it might be possible to strengthen both occupational preparation and liberal learning, particularly by developing programs that integrate academic and professional content and that connect classrooms to the workplace in mutually beneficial ways.

None of the reforms we recommend will have much impact unless the huge structure of inequality within postsecondary education is changed. The endless differentiation of institutions, with their varied student bodies and occupational targets and funding levels, constitutes the most extensive system of tracking in the entire educational system, dwarfing anything in K–12 education. It violates one of the basic conceptions of equal opportunity, the Jacksonian belief that government should not "make the rich richer and the potent more powerful" (see Chapter 8). The most pernicious effect of differentiation is that resources flow so unequally to different types of institutions. Community colleges, with the neediest students, cannot make good on their promise to be teaching institutions, nor can they provide intensive support to their nontraditional students, without more resources. The second-tier comprehensive universities do not receive enough funding to provide the academic support (including learning communities) and the services their students need. Some of the resource differentials among institutions will not be eliminated unless the distribution of income and wealth in this country narrows considerably: high-income families will continue to seek advantages for their children (just as low-income families do and should), and if they want to spend $40,000 a year on an elite college, or on a second-tier private university with the trappings of "college," that will remain their prerogative. But the public support of higher education should recognize the negative effects of such wide differentials in revenue. The basic essentials needed to support students in community colleges and second-tier public universities—financial aid, guidance and counseling in new forms, improvements in basic skills instruction, access to a broader array of support services—are insufficiently funded.

As things now stand, postsecondary education is more like a *filtering system*—where those students with the most promise are selected into elite institutions and have lavish sums spent on them, while those who have not proven themselves and who have the fewest resources are relegated to institutions where they receive the bare minimum of a college education. It is not an *educational system* that takes the progress of all students equally seriously. Without redressing the severe inequity of higher education, the rhetoric of the Education Gospel and the spirit of college for all will remain impossible to fulfill.

3

～ Dilemmas of the Community College

$\mathcal{T}$HE COMMUNITY COLLEGE developed over the course of the twentieth century into a distinctive institution, different from both high schools and four-year colleges though incorporating elements of each. As the community college matured entirely within the century of vocationalism, its trajectory has much in common with the occupational drift of other forms of schooling. In particular, community colleges engage in overt occupational preparation for middle-skilled jobs, and they now provide most vocational education, as high schools have turned almost entirely to "academic" (or pre-vocational) education. In other ways the community college is distinctive. Its ubiquity and its commitment to open access and low tuition have given the community college a relatively egalitarian role within higher education. It has become an alternative or second-chance route into higher education for those seeking a second career or deciding they made a mistake earlier in not continuing to postsecondary schooling. Its combination of purposes or missions, reflecting the American preference for comprehensive rather than specialized institutions, has allowed it to play a unique "bridging" role in the education and training system, at least sometimes.

For all its accomplishments and phenomenal growth, however, the community college remains an embattled and low-status institution, reflecting the dilemmas caused by the shift toward occupational purposes. The development of second chances, while honoring the best tradition of inclusiveness, has been difficult within higher education, with its finely differentiated structure of inequality. The limits of community colleges have made it difficult for nontraditional students to progress, particularly because of what we call the work-family-school dilemma. The community college illustrates better than any other level of the education system the predicament of providing educational equity in an inequitable society, without the social and economic policies to complement educational opportunities.

The Development of Occupational Purposes

Like the high school and the four-year college, the community college began life as an institution without an overtly vocational purpose.[1] Community colleges developed soon after 1900 in two distinct ways: out of efforts to extend high school to grades thirteen and fourteen, and as two-year postsecondary institutions that could relieve research-oriented universities of the need to educate freshmen and sophomores. It is tempting to see in these origins two competing conceptions of community colleges: as egalitarian institutions extending schooling upward for greater numbers of students, and as inegalitarian institutions keeping the masses away from the university. In practice, they are both. In California, where community colleges were established as extensions of high school, the president of Stanford University still justified them in 1913 as a way of relieving the universities of routine teaching functions (Witt et al., 1994, 35): "I am looking forward, as you know, to the time when the large high schools of the state in conjunction with the small colleges will relieve the two great universities from the expense and from the necessity of giving instruction of the first two college years. The instruction of these two years is of necessity elementary and of the same general nature as the work of the high school itself."

Because the earliest junior colleges were designed to provide the first two years of a four-year college education, their curricula were almost entirely academic. But these origins were different from the academic origins of both high schools and four-year colleges. The early community colleges lacked any roots in the common school movement, and did not have the religious origins of many four-year colleges. Therefore moral, civic, and intellectual purposes were never as powerful, and never served as serious alternatives to vocationalism. Community colleges arose somewhat after four-year colleges and universities had developed their research functions and professional schools, so they had to search for another reason for being. As they developed a greater emphasis on direct occupational preparation, even their academic-transfer function became defined by occupational goals, since transfer usually meant moving to another occupationally oriented institution, albeit one of higher status. Like the college-prep track of the twentieth-century high school, the academic track of the community college has become largely occupational, designed to provide access to the baccalaureate degree and its benefits of earnings and status.

Although the curricula of the early community colleges tended to replicate those of four-year colleges, most states allowed "courses of instruction designed to prepare persons for agriculture, industry, commerce, home-making, and such other courses of instruction as may be deemed necessary" (Witt et al., 1994), phrases reminiscent of the Morrill Act. During the Depression of the 1930s, more occupational courses were added as competition for employment became more intense. Much the same occurred during World War II, with short-term vocational efforts to meet war needs. These occupational blips—a common response by academic institutions when a perceived or real crisis makes utilitarian goals more urgent—did not do much to change the community college's academic focus. On the eve of the Depression, fewer than one-sixth of California community college students were in occupational courses, and the proportion was probably lower in other states. Students were evidently voting with their feet, choosing transfer programs with the likeliest access to the baccalaureate and thus to higher status.

At the same time, a persistent argument was laying the groundwork for the subsequent emphasis on occupational preparation. As Alexis Lange of the University of California argued in 1918, "probably the greatest and certainly the most original contribution to be made by the junior colleges is the means of training for the vocations occupying the middle ground between those of the artisan type and the professions." Leonard Koos, an early proponent of vocational education, similarly argued that community colleges should prepare semiprofessionals for occupations "that are to be distinguished on the one hand from *trades*, the training for which is concluded during the secondary school period, and on the other, from *professions*, adequate preparation for which requires four or more years of training beyond the high school" (Witt et al., 1994, x).

The period after World War II was critical for the development of this argument. Despite the growth of four-year colleges before 1940 and the extraordinary success of the GI Bill just after the war, community college advocates sharply criticized higher education. Four-year colleges, they claimed, were mired in traditions of the liberal arts, excessively academic, and unresponsive to the nation's postwar economic needs; they offered little to students unable or unwilling to attend for four years. This view of higher education paralleled the earlier criticisms of high schools, but unlike the efforts at secondary school reform between 1880 and the 1920s, community college advocates did not believe the four-year colleges would change. Instead they proposed creating a large number of public two-year colleges with substantially different purposes. Their rationale lay in the changing national economy—a mid-twentieth-century version of the Education Gospel. In the first half of the twentieth century, the labor market shifted from agricultural and factory workers to service, office, and technology-based occupations; in the second half, the labor market required more technical workers and semiprofessionals. As the Truman Commission wrote (President's Commission on Higher Education, 1947, vol. 1, 68–69): "To meet the needs of the economy our schools must train many more young people for employment as medical secretaries, recreational leaders, hotel and restaurant managers, aviators, salesmen in fields like life insurance and real estate, photographers, automotive and electrical technicians, and . . . medical technicians, dental hygienists, nurses' aides, laboratory technicians." The commission claimed that for each job requiring four years of college preparation, there were five jobs that required only two years. The appropriate preparation was beyond the high school's responsibility, and four-year institutions had other professional purposes. This left middle-level preparation to community colleges (68): "Semiprofessional training, properly conceived and organized, can make a significant contribution to education for society's occupational requirements. In not providing this sort of training anywhere in existing programs, the educational system is out of step with the demands of the twentieth century American economy." By the end of World War II, then, the Education Gospel had been reaffirmed for the community college, with an image of a technologically driven economy that required more occupationally based schooling—college for all, or at least for many more.

Such arguments grew substantially for the next half century, providing the defining vision of the community college. In the 1960s federal officials, fearing that the country's growing needs for technical and semiprofessional workers were not being met, called for more technical training in community colleges "to back up our professionals with more semiprofessional technicians." By the 1980s this view had positioned the community college squarely in the middle of the occupational distribution, providing training for many technical and semiprofessional jobs (Brint and Karabel, 1989, ch. 3; Dougherty, 1994).

These insistent arguments for occupational programs prepared the community college to become more obviously vocational.[2] From the 1960s to the end of the twentieth century, public community colleges became the fastest-growing sector in American education, increasing their share of enrollments in all of postsecondary education from 18 percent in 1965 to 37 percent in 1997. Of the students attending college for the first time in the fall of 1997, 40 percent enrolled in a community college. For two-fifths of students at the beginning of the twenty-first century, college for all means entering a community college, and often there isn't much distinction in their minds between two- and four-year colleges.

Several reasons account for the dramatic expansion in enrollment. The lower tuition of community colleges and the location of most colleges within driving or mass-transit distance of virtually all students (save those in rural areas) mean that both school and housing costs are affordable. With more flexible schedules than four-year colleges, they can accommodate working students, thus reducing the opportunity costs as well as direct costs. In addition, the increase in the employment and economic benefits of postsecondary education below the baccalaureate level has pulled more students in. The proportion of jobs held by individuals with "some college" increased from 13.1 percent in 1967 to 27.3 percent in 1996. Simultaneously, the earnings premium for those with some college increased, suggesting that demand was increasing faster than supply. In the late 1960s and early 1970s those with some college but less than a baccalaureate degree earned slightly less than high school graduates did, but their earnings premium thereafter climbed steadily, and it is now 13.6 percent for men and 16.7 percent for women (Grubb, 1996b, table 1). At the same time, the proportion of students in occupational programs expanded, rising from about 20 percent in 1959 to 29 percent in the fall of 1968, between 40 and 60 percent during the 1980s, and 61 percent in 1992–93.[3] As with high schools and four-year colleges, expansion has always been accompanied by increases in occupational enrollments, where the economic hopes of students are mostly clearly expressed.

While community colleges have become more explicitly occupational, they too—like the high school—are vocational in a more general sense: almost all students attend them for economic purposes, whether to complete occupational certificates and associate degrees or to transfer to four-year colleges. Instructors note that virtually all students are there for occupational reasons: "They're already somebody but they want a decent job, you know—the American dream." Despite a variety of purposes cited by students—becoming better parents, increasing self-esteem—instructors conclude their job is "to help students to get a job; that's what they're coming here for" (Grubb and Associates, 1999). And yet much of the community college curriculum, as in high school, does not appear to be vocational: a great deal of it is concerned with basic skills in reading, writing, and math, with conventional academic courses required for transfer, and with the general education requirements that symbolize a "real college." The disjunction between the occupational purposes of students and the academic form of much of the curriculum often creates problems, particularly the familiar vocational question: "Why do I have to know this?" The problem is especially acute when students who enter college for occupational advancement find themselves in basic English and math courses, doing drills on subject-verb agreement, simple arithmetic, and other exercises far removed from the requirements of work.

The expansion of enrollments in community colleges and the increase in overtly occupational programs for middle-level jobs have had several consequences. One is that the community college has gained a reputation as the "people's college," a democratic or egalitarian institution accepting students who might not otherwise go to college. Tuition and opportunity costs are low, making the schools attractive to students who cannot afford a four-year college or who are unwilling to leave home. They are open-access institutions that admit students without

entrance requirements, making them the dominant postsecondary option for students who have not done well in high school. They are also
increasingly the educational institution of choice for many immigrants,
a low-cost place to learn English, to absorb the customs of a new country, and to find out how American social and economic mobility works.
For these reasons community colleges have relatively high proportions
of lower-income and minority students. In 1995, for example, 40 percent of all African American undergraduates and 54 percent of Latino
college students were enrolled in community colleges, compared with
35 percent of white students.

In the process, community colleges have also become the country's
most important "second-chance" institutions, both in their degree-
granting programs and in noncredit divisions.[4] They provide a second
crack at higher education for older students whose earlier motivation
and performance were inadequate to gain them admission to a four-
year college. Other second-chance students include women joining the
workforce after a divorce or after their children are grown, or dislocated workers whose jobs have been eliminated. Job training, welfare-
to-work, and adult education programs also subcontract with community colleges to provide short-term skills training or basic literacy
courses.

To add to the heterogeneity, many students—both recent high
school graduates and older students returning for a second chance—
are "experimenters" who enroll because they have little sense of what
to do, or they have found themselves in dead-end jobs.[5] As one said,
"When I first came here I had no idea what I wanted to study . . . I
know the only way to have a good life is to get a degree. I didn't really
have much idea of what I wanted to do. I knew I needed to go to
school, though." Another noted the importance of cost in deciding to
enroll: "Realistically, it's economics. I don't want to spend all of my parents' money going to a four-year school when I don't really know what
I want to do yet. So I figure, go to a community college and then find
out what I want to do." Community college offers a low-cost way of ex-
ploring occupational alternatives and possible futures, an antidote to
the prevailing lack of career-oriented guidance. Most instructors accept that helping such "lost souls" find their way in the world is an important (if unacknowledged) function of the community college. But
this role comes at a cost, because it means that some students are there

not to learn but to figure out if they *want* to learn; one instructor complained, "I have some people who want to take the class for information, and [they] don't intend to do any of the work."

Like the high school, most four-year colleges, and the university (the "multiversity"), the community college has inherited the traditions of comprehensive rather than specialized institutions. Although some states have created technical institutes focused entirely on occupational preparation, most have created comprehensive community colleges precisely to preserve an egalitarian image. And in many states that did establish separate technical colleges, the process of "mission drift" has converted those schools into comprehensive colleges.[6] In almost all cases, the push toward comprehensiveness has come from institutions striving to provide the highest-status programs, and from students demanding access to the high-status baccalaureate degree.

With a vision of being comprehensive community-serving institutions, community colleges have come to serve many purposes or missions in addition to transfer and occupational education. One is to provide remedial (or "developmental") education, as a corollary of their role as "people's colleges." More and more students have entered unprepared by high school for college-level work. In regions with large numbers of immigrants, community colleges have been important in teaching English as a Second Language (ESL). While discussions about nontraditional community college students from families with low levels of education have been less charged than the earlier high school debates about the "children of the plain people," the same issue of whether such students should be in public education has emerged. The increased amount of developmental education provided for such students has remained controversial, with legislators resistant to such spending and colleges unwilling to acknowledge how much remediation they provide, in part because remediation threatens to undermine their standing as "colleges."

In some areas, either by state mandate or through entrepreneurial expansion, community colleges also provide short-term programs, often labeled continuing or noncredit education, as well as an array of community services ranging from arts performances to avocational programs to regional planning activities. The most recent expansion of the community college mission has been in economic development, including teaching relatively short-term training courses for the employees of specific companies and offering advice to employers through small-business development centers.[7] And so, along with conventional vocational programs that prepare students to enter the labor force for the first time, community colleges also have a substantial role in providing new skills for existing workers and in retraining individuals who want to change occupations—the vision of lifelong learning.

In many ways community colleges have been overwhelmingly successful institutions. They have expanded substantially, more than any other form of public education in the past fifty years. They are also ubiquitous; there are now community colleges in virtually every community. Like other comprehensive institutions, they serve an enormous variety of purposes, from standard academic goals to occupational education, remediation, workforce development, and community development, and they enroll a corresponding variety of students. In contrast to four-year colleges, community colleges represent the tradition of egalitarian and inclusive public education, with fewer barriers to entry than four-year colleges. Occupational purposes have been central to expanding both enrollments and missions. But these very successes have generated conflicts, and community colleges have been among the most controversial of postsecondary institutions.

The Ambiguities of Success

As community colleges have become increasingly occupational, they have experienced many problems common to other forms of vocationalized schooling. Perhaps the most obvious is caused by the hierarchy in postsecondary education that places research universities and elite liberal arts colleges at the top, the less-selective public and private universities and colleges in the vast middle, and community colleges firmly at the bottom. Community colleges have suffered by comparison with four-year colleges and universities, for failing to offer a truly "higher" education. Ambivalence about them has been reflected in their earlier name, the "junior" college, and in such labels as "high schools with ashtrays." Their lack of admissions standards separates community colleges from colleges that claim to be selective (though selectivity is often a fiction). Their remedial or developmental courses and workforce development programs for specific employers make it even more difficult to recognize community colleges as institutions of higher learning. Under these conditions they generally do not gain the attention given to other sectors of higher education, and they certainly lack funding as a result. The national figures on spending, as cited in Chapter 2, reveal that spending per full-time-equivalent student is $7,665 in community colleges, compared with $11,345 in second-tier public universities granting master's degrees, $17,780 in public doctoral institutions, and $32,512 in research universities. In response to their lack of status, some community colleges have tried to become baccalaureate-granting institutions—another illustration of "institutional drift"—rather than trying harder to define their distinctive identity.

A second problem is that the egalitarian claims of community colleges are hotly contested. More than forty years ago, Burton Clark (1960) argued that community colleges operated to divert or "cool out" underprepared students into low-status occupational programs and away from academic programs leading to baccalaureate degrees. (This charge is similar to the critique of high school vocational education as a dumping ground for students unable to do academic work.) In a slightly different version of cooling out, other critics have argued that community college might divert students who would otherwise earn a baccalaureate degree to lower levels of schooling and less rewarding credentials. "Cooling out"—named after the process by which con artists convince victims that they are to blame for their own losses—intends to persuade students to view their educational attainment as the result of their own decisions, in choosing a community college over a four-year college and an occupational program over a transfer program. Citing a now-outdated 1957 counseling manual used at a single California college, Clark stressed that cooling out occurred when counselors directed students to be more realistic: "Be alert to the problem of unrealistic vocational goals," advised the manual, and "help students to accept their limitations and strive for success in other worthwhile objectives that are within their grasp." Other critics have argued that the very existence and expansion of the community college diverts lower-income students to lower-cost community colleges with low transfer and completion rates.[8]

These criticisms are at the heart of a debate about whether community colleges enhance the education of individuals who would otherwise not go beyond high school—the thesis of "educational advancement"—or whether instead they "cool out" individuals who would otherwise earn a baccalaureate degree. While some cooling out surely occurs, the evidence indicates that community college students are a relatively distinct group who would not have enrolled at a four-year college, because of costs, distance, and unfamiliarity.[9] Furthermore, while guidance and counseling may have been mechanisms for tracking in the 1950s, the guidance community has increasingly rejected this role. Besides, guidance in community colleges is not powerful enough—and fails to reach enough students—to have much impact.[10] There are other practices that discourage the least-prepared students, including traditional teaching methods, remedial or ESL coursework requirements, and the lack of support for low-income students. On the whole, however, community colleges have served to advance the non-traditional students who in previous decades would not have gone on to postsecondary education at all.

Other problems faced by occupational education in community colleges are similar to those of high school voc ed. Academic subjects lead to transfer and the baccalaureate degree, while occupational subjects lead to middle-skilled and subprofessional occupations with less upward mobility; as a result, occupational education has continued to suffer from second-class status. Even more than in the high school, community college programs are structured so that occupational students, concerned with fulfilling a number of specific "skills" courses, rarely meet transfer-oriented students, and in many colleges the physical separation of labs and workshops away from academic classrooms creates a spatial isolation as well, symbolic but powerful. The two kinds of faculty often have different backgrounds—academic faculty wedded to their academic disciplines, occupational faculty coming from the world of work and identified with their occupations—and different perspectives on the appropriateness of work-focused education.

The special teaching conditions of occupational education cause additional problems. In many ways teaching in occupational programs is more sophisticated and varied than academic instruction. An institution that prepares for vocations as diverse as nursing, business management, engineering technologies, golf course management, electron microscopy, automotive repair, zookeeping, and dairy management doesn't fit the image of a conventional college. A dairy barn is so different from the business or academic classroom and the "equipment"— cows—so dissimilar to personal computers and microscopes that it is difficult to imagine all of them existing within the same sphere of instruction. The tools of occupational instruction—cows and electron microscopes, medical instruments and auto diagnostic stations—are also more complicated and more expensive than the materials in most academic courses. The competencies in occupational areas are more varied than they are in academic education: they include not only the verbal and mathematical abilities that dominate academic subjects but also kinesthetic or manual abilities, visual abilities, the interpersonal skills required at work, and sometimes perceptual abilities (smell, the recognition of how things ought to look and feel).[11] In addition, occupational instruction usually incorporates several settings—the conventional classroom, the workshop or lab, and sometimes on-the-job learning in internships or co-op education. So the basic conditions of occupational instruction are unfamiliar within academic education, reinforcing the distance between academic and occupational faculties.

Occupational instructors also serve two different interests, the development of the students and the demands of employers. Often these conflict, particularly when students' long-run interests run contrary to employers' demands for training that is immediately useful. Among occupational instructors, who usually come from the workplace, the influence of external workplace standards is pervasive, rooted in the belief that competence on the job—outside the college—is the ultimate arbiter of success. They often believe in producing what Devenport and Hebel (2001) call "turnkey graduates," employees ready to work at full capacity the first day on the job—even though such short-term, specific preparation may be contrary to the long-run interests of students. Advisory committees of local employers reinforce these views, as do licensing requirements—in health occupations, early childhood, cosmetology, construction supervision, and aircraft maintenance—and voluntary standards in such areas as auto repair, welding, and information technology. But while occupational instruction must incorporate the views of employers to be successful, Americans remain ambivalent about education determined by the demands of the workplace. On the one hand, the notion of learning on the job instead of in school remains attractive, particularly among those who romanticize the history of apprenticeship. On the other hand, schooling to prepare for the technical requirements of occupations appears more utilitarian than intellectual, more an extension of the job market than a real education.

Like high school vocational education, occupational education in community colleges has been constrained by its location in a comprehensive educational institution. Had community college advocates focused on technical and semiprofessional preparation only, the United States might have developed a system of high-status technical institutes similar to those in Europe. But the college's earliest purpose was transfer education, and it always saw itself as serving "the total post-high school needs of its community," as the 1947 Truman Commission expressed it (vol. 1, 67–68). Locating occupational education within a comprehensive institution has to some extent doomed it to second-class status. The highest-status track remains the transfer program; academic faculty dominate internal governing committees, and national debates usually focus on academic concerns. Community colleges are funded with academic education in mind, and the high costs of labs, workshops, materials, and small classes make it difficult to support a wide variety of occupational programs. Once again the preference of Americans for comprehensive institutions—rather than specialized institutions—has made it difficult for occupational education to thrive.

A final problem for occupational education in community colleges is that it targets the middle of the occupational hierarchy, below the professional and managerial jobs associated with baccalaureate degrees, though above the relatively unskilled jobs of high school programs. The vocations in the middle are ones for which formal schooling and credentials tend to be less important, and many jobs can be entered through informal experiences, military training, and other nonschool pathways. Access to such occupations through nonschool routes may lower the economic benefits of community college programs. However, in recent years the evidence about the value of some postsecondary education below the baccalaureate level has become clearer (as we review in Chapter 6).

Perhaps the most promising development affecting community colleges is a distinct shift in the nature of occupations in the middle. Even though the image of vocational education is still dominated by older occupations associated with the Industrial Revolution—metal-working technologies, construction crafts, the automotive trades, and (for women) food service, cosmetology, and other personal services—the fastest growing middle-level occupations now are quite different. What we might call modernized middle-level occupations include many health occupations, computer-related occupations in information technology and Web design, a vast array of business jobs, electronics and other technical and engineering positions, and new occupations like those in biotechnology. The vast majority of current occupational enrollments are in such areas: 29 percent are in business, 22 percent in health occupations, 12 percent in engineering and science technologies, 5 percent in computers and data processing. The traditional vocational areas—agriculture, home economics, marketing, trade and industry—together comprise only 12 percent of all enrollments (Levesque et al., 2000, section 6). Each of the modernized occupations includes a great deal of academic content in math, sciences, reading and writing—we might even call them knowledge-based occupations—as well as occupation-specific content, thereby integrating both academic and vocational competencies. Many of them operate at the juncture of theory and machinery; they meld professional knowledge learned in school and experience-based capacities, and they incorporate both mental and manual skills, both "head" and "hand" (Whalley and Barley, 1997; Barley, 1993). They lead to higher economic returns than do either traditional vocational programs or academic programs (Grubb, 2002a). Most of these modernized occupations have analogues in four-year colleges—in business, engineering, health professions, and computing—facilitating transfer and further movement up the academic hierarchy. These occupations are more likely to enjoy the benefits of professional status, including licensing requirements and the special protection of a knowledge base. When the image of occupational education catches up with this reality, its status in community colleges may increase too and become what it is in four-year colleges, where professional education leads to both higher status and higher earnings.

The community college, a more recent arrival to the American system of education than the high school or the four-year college or professionalized university, has gone through roughly the same process of shifting from an initially academic perspective toward more overtly occupational purposes. Many of the same dilemmas have been replicated: the split between academic and occupational subjects, the fear that educational differentiation will undermine equity, the creation of comprehensive institutions with internal tracks instead of specialized institutions, the low status of occupational education. The dilemmas associated with vocational transformations are general, rather than specific to particular educational institutions, and they have emerged in similar form whenever educational institutions have become vocationalized.

Equity and the Work-Family-Schooling Dilemma

Contrasting community colleges with four-year colleges inevitably leads to some negative comparisons rooted in the basic design of the institutions. Community colleges are less selective, they have fewer resources, and they aim for lower-level occupations. But the flip slide of being less selective is that they are more equitable, enrolling more students from low-income families, more black and especially more Latino students, more immigrants, more older students—the nontraditional students who contribute to the rhetoric of "democracy's open door." Particularly with evidence that "educational advancement" is more pervasive than "cooling out," the equity claims of community colleges give them a special status within postsecondary education.

On another dimension, community colleges look less successful. College for all and our postsecondary policies in general have stressed *access* to college—the right to enroll in some form of postsecondary education. *Completion* is quite another matter, and here inequity creeps back in. Overall completion rates have not been especially strong. Of students entering public two-year colleges in 1995–96, 9.7 percent earned a certificate by June 2001, 15.7 percent earned an associate degree, and 10.5 percent completed a baccalaureate degree; but 46.9 percent were not enrolled in June 2001 and had no credential, and 17.5 percent were still in school. Furthermore, family background mattered a great deal: 43.3 percent of students whose parents held an advanced degree had earned a baccalaureate or associate degree, compared with 22.7 percent of those who parents had not gone to college (Berkner et al., 2002, tables 2.1-A, 2.1-C, 2.2-A). By contrast, of those entering public four-year colleges, 53 percent had completed a baccalaureate degree within this five-year period, 17.3 percent were still in school, and 22.5 percent had no degree and were not enrolled. To be sure, these completion rates from community colleges don't look so bad when we compare them with those of second-tier four-year colleges, many of which have baccalaureate completion rates ranging between 20 and 30 percent. But by most standards community college completion is low, and many students leave with few credits and no credentials.

In response, defenders of community colleges have argued in two directions. One is that students who look like dropouts are really completers, because they have finished enough coursework to find a new job or to get a promotion. If this were true in general, then there would be substantial benefits to small amounts of coursework. This does not seem to be true, however, since increases in earnings associated with small amounts of coursework are often zero and usually no more than 5 percent (Grubb, 2002a, table 4).

Another argument declares that all students are rational, and that "their choices to use a particular institution for a particular purpose at a particular time in their lives are intentional, even if the purpose is 'milling around'" (Adelman, 1992, 22). But there are too many experimenters, too many students who are "ambitious but directionless" (Schneider and Stevenson, 1999, ch. 9), too many for whom barriers, including the requirements of work and family, prevent them from completing their schooling as they might like. Many students do not seem to make well-considered choices; as one commented about leaving the community college (Grubb, 1996b, 79): "It was not a decision at all. Just like you go home, tired from work, you don't decide about 'Oh, I'm just going to go to sleep now.' You just doze off and go to sleep. It wasn't a plan. That's the way [dropping] the class was: it wasn't a plan." The assumption of rationality among "consumers" in higher education may legitimize the huge marketlike system in postcompulsory education, but it isn't true for many students. One response has been to call for increasing resources for guidance and counseling and using them in nontraditional ways, to enhance the ability of students to make informed decisions on their own behalf (Grubb, 2003; Schneider and Stevenson, 1999).

These two arguments do not really explain low completion rates, however. The real culprit, based on several recent studies involving student interviews, is the work-family-schooling dilemma. Almost all community college students work to support themselves, and many carry a full-time academic schedule at the same time. Many have families, including children, and some are also responsible for elderly parents or other members of an extended family. An alarming number of female students suffer some kind of abuse, often by husbands and boyfriends who resent their independence; others have to intervene when violence and abuse affect a member of their family.

For these students, so different from traditional full-time middle-class students without the entanglements of work and family, life is a balancing act. A small change in a work schedule, an unanticipated breakdown in child care arrangements, a health issue that requires attention, or a car that breaks down can unravel their carefully laid plans. As one Latina remarked, "It's a great challenge. You know, having five kids and taking seven units and having to work is a challenge. You wake every day thinking, how or where are you going to get the strength to keep going, every single day?" The obligations of family cannot be postponed, and they particularly affect women. Work is essential for both men and women, since these students have no other means of support. As one described the pressure, "It's like you want to finish up things at work, but you've got to rush off to school, and then when you're at school you've got to do your homework but there's so much to do at work. Sometimes I wish I didn't work, but then I don't have enough money to—my family won't have enough money to live off of." What falls by the wayside in most cases is schooling—and so students withdraw from classes, delay classwork until there is no alternative but to withdraw, or fail to reregister, and then programs requiring several semesters worth of coursework are delayed. When this happens repeatedly, students may be placed on probation, and then the period to completion can become unimaginably long. "Life gets in the way" of even the best-planned education program, as one instructor said.[12]

Community colleges do have some ways to address the work-family-schooling dilemma. Colleges already offer flexible schedules, including evening hours and often weekend classes, for students who cannot attend at the conventional times. Some colleges have special programs for older students, like the PACE program (Program of Adult College Education), a learning community that incorporates evening and Saturday classes. Distance education has reportedly been a boon to such students, as it further increases flexibility. Many instructors sympathize with the "busied up" conditions of their students' lives, and they make allowances for crises. Some colleges provide child care, usually through special-purpose state grants, and while most colleges do not provide much personal counseling for family problems, they usually try to refer students to services in the community. Some student aid is available for low-income students, and virtually all colleges maintain employment offices to help students find jobs—particularly "stay-in-school" jobs compatible with a student's schedule.

Each of these supports could no doubt be improved: child care is often in short supply, financial offices are often weak so that community college students are less likely to receive financial aid, and employment offices don't do much to link jobs to the interests of students. But unless we redefine community colleges as comprehensive social service institutions and provide funding accordingly, they are not supposed to be massive providers of child care, family support services, or income assistance. To be sure, there has been a century-long effort in K–12 education to address the "whole child," and proponents of comprehensive school-based services (or full-service schools) have argued that schools should be the locus of many coordinated services (e.g., Dryfoos, 1994; USGAO, 1993). But such schools have been developed only rarely, for example when an energetic principal has persuaded community-based organizations to locate on a high school campus. This model has not been clearly articulated for community colleges, and the necessary resources are missing. After all, community colleges are by design intended to economize on costs to taxpayers, as compared with four-year colleges and flagship universities, not to increase costs because their students' needs are greater.

The responsibilities for unscrambling the work-family-schooling puzzle lie in other areas of social policy. If we had a universal child care program for toddlers two to five, one dimension of family stress would be reduced. If we had a system of family support centers, or community mental health centers, other family crises might be alleviated. If there were universal health coverage or broad access to community health clinics, then the time required to scrounge health care at emergency rooms would be reduced. If there were greater efforts to reconstruct the low-wage labor market so that young students could earn a decent wage, then the total amount of necessary employment would be reduced. If student aid were expanded and made more available to community college and part-time students, or if student loans could be used to postpone the early costs of schooling to later years of higher earnings (as in Australia; see Gallager, 2003), then another dimension of the work-family-schooling dilemma would be less problematic. None of these is a wild-eyed idea, and each has a following. Each would be valuable in its own right as an extension of basic care to the whole population, but each would be doubly valuable in helping students make their way through college. Making good on the promises of college for all and the use of education to prepare the workforce of the twenty-first century—and providing equal opportunity not only through *access* to postsecondary education but also through a reasonable chance of *completion*—will require the expansion of both college opportunities and complementary social policies.

Building on Strengths

Community colleges have many compelling features but also some obvious flaws. The question is whether future developments can build on the strengths of these institutions, moderate the flaws, and create a "strong" form of vocationalism—a form that serves the interests of students over the long run, that responds to the demands for the workforce of the twenty-first century in the broadest sense, and that conforms to a consistent vision of equality of educational opportunity. Otherwise it is all too easy to imagine community colleges mirroring the problems of high schools: their covertly vocational goal of transferring students to four-year colleges for the baccalaureate failing because transfer rates are too low; their overtly occupational programs leading to mediocre jobs, partly because few students complete coherent programs; increasing amounts of developmental education displacing both the transfer and the occupational missions; and separation continuing between academic and occupational purposes, faculty, and students. Following are six recommendations for building on the strengths of community colleges.

First, to avoid narrow forms of vocationalism, community colleges should strive to be as good as they can be *in their own terms*. If community colleges pride themselves on being "teaching institutions," they should strengthen the institutional mechanisms that support high-quality teaching. These include improved hiring and promotion policies, more instructor preparation and continuing development, teaching loads that allow time for instructional experimentation and improvement, instructional centers to support faculty, administrator support, and perhaps salary structures, like merit pay, based on teaching. If they pride themselves on being "the people's college," providing access to students who otherwise would not go beyond high school, then they need to provide a variety of other supports: improved remedial or developmental education, more coherent guidance and counseling, better tutorial services, better access to student loans and grants. As we have pointed out, the burdens of supporting nontraditional students must be shared by other social programs—child care policies, health and mental health programs, income support programs, and other noneducational policies that might enhance completion, especially for low-income and nontraditional students.[13]

Second, community colleges should make their many different purposes or missions more compatible with one another. One way to do this is to create bridges facilitating movement between academic and occupational programs, between remedial education and college-level courses, between short-term workforce development and longer occupational programs, between noncredit programs and credit programs—rather than maintaining independent islands of disconnected activities. The current structure is what one might call the shopping mall community college, where students choose from an extensive array of unrelated offerings. For students with clear goals, the vast bazaar of options may be fine. But for second-chance students, experimenters who enter the institution without much sense of purpose, or those who enter in casual ways but need access to the economic mainstream, student choice is unlikely to resolve the confusion created by the college's multiple, independent purposes.

Third, community colleges should allow occupational education to fulfill its own goals. This means changing the "academic" funding structures that make it difficult to support labs and workshops, expensive equipment and materials, and the small classes necessary in many occupational areas. It also implies preparing occupational instructors better for their teaching roles, since instruction in occupational areas is so complex. And particularly for modernized middle-level occupations, it requires links between academic disciplines and occupational preparation, because of the extensive academic content required in such occupations.

Fourth, community colleges should recognize that high-quality occupational programs involve a delicate balancing act. On the one hand, the programs need to target those occupations with relatively high wages and decent prospects for advancement, so they must be knowledgeable about labor-market conditions. Because community colleges are such local institutions, they need to work with nearby employers to make sure that the methods and technologies they teach are consistent with local practices. Many colleges do so through advisory committees, though developing cooperative education and internship programs are probably better ways to develop close working relationships with employers (Grubb, 1996b; Villeneuve and Grubb, 1996). On the other hand, it is important not to become overly job-specific, both because it is likely to harm students in the long run as specific skills become obsolete, and because it involves educational institutions in specific training that firms themselves can provide more effectively.

Fifth, community colleges should elevate the status of occupational education. The second-class status of occupational education is not inevitable; after all, professional education in four-year colleges and universities has grown in stature compared with academic disciplines, because of the employment benefits. Here, shifts in the labor market are likely to be a blessing. It is already clear that completing an occupational associate degree and then finding a related job generates higher economic returns than completing an academic associate degree (Grubb, 2002a). With the rise of modernized middle-level occupations linked more clearly to academic content, and to opportunities in four-year colleges, occupational education should no longer be considered a "terminal" program; like the "college and careers" programs now being developed in high schools (Stern, 1999), occupational education in community colleges can be designed to prepare individuals for employment, for further education, or for the combination of employment with later schooling that has become so common. And the need for academic preparation as well as occupational skills presents new opportunities to combine academic and vocational content, through integrated courses, team teaching, and learning communities in which students take several courses simultaneously (Grubb, 1996b; Badway and Grubb, 1997). To the extent that status follows employment patterns and opportunities for further education, the status imbalance between academic and occupational education should correct itself over time.

Sixth, community colleges should support their "collegiate" function—particularly the role of general education—to develop the intellect as well as the marketability of students. Within community colleges, which the vast majority of students have entered for occupational purposes, general education requirements are often viewed as impediments to completing programs expeditiously. Particularly with experimenters undecided about what major to pursue, counselors often advise students to "get gen ed requirements out of the way." One such student said, "I was advised to just plug along, just keep going, and get all the general stuff out of the way"—an unfortunate attitude that suggests general education is primarily an irritating barrier. At the same time, students often recognize that academic and intellectual development defines what it means to go to a "real college." Community colleges have developed strong hybrid approaches to occupational and academic instruction, using occupational applications to examine the large questions from academic and general education. Such courses include variations on classes like Working in America, a literature course relying on fiction and nonfiction about work; courses about the history of technology, its effects on society, and the political conflicts over technical change; courses on technology and the humanities, examining the ways technological change and its social effects have been examined in philosophy, history, and art; and courses examining the moral and ethical issues generated by the changing world of work. Such courses can offer the opportunity to develop critical perspectives—something that is all too rare in community colleges.[14] A business instructor who uses literature along with case studies from business to "teach students that the wisdom of great writers from the past is still pertinent to the solving of contemporary job-related problems" described this approach (Smith, 1991):

> I have also discovered why my business-career students generally falter when faced with complex problems in their business or technical core courses, especially those that deal with human issues. The juxtaposition between the humanities—which always ask questions about life, happiness, and freedom—and the courses that fill their career programs, always focusing on the absorption of accepted processes or pragmatic applications, is so strong. [My course] is a wild mix that asks students to question first, and then to justify their opinions convincingly, rather than to simply accept.

Such hybrid courses follow Dewey's recommendation for "both-and" policies, because they integrate academic, intellectual, and critical concerns with the knowledge and materials of occupational education. Such approaches provide models for an institution that incorporates overtly occupational goals but still respects the academic foundations of modernized occupations and the intellectual traditions of the nineteenth-century college.

The transforming influences of vocationalism have been unavoidable in community colleges, sandwiched as they are between two other institutions—high schools and four-year colleges—that started becoming vocational even before community colleges were founded. Community colleges are relatively young institutions without roots in the intellectual and moral traditions of the common school or the early four-year college, so they have not been as pressured by partisans of nonoccupational goals. But vocationalism need not follow the high school pattern, dominated by outmoded programs and by the "narrow vocationalism" derided even by the business community. Community colleges provide a vision of what a balanced or "strong" form of vocationalism might look like, one that is responsive to the needs of employers and to the longer-run development of students, to the imperative of "learning to earn" as well as to civic and intellectual development, one that recognizes the special instructional conditions of occupational education without denigrating them simply for being different from academic instruction. This kind of middle way provides one of the few paths out of the dilemmas that vocationalism has created for all institutions. If we as a nation decided to make community colleges all that they could be, they would offer a synthesis of broad occupational preparation and general education, reflect a commitment to excellence in their own terms and to equity in both access and completion, and become comprehensive institutions serving many purposes while creating bridges among them. This is a vision worth pursuing in the new century.

4

∼ Second Chances in Job Training and Adult Education

$\mathcal{A}$NOTHER vocational development took shape during the last third of the twentieth century: public support for short-term job training (or workforce development) programs. Such efforts can provide occupational preparation for groups of individuals—the long-term unemployed, welfare recipients, the disabled, dislocated workers—who might not have access to educational institutions. Even more than community colleges, they can give participants a second chance to enter the mainstream of economic life, consistent with the emphasis in the common-school tradition on inclusiveness and equitable opportunities. Job training programs have been created outside the schooling system deliberately, to avoid some of the flaws of formal education, and they represent an intriguing experiment in creating still another form of job preparation—not apprenticeship, not formal schooling, but something else with distinctive goals and methods.

The promises implicit in these second-chance opportunities are remarkable. They have been promoted as efforts to overcome the unemployment created by technological change and job retrenchment, the high levels of poverty in an inegalitarian society, and the economic decline in regions and occupations over which individuals have no control. And yet job training has in practice been so unstandardized and insubstantial that the programs are rarely successful, and neither those needing training nor employers seeking workers know what they are getting. If Americans are unsure what a high school diploma or college degree signifies in terms of competency, the uncertainty of these second-chance programs is even greater.

Part of the problem lies in the failure to develop coherent systems of training. In the decades around 1900, Americans created a system of schooling that flowed from elementary school through college and professional schools. In contrast, job training programs have remained disconnected from one another and poorly integrated into the education system—despite some efforts near the end of the twentieth century to create statewide systems of education and training. The possibilities of second-chance job training are undermined by the historical dualism of *education* versus *training*. Without modifying that dualism, we suspect that efforts to reform job training will continue to fail.

In the early twenty-first century, the experiment with job training is just about over. The programs never worked well, and they are now being replaced with increased labor-market information and "self-service" approaches to training, not by any form of skill development. The failures of job training illustrate just how hard it is to develop alternatives to formal schooling as ways to prepare for work.

Multiple Strands of Job Training

The modern history of public job training programs begins during the 1930s, when President Franklin Roosevelt created a series of public employment programs that included the Works Progress Administration (WPA), the Civilian Conservation Corps (CCC), and the National Youth Authority (NYA). Many educators hoped that such programs would be run through school districts, allowing them to employ schoolteachers as instructors and reinforcing local control. However, the Roosevelt administration did not trust the public schools to educate low-income youth—particularly in the South, with its history of racism—and feared that school districts would use federal money in place of declining state resources. As a result, the major job training programs were set up outside the Office of Education, and at the local level were generally operated by community groups rather than school districts (Tyack, Lowe, and Hansot, 1984, ch. 3).

Roosevelt's New Deal programs were the most extensive experiment with work-based learning the United States has ever conducted. As one of the planners described them, the programs pioneered "a new technique in education . . . that is, education through work." Youth in the NYA seemed to like this approach: they described regular school as being "like prison," where "they treat you like babies." One posed the central dilemma of the vocationalized high school: "I got to make myself a living. I want to be an auto mechanic. What's French got to do with that?" (Lindley and Lindley, 1938, xiii, 196). But these programs were especially controversial where they provided public employment—jobs that were often attacked as "make work" or "leaf raking," and that smacked of incipient socialism. Educators continued to fight the use of such public funds outside the schools, and the New Deal programs faced hostility over their federal control and their excessive involvement in local labor markets. With few friends and many enemies, these experiments in work-based education had died a quiet death when the onset of World War II replaced the crisis of the Great Depression.

Job training reemerged in public policy in the 1960s, initially in the Kennedy administration's response to the 1960–61 recession, and afterward as part of the Great Society's employment programs under Johnson. While it's tempting to see a direct legacy from the New Deal—Lyndon Johnson had been the Texas director of the National Youth Administration—this connection was probably less powerful than the fundamental idea that preparation for work could take place outside of schools (especially for individuals whom the schools had failed), and that short-term efforts might be sufficient to resolve unemployment problems.[1] Congress enacted the Manpower Development Training Act (MDTA) of 1962 to reduce unemployment through job training programs outside the schools, independent of federal funding for vocational education, partly because of the poor reputation of vocational education and partly because of the conviction that secondary schools were ill-equipped to provide nontraditional training for adults. MDTA programs were usually short-term (ten- to fifteen-week) job-specific training courses focused on entry-level jobs, intended to get the unemployed back into the labor force in a hurry. Many of them were operated by community-based organizations (CBOs), under the assumption that such groups were in better contact with the unemployed. And so a pattern and a constituency evolved in favor of short-term, job-specific, entry-level programs operated largely by CBOs.

A second strand of workforce training also emerged in the 1960s as part of the Great Society's War on Poverty—the beginning of a link between job training and welfare. The main federal program for welfare, Aid to Families with Dependent Children (AFDC), stressed the importance of supporting *children* and was initially intended to aid mothers caring for their offspring at home. However, as working became more common for all women, pressure increased to move welfare mothers (and fathers) into employment. A series of programs to encourage work culminated in 1967 in the Work Incentive Program (WIN), which made work mandatory for certain welfare recipients. At the same time, the Great Society initiated a "services strategy" that included child care and transportation, enabling recipients to work their way out of poverty by enrolling in short-term job training.

During the 1970s and 1980s, training programs were consolidated, states gained greater control over federal training funds, and public service employment (PSE) was introduced in the Comprehensive Employment and Training Act of 1973 (CETA). PSE was especially intriguing, since it combated unemployment directly, rather than assuming that training alone could increase employment. It also responded to the glaring mismatch in cities, where housing, transportation, safety, and maintenance needs were substantial and yet a vast pool of individuals could not find employment (Lafer, 2002, ch. 5). The PSE share of the CETA budget rose from 34 percent in 1975 to 60 percent in 1978, supporting 725,000 jobs. While this number was a proverbial drop in the bucket—after all, there were 6.2 million unemployed individuals that year—it still represented a new direction for training programs.

Like public employment in the 1930s, PSE was always a target of opposition. As one conservative critic argued, such jobs "deprive the poor of an understanding of their real predicament: the need to work harder than the classes above them in order to gain upward mobility." When President Reagan introduced the Job Training Partnership Act (JTPA) and eliminated PSE in 1982, he invoked the underlying philosophy of job training in opposition to public employment: "This is not another make-work, dead-end bureaucratic boondoggle. This program will train more than one million Americans every year in skills they can market." His version of the Education Gospel reaffirmed that solutions to poverty and unemployment lay in the provision of skills, not the provision of jobs (Lafer, 2002, 156, 164).

At the same time, training for welfare recipients went through its own changes. In 1981 the Reagan administration allowed states to develop programs for getting welfare recipients back to work. The resulting efforts varied enormously. They all tended to provide help in searching for work, but even the most basic forms of education, like remediation for those lacking basic skills, were rare. Building on the state initiatives, the Family Support Act of 1988 provided federal matching funds for remedial education, vocational education, and training, along with other social services. This approach combined the social services strategy of 1960s welfare reform with the employment emphasis of WIN, and reinforced decentralized state responsibility.

By the 1990s, a vast array of job training programs had been established. In addition to programs for the unemployed and for welfare recipients, other federal legislation supported training for dislocated workers who had lost their jobs because of sectoral changes (like the decline of logging in the Pacific Northwest), for veterans, and for disabled individuals. The federal government has repeatedly responded to new problems with new programs—rather than by incorporating new purposes into existing programs (or into educational institutions)—and by piling on new initiatives without asking how existing structures could do the job. When the General Accounting Office counted the number of education and training programs in 1995, it found that about 163 separate programs, located in virtually every department of the federal government, spent a total of $20.4 billion that year (USGAO, 1995, appendix table II).

The array of job training programs did not constitute a coherent system in any sense. A favorite critique of job training has cited the lack of links among programs, the inconsistencies in local offerings, and the waste and duplication. *America's Choice: High Skills or Low Wages!* expressed this common sentiment (CSAW, 1990, 53–54): "The various and often unintended origins of our adult training and employment 'system' have created a bewildering array of services, programs, and providers . . . a crazy quilt of competing and overlapping policies and programs, with no coherent system of standardization or information exchange services on which various providers and agencies can rely."

Driven in part by this "crazy quilt" and in part by persistent rhetoric about the need for greater skills, many states began to develop more coherent systems of workforce development during the 1980s and

1990s, just as schools and colleges did a century earlier (Grubb et al., 1999). In some cases, referral mechanisms created "ladders" of opportunity for clients to move from shorter, lower-level programs to more intensive and sophisticated programs, from *training* into *education*. Indeed, a rags-to-riches myth developed, that a welfare mother could enter a welfare-to-work program for remedial education, move into job training for an entry-level health occupation, enroll in a community college while working in entry-level jobs, transfer to a four-year college, graduate, and go on to medical school! Unfortunately, this potential pathway was in practice mostly a legend because the nonsystem of job training was only rarely articulated with the system of education.

Recently, changes in both welfare and job training legislation reshaped job training once again—entirely for the worse.[2] In welfare, the Personal Responsibility and Work Opportunity Reconciliation Act of 1996 (PRWORA) largely replaced training with the ethos of Work First, the idea that dependent individuals should be put to work as a way of returning them to employment. This assumes that any job, even the most menial, has the potential to teach people the skills and personal habits necessary to succeed. As the conservative American Enterprise Institute argued, "Any entry-level job teaches the important skills of showing up for work, regularly and on time, suitably clothed and prepared to cooperate with other workers, and to attempt to please customers." A legislator in Michigan, a state with a particularly virulent form of Work First, declared that welfare recipients should "get a job or hit the road," a statement that recalled the jobless hoboes of the Great Depression.[3] In this spirit, many states have chosen to bar welfare recipients from education and training. Others have created a series of steps that recipients must go through before they are eligible for training, again reducing the amount of skill development they are offered. While the booming economy after 1996 allowed many welfare recipients to find jobs, these were largely unskilled positions vulnerable to economic downturn cycles. The recession after 2000 was disastrous, for example: many former welfare recipients—still lacking skills, in poorly paid jobs with little on-the-job training and few prospects for advancement—were the first ones dismissed.[4]

The Workforce Investment Act (WIA) of 1998 further undermined the possibility of well-conceived workforce development programs. Congress seemed to run out of ideas about reforming job training, since its prior efforts—consolidation and state control in CETA, and employer control with performance standards in JTPA—had not been successful. WIA abandoned the effort to devise effective training, even as it repeated the comforting rhetoric of the Education Gospel: Secretary of Labor Elaine Chao declared WIA "a new roadmap . . . to help us prepare the 21st century workforce," even though its predecessors had concentrated on training clerical workers and janitors. Instead of even trying to prepare a twenty-first-century workforce, WIA incorporates a Work First philosophy, providing training only to those individuals unable to find employment after two initial stages of information gathering and job search in the program's One-Stop Centers. This guarantees that the majority of services provided by WIA are little more than informational; WIA provides training only to applicants with the least schooling and employment experience, a form of negative selection that makes it difficult to devise effective programs.[5] WIA also introduced voucherlike mechanisms by providing funding through what are called Individual Training Accounts (ITAs). Despite the conventional rhetoric about individual choice and consumer sovereignty, WIA fails to provide its clients with the most basic prerequisites for markets to work well—accurate and timely information, and a clear understanding of the consequences of choices.[6]

WIA has provided very little job training. An early examination of participation found that only 42,000 adults participated in training in 2000 under WIA, compared with 163,000 in 1998 under JTPA (Frank, Rahmanou, and Savner, 2003). As of 2002, only 242 individuals in Boston had received Individual Training Accounts, in a city where perhaps 6,000 individuals enroll in community college occupational programs; in San Francisco, where City College provides occupational education for about 60,000, there were only 1,090 ITAs (Javart and Wandner, 2002, table 3; Macro et al., 2002); and a study of six states found that participation in training had plummeted in all of them (Shaw and Rab, 2003). Finally, WIA has made the creation of coherent workforce development *systems* much more difficult, particularly by relying on individual choice and Individual Training Accounts; community colleges, which often serve as bridges between job training and mainstream education, have reduced their participation in WIA dramatically because of burdensome performance standards and inadequate numbers of referrals (Barnow and King, 2003; Shaw and Rab,

2003). The long legacy of job training since the early 1960s has finally ground to a halt, with training reduced to a trickle and replaced by Work First and One-Stop Centers that provide little more than information of unknown effectiveness (USGAO, 2003).

At the beginning of the twenty-first century, forty years of effort—seventy years, if we count the early programs of the New Deal—have produced a wealth of job training experiments.[7] A few of them even seem promising: the Job Corps, an intensive residential program, though too expensive for large-scale replication; the Center for Employment Training in San Jose, California, with its combination of classroom instruction, work experience, preferential hiring within the community, and supportive services; the Youthbuild program that provides training in construction skills while youth rebuild inner-city housing; and some forms of public service employment that give jobs to the unemployed while providing needed urban services. But there have been very few effective programs, nothing like a coherent system, and there is certainly no institutional alternative to formal schooling as the dominant form of occupational preparation. Many states were moving in the direction of a system of job training and education during the 1990s, but federal interventions—welfare "reform," WIA, and Work First, all reflecting extreme hostility toward the poorest members of our society—have effectively annihilated that option. Instead we have seen a long retreat from public responsibility, particularly in the past twenty years: from reestablishing the idea of training during the 1960s and the concept of enhancing demand through public service employment in the 1970s, to the demolition of PSE, the replacement of real training with pallid forms of work experience and job-search assistance, and finally the triumph of Work First, which provides almost nothing to the individuals most in need. Publicly supported job training has essentially vanished from the system of vocational preparation.

Legacies of Job Training

While the public commitment to job training has disappeared, the idea of job training is still with us, and it will probably reemerge at some point. Job training is part of the Education Gospel, with training and low-level skills (rather than "higher-order" skills) seen as solutions to economic swings, technological unemployment, poverty, and dependence. It therefore experiences dilemmas similar to those of occupational preparation within education. Like community colleges, job training has been promoted as a second-chance effort. As in other forms of professional and occupational education, there has been continuing debate about broad versus narrow training: Many providers want longer and more intensive programs, while others take pride in running short programs, claiming they provide "Chevrolet" rather than "Cadillac" projects that get clients to the same place.

Job training also suffers from a problem common to community colleges: the problems of many clients are so complicated that mere training is inadequate to help them advance. The work-family-schooling dilemma plagues job trainees as well as college students. Many clients have difficult family situations, health and mental health issues, housing and transportation problems, a lack of motivation and direction—a complex situation usually described bloodlessly as "multiple barriers to employment." Perhaps the clearest example was the New Chance program, which provided a wide range of intensive services to young mothers, most of them high school dropouts. But New Chance made almost no difference in the lives of those mothers, and may even have had *negative* consequences by increasing pregnancy and reducing employment. A qualitative analysis revealed that many of the women suffered from depression, and that others were subject to abuse or to substantial family demands (taking care of siblings, for example)—problems the program could not address (Quint, Musick, and Ladner, 1994). Once again, complementary policies—in this case, mental health and family support programs—were needed in addition to job training. But job training programs, especially conventional inexpensive ones rather than demonstration programs like New Chance, have routinely provided even fewer support services than community colleges, and for individuals who have even more complicated lives.

The move toward Work First has also clarified the fact that job training has extended the structure of inequality in postcompulsory education to even lower levels. At the top, some individuals—largely those in the upper-middle and middle class—benefit from the best professional schools in the world, partly supported by state subsidies, federal aid, and now tax credits. In the middle, other students—more likely to be working class—attend less-selective comprehensive universities and community colleges, with smaller subsidies and fewer resources. Below

Table 4.1. Impacts of Job Training Partnership Act after 30 months, by target group

	Mean earnings		Impact per assignee		Impact per enrollee in dollars
	Treatment group	Control group	In dollars	As % of control-group earnings	
Adult female	$13,417	$12,241	$1,176[a]	9.6%	$1,837[a]
Adult male	19,474	18,496	978[c]	5.3	1,599[c]
Female youths	10,241	10,106	135	1.3	210
Male youth non-arrestees	15,786	16,375	–589	–3.6	–868
Male youth arrestees					
Using survey data	14,633	18,842	–4,209[b]	–22.3	1,804[b]
Using scaled Unemployment Insurance data	14,148	14,152	–4	0.0	–6

Statistical significance: a = 1%, b = 5%, c = 10%.
Source: Bloom et al. (1994), exhibit 5.

them are high school graduates who receive no postsecondary subsidies, whose real income has been eroding, and whose employment is precarious, particularly during recessions. And then the poorest and least-educated individuals, those with the most "barriers to employment," get the shortest and cheapest programs;[8] under Work First they get little more than imperatives to search for work, to attend job assistance and self-esteem seminars, and, at the end of the day, to take transient, low-paid jobs.

But while job training and mainstream education share some features, they are nonetheless quite different. Most obviously, job training has been largely confined to relatively low-skill occupations—copyshop operators, word processors and file clerks, assembly-line operators, janitors. These are hardly the jobs associated with the Knowledge Revolution, and it is misleading to promote such low-level programs with the rhetoric of the Education Gospel. With its focus on low-skill labor markets, the economic benefits of job training have consistently been paltry.[9] On the whole, programs have been ineffective for both men and women; for male youth they have often had negative effects, since they reduce the labor market experience that might help them advance. The results for JTPA, shown in Table 4.1, are typical: while women benefited more than men (as in high school vocational programs), even for them the increase in earnings of 9.6 percent after completing a program was insufficient to escape poverty or move out of welfare. Even where there are benefits in the first few years after a program ends, these benefits tend to vanish after four or five years (Friedlander and Burtless, 1995). Federal policy has worsened the situation by consistently forcing local programs to be shorter, usually only ten to fifteen weeks, and by replacing any real training with job search assistance and work experience. Under Work First, there are almost no services of any kind—and certainly no training to prepare the twenty-first century workforce.

The contrast between training and education extends to instructional issues as well. Training has developed the connotation of instilling relatively routine skills for specific jobs through simple drill and repetition. In contrast, education implies teaching individuals the larger systems of work within which those skills fit and higher-order competencies (like "industrial intelligence" or SCANS skills) to prepare individuals for upward mobility, as well as general education and other nonvocational learning. In job training there is little attention to teacher training, almost no discussion of pedagogy, and certainly no room for general education. The governance of job training has also separated it from education. The initiatives and funding for most job training have come from the federal government, while the primary responsibility for education comes from states and localities. This separation makes it difficult to integrate education and training, in turn complicating efforts to move from one into the other. Those enrolled in short-term job training and welfare programs have had no obvious way to move from training into the mainstream of education, except where community colleges have provided explicit bridges between the two (Grubb and McDonnell, 1996).

In both welfare reform and job training, Work First has undermined the human-capital assumptions embedded in the Education Gospel: that education and training increase job-related competencies to give the poor an avenue out of poverty, and also benefit the nation at large. The new assumption is that work, even in poorly paid, low-skill, and highly transient jobs, is the best way to improve human capital—despite the long history of failures in apprenticeships where work proved to be noneducative, despite evidence of the lack of much real training within JTPA work experience (Kogan et al., 1989), despite the lessons of the 1970s and 1990s from work-based learning, about how often work is discouraging rather than educative. Abandoning human-capital assumptions has further widened the distinction between education and training.

The final characteristic distinguishing training from education is perhaps the most dismal. While training has consumed substantial resources—$5 billion in 1999, and perhaps $85 billion since the early 1980s—and a great deal of research energy, it has been a largely symbolic effort. It has often been intended to convince the population that the government is doing something to address social problems, even when those actions have been ineffective. Summer youth programs, consistently shown to have no effect on subsequent employment, have been funded year after year because of the pleas of mayors who want to be seen as doing something to get young people off the streets. The efforts of Ronald Reagan to enact JTPA had less to do with any commitment to the poor—never Reagan's interest—than it did with the political specter of increasing unemployment. Dan Quayle, then a senator and the sponsor of the JTPA legislation, commented, "I kept saying to myself, [the Reagan administration] can't veto the bill—not with 10.1 percent unemployment." In the early 1990s, the rising unemployment associated with the 1990–92 recession again demanded some response, which took the form of amendments to JTPA. The passage of PRWORA in 1996 was due largely to the Clinton administration's efforts to seem more moderate and politically acceptable, especially after the disastrous congressional elections of 1994. The enactment of WIA proclaimed its commitment to the Education Gospel—the "roadmap to help us prepare the 21st century workforce"—while reinforcing the doctrine of Work First. The amount of funding available has been sufficient to support about 5 percent of the eligible population—hardly enough to make a dent in poverty or unemployment. Job training is largely a sideshow, creating the impression of acting on social problems without sacrificing much political capital or, conversely, gaining much credit. As Quayle's chief staff member said, "There are some issues that most people just don't care about. Job training is an issue nobody's going to give you a PAC contribution over." Once again, this political reality distinguishes *training* from *education:* people do care about education, and politicians want to be education governors and education presidents, but no one has ever wanted to be the job training president (Lafer 2002, chs. 5 and 7).

Overall, the forty-year effort to develop job training outside schools and colleges as a second-chance alternative to education programs has worked poorly. One reason is simple: since the best occupational areas were already dominated by professional and occupational education, job training had to emphasize the least skilled jobs, and this contributed to trivial employment benefits. Another reason is the screening process operating in education and training: job training programs concentrate on those individuals with the greatest barriers to employment, but offer them shorter and cheaper programs, with inadequate support services and almost no links to education. And the connection to welfare recipients, in a country so malevolent toward the poor, has contributed to the political vulnerability of training, leading in the end to Work First. The effect has been to abandon those most in need of the second-chance opportunities that job training is supposed to provide.

The difficulties that job training has faced illustrate once again how profoundly the institutions supporting job preparation influence its quality, effectiveness, and equity. When employers sponsor job training—whether in the apprenticeship practices of the eighteenth and nineteenth centuries, in work experience under JTPA, or in current training programs for their own employees—training tends to become overly specific, the tension between production versus training becomes obvious, and inequality emerges in various ways, including a focus on upper-level employees. When schools and colleges sponsor job preparation, the older practices of "academic" education and the distance between school and workplace hamper the effectiveness of occupational education. When training shifts outside the schools, the result has been a set of inadequate programs that segregate the worst-off individuals, provide them with overly short training with much fewer resources, and have little effect on their long-term employment, earnings, or independence. Each way of structuring job preparation has come with its own distinctive problems, but the most recent attempts in job training have been a particularly egregious failure. We suspect that the United States has not seen the end of job training, and that it will be resurrected in another recession, another employment crisis, when its symbolic value is too powerful to resist. But unless the distinctions between education and training can be bridged, future job training outside of educational institutions will not work any better.

Adult Education in the Second-Chance System

Adult education has been another second-chance opportunity. Sometimes referred to as continuing or recurrent education, in its broadest definition adult education incorporates all forms of education that adults pursue after they have left their initial period of schooling. These include public job training programs; the training offered by firms to their employees; the education of adults seeking to complete high school, in community colleges, and in university extension programs; the continuing education programs connected to licensing and professional development; and all kinds of instruction by religious organizations, self-help groups, community-based organizations, book clubs, language schools, and sports organizations.

In this broad sense, adult education has a glorious history. Adult self-learning has been a feature of American education since the colonial period. In the nineteenth century and well into the twentieth, the United States was filled with itinerant speakers, entertainers, and informal summer recreational and learning excursions for families and adults. The Chautauqua movement, of summer encampments and month-long retreats, was for many adults the center of their learning activity. Members of workingmen's clubs and trade unions debated important public and economic questions. Women's clubs met to discuss literary works; teachers learned the newest pedagogical techniques in summer "normal" schools. The YMCA and YWCA provided educational activities, especially for young men and young women leaving rural America to enter life in the big city. Immigrant adults attended English-language and citizenship classes. And a host of correspondence courses and proprietary schools provided opportunities for adult learners almost anywhere in the United States. These activities tended to be voluntary, informal, antibureaucratic, participatory, and democratic. They drew on the experiences of students and involved adults in discussions that mattered to them. They usually took place outside of schools, reflecting a mistrust of bureaucratic education and government intervention (Kett, 1994).

Adult education today has retained many of these characteristics; the innovations of modern technology, including most recently Web-based learning, have added to the range of possibilities. Nonetheless, over the course of the twentieth century adult education in the United States underwent three related shifts that made it more like the rest of the educational system. It became increasingly vocational, increasingly centered in schools and connected to degree-granting institutions, and increasingly publicly funded.

The first shift—not surprisingly, given general trends in the educational system generally—has been the redirection toward vocational purposes. Many forms of adult education still focus on culture and moral uplift, but they have been joined by and subordinated to learning for utilitarian purposes. The two fastest growing sectors of adult education are proprietary schools and distance education or Web-based courses. The former are explicitly vocational; students enroll to enter specific occupations or jobs. The latter are often sold as a way to become certified in a particular occupation, to learn specific skill sets and improve job opportunities, or to get a degree for use in the labor market. An entire industry wrapped around professional development is almost always connected to improving the vocational position of professionals. Even though buzzwords like "lifelong learning" and the "learning society" imply a broad range of self-improvement purposes, such slogans are usually tethered to the Education Gospel, to reports about the number of job changes individuals make, or to the importance of reinventing oneself to find work in a fast-changing economy.

The second shift in adult education has been the drift from informal and nonschool settings into formal educational institutions, particularly community colleges, four-year colleges with more older students, and university extension programs. The notion that individuals would not return to school once they left for the workplace has been replaced by lifelong learning, epitomized by upgrade training, retraining for those who want to change jobs, and second-chance opportunities—most of which take place in educational settings. The increasingly dominant role of formal institutions in adult education is obviously linked to the broader vocationalization of schooling and the idea that schools are the best places to prepare for the labor market. The trend is also linked in more concrete ways to the growth of school-based credentials and the growing number of jobs that require "school skills."

The third shift, toward government support, is an extension of job training and workforce development efforts. Publicly funded adult education now includes a variety of remedial and English as a Second Language (ESL) classes for adults with low basic skills who want to enter the workforce.[10] Adults have been routinely referred to adult literacy programs by job training and welfare-to-work programs when they fall below minimum levels on basic skills tests, and federal funds for adult education are now embedded in the Workforce Investment Act of 1998.

Many of the problems associated with job training appear in adult education as well. Enrollments in adult education programs are relatively brief, are usually disconnected from job training programs (even when individuals have been referred by those programs), are rarely evaluated, and are reputed to produce mediocre results. Job training and welfare-to-work providers frequently look on adult education programs with dismay; one welfare program director bemoaned the problems of referring welfare recipients to the "black hole of adult education" from which they never emerged (Grubb et al., 1989). And, like job training, adult education is almost never connected to mainstream educational opportunities, so there are no obvious pathways into education that might enhance individuals' options. Programs leading to the general equivalency diploma (GED) typify these problems. Relatively few adults stay in them long enough to receive the diploma. While the GED is intended to be the equivalent of a high school diploma, in practice it is worth very little in terms of either employment or access to further education. The test required to receive the diploma—conventional multiple-choice questions on decontextualized reading, writing, and math skills—encourages the simplest forms of "skills and drills" instruction, usually from untrained part-time instructors with no background in alternative pedagogies.

With almost no evaluation evidence available about the effectiveness of adult education, a wide variety of claims abound, as do anecdotes about the full and successful lives lived by those who have successfully emerged from GED and other adult education programs. However, the limited evidence on effectiveness suggests that the outcomes are meager and discouraging.[11] One comprehensive review of the data concluded (Diekhoff, 1988, 629):

> Adult literacy programs have failed to produce life-changing improvements in reading ability that are often suggested by published evaluations of these programs. It is true that a handful of adults do make substantial meaningful improvements, but the average participant gains only one or two reading grade levels and is still functionally illiterate by almost any standard when he or she leaves training. But published literacy program evaluations often ignore this fact. Instead of providing needed constructive criticism, these evaluations often read like funding proposals or public relations releases.

The evolution of adult education in the United States has been a journey from extraordinarily rich, varied activities initiated by voluntary organizations rooted in self-help and self-development toward publicly funded, vocationally oriented, school-based programs that concentrate largely on remedial education. Like job training, public adult education has been disconnected from other educational opportunities, so that even if individuals complete adult courses, there is no obvious next step, no bridge to other programs. It is difficult to find evidence on the proportion of adult education students who progress to either training or mainstream education, and most programs are not structured with such goals in mind. As with job training, the result is another sideshow, a set of programs appended to and yet disconnected from the mainstream educational system, with great potential but little evidence of effectiveness.

Expanded Programs, Expanded Possibilities

In the best of all worlds, second-chance systems such as job training, adult education, and some aspects of community colleges (like remedial education) would not be necessary. The first-chance education system would prepare all its students to be active citizens, competent workers, and lifelong learners able to undertake their own educational upgrading as circumstances require. Indeed, there's every reason to reform first-chance programs with these goals in mind, as we have indicated. But even if we could improve formal schooling, we would still need second-chance institutions. Many recent immigrants without access to first-chance education need these programs; our relatively unconstrained market economy leads to business closings, dislocated workers, job changes, unstable employment, and therefore the need for retraining and upgrade training; and in a liberal society where young people are free to make their own choices about schooling and work, many individuals choose paths that they later regret and then need a second chance.

The question is how to enhance access to education and training opportunities without simultaneously undermining the efficacy of these efforts. A hopeful approach starts from recognizing that it is easier to reform existing programs than to develop them from scratch. We should not engage in the typically American process of adding new programs, as if novelty always implies improvement. Many principles implicit in the best education and job training should be preserved—the concept of relatively broad preparation, the notion of developing second-chance programs (including remedial education), the idea of providing support services in addition to classroom instruction, the need for concern about outcomes, including completion rates and placement.

An immediate problem is that separating job training and adult education from mainstream educational institutions has proved to be, after nearly forty years of experimentation, the wrong way to go—particularly in a world where formal schooling monopolizes routes to middle-level and professional employment. Every effort should be made to integrate any short-term job training and adult education into the mainstream of education, to create links so that the best practices of formal schooling can influence job training. Several concrete mechanisms can accomplish such integration.

- In some cases, community colleges offer noncredit courses and programs that serve the same function as job training and adult education, but also provide subsequent access to their conventional programs. Most colleges have noncredit divisions on which they could build, along with state funding mechanisms to support such efforts (Grubb, Badway, and Bell, 2003).

- Job training in community-based organizations could create transition mechanisms so that those completing short-term job training could, as their life circumstances permit, move into longer-term certificate and associate degree programs in community colleges.

- Some successful programs have coordinated the efforts of community-based organizations with those of formal educational institutions, to combine their complementary strengths. For example, the widely cited Communities Organized for Public Service program in San Antonio has combined the efforts of CBOs to recruit Latino students, to provide them with counseling and support of various kinds, and to act as advocates on their behalf, while local community colleges provide classroom instruction in basic English and math as well as occupational preparation.[12]

- In some localities, community colleges have operated JTPA programs, taken on adult education responsibilities, and operated One-Stop Centers funded by WIA. Such organization facilitates—though it certainly doesn't guarantee—linkages between job training or adult education and community colleges as entry points to further education.

A second challenge is that basic skills instruction continues to be ineffective in adult education and job training programs. Most programs teach basic reading, writing, and mathematics in isolation from any other instruction, so that participants intending to move into employment instead find themselves drilling on subject-verb agreement and arithmetic facts, or reading short and irrelevant texts. Instructors are usually part-time and untrained, and the dominant pedagogy relies on the most routine skills and drills, repeating the very teaching methods that did not work for participants in their earlier years of schooling. Fortunately, there are some promising practices that could reshape basic skills instruction in job training and adult education programs, as well as in many community colleges.[13] Some adult education programs and community colleges include divisions of basic skills instruction that have adopted more effective teaching philosophies, rejecting behaviorist and skills-oriented teaching in favor of hybrid methods incorporating more constructivist and student-centered pedagogy. In some institutions basic skills instruction is "contextualized," teaching basic language and mathematical competencies in a context meaningful to students. These can take the form of "applied" courses—business English, business math, applied math for HVAC technicians—that use the specific forms of reading, writing, and math required in a broad occupational area. In addition, a number of institutions have developed learning communities—linked programs in which two or three courses in remedial English or math are taken simultaneously with occupational or academic subjects. The content of the various courses can be integrated, projects can be shared across courses, and the more frequent contact among students creates communities of learners who work together.

A third reform requires reversing the trend toward voucherlike mechanisms, including Individual Training Accounts. Market mechanisms require not only that consumers be well-informed—something that is itself quite difficult, given the number of programs available and the varying quality of information about them—but also that they be sophisticated in the use of uncertain information (Grubb, 2002c). Yet almost by construction, individuals in job training and many adult programs, especially in second-chance institutions, are relatively unsophisticated in their use of information. Many have found their way into these programs almost by accident, and many don't seem well-informed about the alternatives they contemplate.[14] Market mechanisms also make it difficult to shape institutional improvements, like the linking of short-term training with longer-term education and the improvement of remedial instruction. Marketlike mechanisms may be appropriate in some areas of the education and training "system," but not at the lowest levels.

A fourth problem is the link between job training and welfare, since that link has contributed to attacks on training and to the steady shift away from training to job-search assistance and finally to Work First. Job training illustrates why it is better to provide universal programs—as educational institutions do—rather than targeted programs for specific populations, since targeting welfare recipients and the long-term unemployed has stigmatized training and contributed to its demise. It will remain necessary to provide short-term occupational programs for several good reasons—the need of some individuals (including dislocated workers and immigrants) for immediate employment while they plan for the longer term, the requirements of upgrade training for those changing jobs, the desire to explore new opportunities among "experimenters" and curious individuals everywhere. But short-term programs can be provided in many ways—in noncredit divisions of community colleges as well as credit programs, for example—and should be more carefully linked to further education and decent employment, without creating an exclusive link to welfare recipients and the long-term unemployed. Destigmatizing job training by embedding it in multipurpose institutions would give it greater acceptance in the employer community, among policy makers, and among prospective students.

Finally, we have to abandon the fiction that training by itself can correct the serious problems of unemployment, poverty, racial and gender discrimination, and other dislocations in the economy. The assumption embedded in the Education Gospel—that efforts to improve the skills of potential workers can resolve all social and economic problems—is most obviously false in job training, where the combination of multiple barriers to employment among clients and virtually nonexistent support services clarifies how impossible this approach has been. As with the work-family-schooling dilemma among college students, other complementary social and economic policies are necessary: guidance and counseling, to enable individuals to chart life courses for themselves; physical and mental health programs to reduce barriers to participation; child care and other family supports; the direct reduction of unemployment through fiscal and monetary policy as well as targeted economic efforts, especially in central cities. Without other policies related to equity, the ideal of equal educational opportunity has been even more unrealistic for short-term job training than it has been for education.

The development of job training opportunities over the past forty years provides another perspective on the efficacy of schooling as a means of job preparation. Whatever qualms we have about vocational purposes in education—and vocationalism has had distinctly mixed effects, as we document more fully in Chapters 5 through 8—at least educators have tried to provide serious amounts of preparation, more broadly constructed than narrow training. Whatever misgivings we might have about the inequality of the education system, at least it has provided access to many occupations rather than concentrating on only poorly paid work. Whatever doubts we may have about business control in education institutions, it pales beside the dominance of small and marginal employers in JTPA and WIA. Job training provides a vision of vocationalism in extremis, under the worst possible circumstances. The reasons for its failures—the focus on low-skill jobs; the low cost and short duration designed to economize on the preparation of the poor; the distance of *training* from the greater breadth and pedagogical advantages of *education*—are likely to be replicated in any other alternative to formal schooling. In critiquing occupational preparation within schools and colleges, therefore, we need to be careful lest we understate the accomplishments and possibilities of formal schooling relative to nonschool programs.

At the beginning of the twenty-first century, job training represents both failure and opportunity. Training programs have dwindled to almost nothing, and the underlying idea—providing short and cheap solutions to deeply rooted problems like unemployment and poverty—is pernicious, because it claims to offer solutions to those in great need. And yet the idea of second chances remains so central to American values, and the attractiveness of job preparation outside formal schooling remains so powerful, that job training will probably be resuscitated in the future. When this happens, its success will depend on connecting training to education and narrowing that gap so that individuals and society can benefit from a better-prepared workforce.

5

⌒ The American Approach to Vocationalism

$\mathcal{B}$ʏ ᴛʜᴇ ᴇɴᴅ of the twentieth century, Americans had built a huge edifice of education and training. In 1900 only 6.3 percent of each age group finished high school; this proportion increased to a high of 79.1 percent in 1969 before dropping back to 70.6 percent in 2000. In 1900 only 2.3 percent of those aged eighteen to twenty-four were in college; by the close of the century 58 percent of this group attended college—short of college for all, but still a majority. In 1940, on the eve of World War II, only 14 percent of the entire population had completed high school, and 4.5 percent had completed four years of college; by the end of the century these proportions had increased to 83.4 percent for high school, and 25.2 percent for college.[1] Today the high school, a small and elite institution in 1900, has become a level of schooling that everyone takes for granted. College and university education, an essentially negligible enterprise in 1900, has expanded to the point of being a mass institution, one large enough to approach the ideal of college for all. At the end of the nineteenth century the principle of inclusivity, dating from the common school movement, applied only to grammar schooling through grade eight; now inclusivity and concern over access extend to all levels of the education system, including the university. Moreover, second-chance institutions—community colleges within the education system, job training programs and adult education outside it—have been added for those who lost their way the first time around. In comparison with most other developed countries, the expansion and elaboration of formal schooling in the United States started earlier and has taken place over a longer period of time (Goldin, 1999; Wolf, 2002, fig. 6.2).

The expansion of enrollments was part of the shift to more overtly occupational purposes. In the American approach,[2] vocational transformations have always been *precursors* to the expansion of enrollments, rather than consequences. The high school became vocationally differentiated by about 1915, when only 12 percent of the cohort graduated from high school; as high school enrollments burgeoned in the next four decades, students entered an institution with clearly occupational purposes. The development of land-grant institutions dedicated to a "liberal and practical education" and of universities with professional schools had been accomplished by 1900, when only 2.3 percent of the age group attended college; when enrollments increased in the 1920s and in the 1960s and thereafter, they again expanded within collegiate institutions that were already professionalized. The arguments for occupational purposes in community colleges, first developed in the 1930s and 1940s, led to the creation of comprehensive colleges in the 1950s and early 1960s; when enrollments boomed in the late '60s and '70s, community colleges were already comprehensive rather than primarily academic or transfer institutions. Conversely, no level of schooling in the United States above the middle school has ever been expanded appreciably for only intellectual or civic or moral purposes.[3] The segments of education dedicated to purely intellectual or moral traditions—elite liberal arts colleges, a few private religious colleges, a few selective public high schools, and some private high schools dedicated to an older academic tradition—have dwindled in relative importance as vocationalized high schools and enormous public and professionalized universities have grown up around them.

The American version of vocationalism is also notable for its emphasis on formal schooling as the dominant mode of preparation for work, rather than a broader variety of institutions.[4] Apprenticeships were weak as early as the eighteenth century, and the various efforts to revive them have not succeeded. The other institutions that developed around 1900 to continue work-based learning—corporation schools, private trade schools, and cooperative education—have survived only in small numbers, or in institutions like proprietary vocational schools of varying (and mostly dubious) reputation. The continuation schools envisioned in the Smith-Hughes Act of 1917, intended to provide continuing education past the age of compulsion to youth who had to go to work, in practice became dumping grounds for students unable to make adequate progress in conventional high schools, rather than innovative ways of combining schooling and employment. The efforts to revive work-based learning as part of job training, in the 1930s and again in youth programs like the Job Corps and the Youth Conservation Corps, have been marginal. Moves to combine work-based learning with schooling failed in both the 1970s and again in the 1990s. Experiments with job training in a variety of locations, including community-based organizations, have dwindled virtually to nothing. Adult education, historically a distinct alternative to formal and bureaucratized schooling, has itself become vocationalized and institutionalized, and in the process has been reduced to a pastiche of remedial and ESL programs, ineffective and disconnected from mainstream education. Instead of the rich variety of occupational preparation available in some other countries, the United States has been dominated by formal schooling, for better and for worse.

Vocationalism in the United States has also developed within comprehensive educational institutions—not, as in many European countries, in vocational high schools, technical colleges, or specialized universities. While there remain a few specialized high schools in large cities, a few technical institutes, and some specialized postsecondary organizations in the arts and psychology, overall the institutions in the United States have been comprehensive, especially the expanding institutions like high schools, community colleges, and second-tier universities. The American preference for comprehensive institutions partly reflects an equity issue, as specialized schooling has consistently been attacked for segregating some students—the "manually minded" in high schools, professional aspirants in colleges—from others. In addition, students have voted with their feet, preferring comprehensive institutions that maximize choice and keep the promise of further education open—important features of the *system* of education created in the twentieth century. And vocational institutions themselves have tried to become comprehensive as a way of reaching for the higher status of academic programs and access to yet further education, leading inevitably to "institutional drift." The resulting comprehensive institutions have had mixed effects: on the one hand, their academic programs have often overshadowed vocational and professional programs, and sometimes degraded the quality of occupational efforts; on the other hand, they have made it easier to move between academic and vocational programs, and to integrate academic and vocational learning. In any event, they are a permanent feature of the American landscape.

Vocationalism has influenced every level of the American system from the high school on up. What is less often noted is that, after a century of development, the American approach to vocationalism now emphasizes postsecondary over secondary education. Traditional vocational education, which has almost disappeared from high schools except in the reforms for "education through occupations," now takes place in community colleges. Unlike in European countries following the German tradition, there is no well-developed vocational path through secondary education in this country. Currently the greatest emphasis of reformers seems to be on college for all, not reductions in high school dropout rates, and the real battles over access now take place for postsecondary education. The United States spends much more than other countries on postsecondary education relative to K–12 schooling.[5] The comparative growth of postsecondary education—historically rooted in the preparation of an elite—has displaced the more egalitarian ethic of K–12 education that arose from the inclusiveness of the common schools, and when one examines the contributions of education to growth and its links to employment, the most powerful and effective examples come from postsecondary institutions (see Chapters 6 and 8). The postsecondary emphasis is a distinctive feature of American-style vocationalism, particularly in contrast to countries with intensive secondary vocational education and postsecondary institutions that have remained largely academic.

The process of vocationalizing American education has created a *system* of education in which the links among different levels are formalized. These links in turn mean that some levels of education that appear to be academic—the college-prep tracks in the high school, the transfer programs of community colleges, or liberal arts majors in elite colleges—are really forms of pre-vocational preparation for the higher levels of schooling where professional education takes place. This forces us to recognize that vocationalism has never been complete. Even when the major purpose of most schooling is occupational preparation, there is still room in the system for moral, political, and intellectual education, and it is rare to find public forms of work preparation that are single-mindedly vocational (with the exception of job training). Vocationalism is incomplete in another sense as well, because there are different conceptions of vocationalism, and different forms of schooling may adhere to one or two but not all of them, an idea we will explore later in this chapter. Perhaps not surprisingly, vocationalism proves to be most complete in preparation for the high professions, again reinforcing the postsecondary and professional emphasis of American vocationalism.

Despite the many dissenters, vocationalism has been powerful enough that once underway it has become self-reinforcing, so there is no reason to think that vocationalism as a mechanism of expanding schooling has run its course. Our inability to develop successful non-school forms of preparation, illustrated by the failure of job training and the difficulty of resurrecting apprenticeship-like practices, suggests that there may not be any powerful alternative to a vocationalized educational system. Indeed, when new institutions were created in the twentieth century, they followed the pattern of established institutions: the second-tier comprehensive universities adopted the patterns of research universities, and most aspired to develop full professional schools and PhD programs; community colleges, for all their efforts to enroll nontraditional students, have remained part of the education mainstream and often hope to become baccalaureate-granting colleges; and the newer profit-oriented organizations like the University of Phoenix fit well into a system of vocationalized institutions. So vocationalism will endure; the important question is, *what kind* of vocationalism will we develop in the twenty-first century?

The process of converting prevocational schools and colleges to occupational preparation has led not only to the expansion of enrollments but also to the reinforcement of marketlike practices in high schools and especially in postsecondary education, where consumer choice has always dominated. Some segments of the educational marketplace work relatively well, when consumers are sophisticated about the choices, providers respond to appropriate incentives, and the quality of educational credentials is unambiguous. But markets are likely to work poorly when consumers are unsophisticated, providers respond to inappropriate incentives, market-making mechanisms (like educational credentials) are ambiguous, or the nature of the "product" is uncertain. The differing kinds of education markets allow us to see how public policies might be altered to create the conditions necessary for markets to work well.

Raising the issue of public policy clarifies that any system of schooling operates within a context of broader government policies. Unfortunately, in our country the inadequacies of a broad range of social and economic policies undermine the capacity of the education system to achieve its goals, including its vocational goals. Many developments associated with the welfare state—the regulatory mechanisms of the period after 1900, the social programs of the 1930s, the Great Society initiatives of the 1960s—have been potentially complementary to education and training. But over the past thirty years opponents of social programs have transformed the notion that government is responsible for the well-being of all its citizens into the view that "welfare" should be only grudgingly offered to the (undeserving) poor (Katz, 2001; Piven and Cloward, 1997). This ideological shift has had disastrous consequences, not only for large numbers of Americans without basic material resources but also for education. It has undermined progress through K–12 schooling for low-income children, made it difficult for postsecondary students (particularly in community colleges) to finish their programs, subverted the effectiveness of second-chance opportunities including job training, and weakened any program touched by the stigma of welfare. When we turn in subsequent chapters to appropriate reforms, we will argue the need to create a Foundational State recreating the foundations or preconditions necessary to fulfill the expectations of the Education Gospel and to develop a more equitable form of vocationalism.

A distinctly American system of vocationalism is now firmly in place. This system, constructed over slightly more than a century, draws much of its justification from the Education Gospel, which gives schools and universities crucial responsibilities and stalwart defenders. It has had many consequences, both positive and negative—in its effects on earnings, status, and economic growth, on the effectiveness of school-based preparation for work, and on equity and opportunity. This approach to vocationalism is both historically rooted and widely accepted, and it must be the starting point for recommendations that will carry us forward in the twenty-first century.

Linking Institutions in a Vocational System

Our current educational institutions—particularly high schools, colleges, and universities—were developed during the nineteenth century. In the twentieth century they became increasingly occupational in their purposes and also more clearly connected, resulting in an educational *system* that now extends from the lowest level (including early childhood programs) to the pinnacle of graduate school. These links mean that, regardless of the content at any level, each stage is also a mechanism of advancement to a higher stage. This has made the system as a whole more instrumental and more vocational, even as it has allowed some levels to appear entirely academic.

The link between secondary school and college is archetypal. In the nineteenth century, no clear progression existed, since there were multiple routes into college—sometimes passage of an entrance exam, sometimes just an interview or a personal recommendation. No occupation required high school or college graduation, so the lack of formal schooling was not a barrier to upward mobility. Toward the end of the century, some college administrators, concerned about the low level of student preparation, moved to create a more orderly transition. Midwestern universities led the way by establishing certification procedures that automatically admitted graduates of certified high schools. In 1894 the Committee of Ten, chaired by Harvard's president, Charles William Eliot, articulated the view that there ought to be one standard approach to the high school curriculum as a precursor to college entrance. The practice of completing high school before entering college became part of the emerging system. The College Entrance Examination Board (CEEB), later known as the College Board, initiated the movement for standardized college entrance examinations, leading to the Scholastic Aptitude Test (SAT) in the 1920s. The Carnegie Foundation for the Advancement of Teaching introduced the "Carnegie unit" in 1909 as a way to standardize the amount of academic coursework necessary for entry into college. These developments ultimately linked high schools and colleges in both orderly and (apparently) meritocratic ways (Johanek, 2001).

A similar link has been established between two- and four-year colleges. Because community colleges are local institutions, they typically have articulation agreements with local four-year colleges, where students with certain courses and grades are accepted for admission. Transfer rates, a crucial measure of success for community colleges as multipurpose institutions, are both symbolic and real, since they link two-year colleges to the upward vocational sweep of the education system.

The process of creating an orderly and meritocratic system has been repeated for admissions to graduate school, where the baccalaureate degree plus an external examination—the Graduate Record Exam (GRE), the Law School Admissions Test (LSAT), and so on—are absolute prerequisites. These processes have been contested, for both graduate and undergraduate admissions, in technical debates about the predictive validity of grades and test scores, in political charges of inequity and in demands for affirmative action, and in arguments that competencies other than cognitive ability make good doctors and lawyers and businesspeople. But such controversies have been sideshows to the main event: developing regular procedures for moving from one level of schooling to another via an education credential plus grades plus a related entrance exam. In the process, every level of schooling has become crucial for attaining the next higher level.

Many other formal and informal mechanisms articulate different levels of the educational system. These include university outreach programs for low-income and minority students; "2+2" and tech-prep programs connecting high schools and community colleges; subject-specific projects to make high school courses consistent with collegiate expectations; summer "bridge" programs before the freshman year; articulation agreements and transfer centers; academic counseling; common course-numbering systems and general education requirements that allow students to move easily from one institution to another. Some states have formalized the transition between K–12 and post-secondary education by devising K–16 master plans. All these efforts are part of the extended process, initiated more than a century ago, to facilitate upward movement in the overall system.

The big exceptions to the development of an articulated system have been job training and adult education. Their disconnection from mainstream education, rooted partly in their historical origins as alternatives to conventional schooling (Kett, 1994), undermines their effectiveness as forms of work preparation, since they are rarely adequate by themselves for gaining access to good jobs, and since they do not provide access to further education. While job training and remedial learning in adult education could potentially play important roles, they remain marginal and unsystematic, leading neither to real employment nor to further education—a warning to any form of workforce preparation that fails to create links to mainstream education.

One desirable consequence of creating an educational *system* is that American educational institutions usually allow upward progress, unlike the "terminal" technical schools created in many European systems. When upward routes seem blocked—for example, when too few students from certain high schools progress to college, or when transfer rates from community colleges appear too low—there are inevitably outcries, followed by efforts to increase access to further education.

Another consequence is that many apparently academic programs have become, at their heart, pre-vocational. The academic track of the high school, the normal route to college and then professional and managerial occupations, effectively serves a vocational purpose, and the largest number of students recognize the high school as inescapably vocational (Goodlad, 1984, ch. 2). For middle-class students, college has long been a place to "find oneself," which increasingly has meant finding a career to pursue and a graduate school to enter—often through a nominally academic major such as science, English or history (for law), or economics (for business). Inadvertently, perhaps, community college has become something similar for working-class students: the "experimenters" who enroll in courses as a way of learning about alternative occupations are also "finding themselves," if with fewer resources and less familial support than students in four-year colleges. Along the way, there is adequate room for purely intellectual pursuits, for the humanities and the general education requirements that invoke the grandest intellectual traditions and define a "real college." But we might call these forms of education pre-vocational rather than academic, because student goals are vocational. Furthermore, the *system* is more vocational than its components, since students are usually aiming for vocational or professional programs after their academic coursework.

Having a schooling system explicitly tied to vocational purposes means that knowing how to progress through the system becomes critical for upward mobility. On the one hand, the creation of systematic linkages has made progression through the system *relatively* transparent, at least compared with a nonsystem—as in the nineteenth-century world of unsystematic routes into college, or family-based apprenticeship routes, or job training and adult education where programs are unrelated to one another either vertically or horizontally. The mechanisms of upward mobility are in one sense well known—the subject of guidance and counseling, of a small library of advice literature and Web sites, and of an industry of test preparation programs for such exams as the SAT and LSAT. On the other hand, the system is still not well understood by many students and their families, particularly those without much schooling and those who are new to this country. A new form of inequality has arisen in this vocationalized system of education, in which the lack of knowledge about mobility within the education system and about its articulation with employment presents a barrier. The *potentially* more transparent system in practice remains opaque to many participants, a subject we address later in examining guidance and counseling.

Furthermore, even if mobility within the education system seems relatively transparent, mobility from schooling to work is not as clear. To be sure, in professional education the relationship is unambiguous: lawyers must go to law school, take bar exams, and then apply for positions that usually require law degrees; doctors must go to medical school and pass medical boards before starting up the ladder of internships and residencies. In the semiprofessions, however, these relationships start to break down. For example, teachers must go through education school and earn credentials, but in periods of shortages (like the present), many individuals earn emergency credentials and alternative credentialing programs spring up that are primarily on-the-job learning, blurring the relationship between formal schooling and employment. In social work, despite efforts to professionalize social workers through increasing education, many individuals have entered the profession through other means, and the debate about educational credentials and licensing is fierce and never-ending.[6] In midlevel occupations accessed through community colleges, a few (those in nursing and other health-related occupations, aviation mechanics, and electrical work) are subject to licensing requirements, but others may be entered through nonschool training (from the military or union-based apprenticeships, for example), through experience, or even through avocational learning, again blurring the role of school-based preparation. The mechanisms linking schooling to employment are relatively weak, as we will examine further in Chapter 7, compared with those in other countries, like Germany, where elaborate credentials clearly define the connections between education and employment (Buechtemann, Schupp, and Solof, 1993). If Americans created a relatively transparent *education* system over the twentieth century, they failed to create a transparent *education and employment* system. The result has been to generate serious ambiguities about school-based preparation for work.

Alternative Conceptions of Vocationalism

Despite the triumph of vocationalism, the rise of occupational purposes has always been contested. Opposition comes from, among others, the defenders of a more traditional education rooted in the civic purposes of the nineteenth-century common schools or the piety and discipline of the early religious colleges, or simply in the view that education should be more than narrow "trade training." As a result of this dissent, vocationalism has remained incomplete. Avowedly civic purposes persist in several high school subjects (particularly social studies and history), and intellectual goals live on in the general education requirements of community and four-year colleges. The academic track in the high school and academic majors in colleges have endured, even if they should sometimes be called prevocational. And academic subjects continue to be included in every specification of what should be taught, including the New Basics of *A Nation at Risk* (1983) and the subjects—English and math—of the accountability movement. Old purposes in education never die; instead they are augmented and sometimes superceded by new goals and new allegiances.

Vocationalism has remained incomplete in a different sense, as well, because people have more than one goal in mind when they discuss the vocational purposes of education. Americans seem to use this term in at least four different ways. The first involves *occupational intentions*, when a school or college—or its student body—views its purpose as vocational preparation. This obviously happens in professional schools of law, medicine, and education, but it also occurs in less obvious ways when students expect that completing high school will get them better jobs, or when they enter college hoping to gain access to better jobs.

This expression of vocational intentions is neatly summarized in the words of one student (Grubb, 1996b, 68): "I didn't have much idea of what I wanted to do; I knew that I needed to go to school, though." Occupational intention can be quite controversial when an institution's participants differ about purposes. For example, teachers often view the high school as primarily intellectual and hope their students are motivated by the love of their subjects, but students view it as vocational and see their grades only as a way of getting into college (Goodlad, 1984, ch. 2). College professors and their students, particularly their credential-driven students, exhibit the same conflict, exemplified in questions like "Will this be on the test?" and in the incessant quest for "relevance." In practice, then, an institution is fully vocationalized in terms of *intentions* only when students, instructors, administrators, parents, and policy makers agree about its occupational purpose. In this sense the high school is incompletely vocationalized because participants are still divided over its purposes, while medical schools, business schools, and truck-driving schools are fully vocational.

A second conception of vocationalism depends on whether an institution's subject matter is directed toward overtly vocational ends—the criterion of *occupational curriculum*. Like occupational intent, this concept at first seems simple: professional schools, high school vocational education, and community college occupational programs all have occupational curricula, with courses like Accounting I, Computer Architecture, Dairy Herd Management, and Fashion Merchandising. But here, too, occupational curricula have been contested. Except in narrowly defined job training, differences exist over what curriculum produces the most effective workers—over the appropriate skills to teach, the appropriate mix of academic (or theoretical) versus vocational (or applied) coursework, the balance between school-based learning and work-based learning in internships, and sometimes the best pedagogies for teaching vocational competencies. The simple idea that an institution or program is vocational when its curriculum emphasizes occupational competencies becomes murkier when disagreement persists over the precise content of that curriculum—as in the disagreements over professional education reviewed in Chapter 2, or in the difference between *A Nation at Risk*, which promotes academic courses, and the SCANS Commission's recommendation for teaching the varied SCANS skills. Institutions may also be vocational in the sense of student intentions without changing their curricula, leading to inevitable complaints about the lack of "relevance" for academic coursework. When the obverse happens—when a curriculum is explicitly vocational but students have higher schooling aspirations, as happens when students are tracked into dead-end vocational programs—then complaints about tracking, inequity, and "cooling out" proliferate. Only when occupational intentions and occupational curricula are aligned is there an equilibrium of motive and content.

A third conception of vocationalism, *related employment*, involves the connection between education and employment. We think of a fully vocationalized program as one in which the large majority of its graduates find employment in the occupational area for which they have been trained. This is usually the case, for example, in high-demand areas like health occupations, in many computing fields (at least until the collapse of the high-tech market in 2000), and in engineering (again with the important exception of cyclical fluctuations). But when a program's completers enter diverse occupations, as do college students in the humanities, then we tend not to consider the program vocational. Sometimes a program can be vocational in intent and curriculum, but its completers fail to find related employment because of a misdiagnosis of the labor market or because the program lacks any links to local employers. The failure to find related employment gives vocational education a bad reputation: low placements in related occupations undercut a program's economic benefits (as we will discuss in Chapter 6) as well as its students' occupational intentions. This occurs so often, especially in lower-level programs, that both federal and state accountability requirements have used related placement as a measure of effectiveness. Such efforts to connect occupational preparation more tightly to employment also signal a substantial gap between schooling and work—an effect of creating a vocationalized education system, but not an *education and employment* system.

A fourth conception of vocationalism involves *required schooling*, when a particular kind of schooling is an absolute requirement for entering an occupation: medical school for doctors, PhD programs for professors, engineering school for engineers, and pre-baccalaureate degrees for radiological technicians, aviation mechanics, and those in other licensed occupations. Educational institutions benefit enormously from such requirements, which guarantee continuing demand.

Unless these institutions have misjudged the labor market and over-enrolled students, occupational placements are virtually assured. Required schooling dominates where there is formal licensing, and in other cases where hiring practices have come to require a specific level of schooling; many jobs, even quite unskilled jobs, mandate a high school diploma. But where neither licensing nor hiring practices require a specific level of schooling, educational institutions have to compete with other sources of preparation, and placements are not assured; if placement rates are low, they may be considered weak forms of occupational preparation.

When education or training programs fail to satisfy all four of these criteria, conflict is almost inevitable. Some institutions are clearly vocational by all of these criteria: medical schools, nursing programs, many technical programs at both the two- and four-year college levels. Others are vocational through only one or two criteria: for example, their students may intend to prepare for specific jobs and their curriculum may be driven by the apparent demands of employers, but students are unable to find related employment—a situation that dooms many vocational programs that fail to assess the state of the labor market, and many short-term job training efforts. Alternatively, students may view programs as vocational even though the curriculum does not incorporate job-related competencies—as in academic tracks in high school, for example, where many students fail to see the point of their coursework. In still other cases, school-based content lags behind the requirements of work—a problem of occupational curricula in a fast-changing world—and despite high rates of related employment or even required schooling, employers complain about their new hires. Or a curriculum may include material apparently unrelated to employment—like general education requirements in business school—and cause students to complain about the "relevance" of their coursework. The alignment of all four conceptions of vocationalism is rare precisely because nonvocational components persist, because participants disagree about the purposes of education, because aligning educational programs and employment requirements is difficult. And so it should not be surprising that even as schools and colleges have become increasingly vocational, conflicts have emerged—not only with older, pre-vocational conceptions of schooling, but also among the different strands of a fully vocational form of education.

A different consequence of the varied conceptions of vocationalism is that the distinctions between *vocational* education and *professional* education are overdrawn, and sometimes pernicious. Most Americans think of vocational education as pre-baccalaureate occupational training in high schools and community colleges and, in even more narrow forms, in job training programs. Professional education, in contrast, requires baccalaureate and postgraduate schooling, presumably because professional expertise is heavily dependent on school-based skills, while vocational expertise might be learned on the job. While there is some truth to this distinction, vocational education and professional education confront many of the same issues. Each faces the dilemma of establishing an occupational curriculum, with endless debates about appropriate content and pedagogy, narrow versus broad preparation, the "skills" that should be included in schooling rather than left to practical experience, and the connections of schooling to employment—issues we examine in Chapter 7. And both vocational and professional education have been driven by efforts to increase the status of occupations, as well as their earnings, by adding more years of required schooling. The similarity between vocational education and professional education is important in part because it helps us understand how pervasive vocationalism has become.

At the same time, professionalism does have some important advantages over vocational education. The most obvious are the higher earnings and higher status of occupations that we consider professional. But professionals are also more likely to have developed an ethic of special contribution to society based on their command of specialized knowledge, thereby justifying school-based preparation over other forms. In contrast, vocational education often includes skills that are more readily developed on the job. The claims of professional education rest on special contributions and moral roles—doctors heal the sick, lawyers preserve the rights of the innocent and the property of all, engineers make buildings safe, teachers prepare the next generation. The parallel claim among vocational educators about the inherent dignity of all labor has had little appeal in an era when many jobs have been deskilled, when workers have little control over their employment, when real wages and employment stability have been falling for modestly skilled (or modestly *schooled*) jobs. While both unions and professional associations try to restrict entry and enhance wages, professionals can justify such actions by the need for advanced knowledge. No one, after all, wants an untrained doctor or engineer, while an untrained sales clerk or carpenter might be less dangerous.

Overall, professional preparation is more likely than other occupational schooling to adhere to all four conceptions of vocationalism, while vocational education is more likely to fail on the criteria of related employment and required schooling. The academic education we have labeled pre-vocational—the college-prep track in high school, the transfer track in community college, academic majors for students preparing for graduate school—is vocational only in the sense of student intentions. Professionalism is therefore the most complete expression of vocationalism, and it is not surprising to see that it expanded throughout the twentieth century.

Continuous Reinforcement of Vocationalism

Once a system of vocational schools and colleges began to emerge, the process of vocationalizing became self-reinforcing. Both older occupations and new occupations (like computer programming) have shifted their preparation into formal schooling. This process has taken place not, by and large, through government action but through much more decentralized and private mechanisms, driven by the continued weakness of work-based methods, the economics of job preparation pushing costs onto the public sector or onto individuals, and the norms requiring more schooling for professional status.

In a complex economy with varied occupations, the vocationalizing process has followed several different patterns. One involves the shift away from the "school of hard knocks" into formal schooling. Particularly vivid examples of those affected include individuals in artistic occupations, such as visual artists, actors, dancers, musicians, and filmmakers.[7] Traditionally, visual artists made their way by painting on their own, living in the proverbial garrets, and learning from each other—like the Impressionists working in Paris around 1900, or the color-field painters and abstract expressionists in New York during the 1950s. In contrast, "academic" training in formal art schools had a pejorative connotation, as it was seen as a form of preparation devoted to mastering old art—classroom copying rather than creating new art forms. In the past two decades, however, most artists have started by earning a bachelor's or master's degree in fine arts from a conventional university or art school, as have increasing numbers of actors, musicians, and dancers. Such schooling provides access to knowledge about methods, access to complex tools (kilns and printing presses), a community of fellow artists, and education in the history and theory of art, including ways of thinking that are newly important in conceptual art. In a highly competitive profession, the art degree opens doors to employment in the art world, including jobs in museums, galleries, and management that do not involve making art but do keep aspiring artists in touch with current developments. The master of fine arts (MFA) degree is also necessary for teaching jobs in the arts, which are infinitely better than waiting on tables as a way of earning a living while trying to become famous—or at least self-supporting—in one's craft. And so certain occupations that once epitomized freedom from formal schooling have become credentialed, just as accounting and dentistry and law have been.

Other examples of the shift to school-based preparation involve occupations that seem—at least to old-school proponents of college— odd additions to higher education: horticulture service operations; poultry science; apparel and accessories marketing; hospitality services; broadcast journalism; medical records administration; parks, recreation, leisure, and fitness studies.[8] Many middle-level occupations have striven to develop the status of professions, with required levels of education and certification by industry groups: farmers and foresters (reviewed in Cheit, 1975); real estate agents; auto mechanics, now regulated by the National Automotive Technicians Education Foundation; workers in the hotel and restaurant industry, with standards formulated by the American Culinary Federation and the American Hotel-Motel Association, among others; ski guides, certified by the American Mountain Guides Association, a member of the International Federation of Mountain Guides Associations. Recently manufacturer's representatives have proposed a three-year, three-level, school-based certification program for their field, citing reasons straight from the Education Gospel: "to remain globally competitive, many industry experts believe America must have a work force whose members are highly trained and knowledgeable enough to respond to rapidly changing skill demands" (Weinrauch, Stevens, and Carlson, 1997). And youth-serving (or "youth development") agencies have recently stated that their workers should have baccalaureate degrees, "necessary to an emerging profession's identity" (Alexander, 2002), even though youth work is built largely on street skills. These efforts extend the logic of professionalism to many more occupations, including those dominated by small employers (like hospitality services and auto repair), who are notoriously difficult to organize but nonetheless have been moving toward industry associations. They have also enlarged the conceptions of "skill" well beyond those conventionally associated with schooling to include interpersonal skills, manual and visual skills, and nonstandard forms of literacy. As school-based preparation has become the route into professions, occupations seeking to enhance their professional status have been pressed into colleges and universities.

New occupations have evolved in much the same way, proceeding through a cycle that ends with formal schooling. The occupations of the "new economy" based on computers and electronics began with computer programmers, whose preparation in the 1960s and 1970s was informal: early programmers learned by reading manuals and by doing (Greenbaum, 1979). Gradually, however, programming moved into formal schooling, with baccalaureate programs for programmers, subbaccalaureate programs for those working with applications (e.g., word processing and spreadsheet programs), and graduate programs for those aiming to enter research and development. This cycle of informal preparation superceded by formal schooling is now being replicated in Web-related occupations, where at first individuals prepared by learning HTML and Web-site design on their own. In the past five years, a new kind of program has been created in community colleges that incorporates elements of design, programming, and marketing, often labeled a multimedia program (Villeneuve, 2000). Similarly, in biotechnology new programs are being developed in both two- and four-year colleges to prepare students for jobs ranging from researcher to production worker. Of course, talented individuals can still find their way into computer programming or art or culinary occupations without formal credentials; the criterion of *required schooling* is not an absolute factor, as it is in licensed professions. But for all of these occupations formal schooling is increasingly the dominant path of entry.

A second pattern of self-reinforcement involves the reorganization of work, generating new specialties that become distinct occupations with their own educational requirements. Business has created sub-occupations with specialized programs, including those for purchasing agents, sales representatives, accounting, insurance and actuarial science, hospitality services management, real estate, and apparel and accessories marketing. Medicine has become increasingly fragmented, partly as a result of efforts to de-skill some occupations, with school-based programs emerging for physicians' assistants, certified nurse practitioners and nurse's aides, midwife-practitioners, cardiac technologists, radiological technicians, and physical therapists. The law has spawned paralegals and legal secretaries; engineers have begotten engineering technicians; architects have sired architectural drafters; and accountants now rely on para-accountants and spreadsheet specialists trained in community colleges. As the shift toward de-skilling creates new occupations with schooling requirements, it reinforces the trend toward required schooling for all occupations.

A third mechanism reinforcing vocationalism comes from the competition among educational institutions for additional students. The most typical form of institutional competition is opening new programs of study. Almost every suggestion for a new program comes with an assessment of the anticipated job market, and state agencies typically ask for demand data before approving new programs in public universities. In addition, education institutions strive for higher status through "institutional drift"—by offering degrees for jobs higher in the occupational hierarchy. Most public comprehensive universities used to be normal schools designed to prepare teachers; many subsequently became comprehensive state colleges serving undergraduates with a few master's-level programs. Some of these, as in California, are now pressing to offer the PhD, the mark of the true research university; others have established honors colleges as ways of competing with elite universities (Selingo, 2002). At the sub-baccalaureate level, regional vocational schools, established in the 1970s to provide secondary vocational education to clusters of high schools, have adopted adult vocational programs and then become technical institutes granting associate degrees. These technical institutes have in turn become comprehensive community colleges in many states (most recently Minnesota, South Carolina, and Louisiana). The pressure from community colleges now is to provide baccalaureate degrees, as add-ons to their associate-degree programs.

A fourth mechanism of reinforcement comes from students seeking to amplify their professional qualifications. Once vocationalism is under way, additional schooling becomes increasingly necessary for students as a form of self-defense, particularly if they want access to the best professions. And so we see high-status professional schools and four-year colleges oversubscribed, with battles ensuing over access, the validity of standardized entrance tests, and affirmative action. While it might seem that the education system would run out of places for students to go—that they would max out at the PhD—those seeking academic positions routinely complete postdoctoral programs, extending their preparation by several years. Doctors may serve multiple residencies to gain specialty degrees; MD/PhD, MD/JD, and JD/PhD combinations seem to be thriving. Increasingly undergraduates are earning credits for two, three, or even four majors as a way of gaining an advantage in the labor market; as one student noted, "I thought four majors would be good when I was looking for a job" (Lewin, 2002). As of 2000, only 8.4 percent of the labor force had more than a baccalaureate degree (see Table I.1), so there is still considerable room to expand educational credentials—to proclaim graduate school for all! There's no reason why the escalation of schooling and credentials should stop anytime soon, since the members of the Education Coalition, particularly students and educators, support the process.

In contrast, there are few examples of what we might call de-schooling,[9] efforts either to reduce educational requirements or to transfer occupational preparation back into apprentice-like forms. While Florida tried in the early 1990s to implement a "leveling process," allocating specific levels of occupational preparation to adult education and community colleges to prevent institutional competition and education inflation, no other state has followed its example (Grubb and McDonnell, 1996). And we know of no occupation for which schooling requirements have been dropped.[10] Formal apprenticeship mechanisms have failed to expand appreciably: the number of registered apprentices has grown from about 300,000 in the late 1970s to about 440,000, roughly two-thirds of whom are in the building trades, but this is a small fraction of the number of students (perhaps 3.2 million a year) enrolled in credit-bearing postsecondary occupational programs in community colleges, with a great deal more in noncredit programs. The efforts to increase apprenticeship have been undermined by the lack of public subsidy and by lax efforts in state and federal agencies; furthermore, apprenticeships usually require funding and support from employers, something many are unwilling to provide when they fear their trained workers will be "poached" by other employers.[11] In the 1990s there was a flowering of interest in work-based apprenticeships like those in the German system (Hamilton, 1990), but the School-to-Work Opportunities Act ended with dismal results (Hershey et al., 1998), essentially killing any further discussion of apprenticeships. The process of changing schooling requirements, then, has operated only to increase education levels, never to reduce them.

It is easy to be cynical about the expansion of education require-ments. The critics of credentialism have often argued that schooling is an empty exercise in which students learn very little related to their fu-ture work. Overschooling—more schooling than necessary to do the job—is a common problem in the American economy, as we will docu-ment in Chapter 7. Other problems with credentialism include high costs, the inequities of school-based programs, and the mismatch be-tween the competencies taught in school and those required on the job (Collins, 1979). But school-based forms of preparation have a number of obvious advantages. They are *potentially* more transparent pathways into jobs than are experienced-based routes, which have unclear crite-ria for hiring. Educational institutions are more inclusive and more susceptible to open debate and reform than a system of job entry through personal contacts or familial relationships. Equity issues—the lack of women in stereotypically male occupations, discrimination against racial minorities, the barriers to disabled individuals in employ-ment—can be debated and *potentially* rectified within the educational system. The wrangling over curricula in professional programs and the arguments about broader preparation ("education") versus shorter, specific preparation ("training") are examples of public debate over is-sues that would otherwise be decided by individual employers. And anything that can improve working conditions and enhance the control of workers themselves—which *may* happen as part of professionalism —is surely hopeful. So there are good reasons, aside from the self-in-terest of the Education Coalition, for the self-reinforcing shift of prep-aration into schooling.

Education Markets and Their Limitations

Vocationalism continually recreates forms of schooling that are useful because they have value in the labor market. As a result, vocationalism has contributed to thinking of schooling in marketlike terms. The movements for vocational and professional education helped shift the purpose of education from collective goals—the maintenance of democracy, the preparation of moral leaders—to private goals like access to valued occupations. Mechanisms of consumer (or student) choice entered the high school, first with the development of vocational tracks, then with the explosion of electives starting in the 1920s, ending up with the shopping mall high school (Powell, Farrar, and Cohen, 1985). Marketlike mechanisms have been growing in other ways too, as proposals for expanding school choice through vouchers, charter schools, and subcontracting to private organizations like Edison Schools have proliferated.

At postcompulsory levels, consumer choice among colleges has always existed, and most providers are motivated by (or constrained by) consumer demand. The dominant federal subsidies in higher education—grants, loans, and tax credits—take the form of lightly regulated vouchers that students carry with them. Most states have created systems of public universities that provide substantial choice, and the private sector expands this choice with elite colleges, religious colleges, some low-quality institutions open to anyone who can pay, some specialized institutions, and now proprietary universities like the University of Phoenix aimed at working adults. The choices *within* institutions have also been enormous as specialized institutions have given way to comprehensive ones, usually including a dozen or so relatively autonomous colleges and graduate schools with course offerings in the thousands. The student as consumer has displaced earlier notions of prescribed and coherent programs of learning, and the shopping mall university has triumphed over earlier versions of collegiate education.

However, quasi-markets in education remain controversial, since various imperfections may lead to suboptimal outcomes. The nature of the "commodity"—education and training—is uncertain in its future effects and variable among participants. Individuals are often poorly informed about the choices they must consider, or are unprepared to make choices for themselves. Education institutions, with their own interests, stand between the ultimate demanders (employers) and the suppliers (students) of skilled labor. Some institutions are concerned for their reputation, and generate strong programs and high rates of related employment; others are concerned more with enrollment and "profit," and may neglect the quality of their offerings—a charge often leveled against proprietary schools and less-selective universities. Credentials, central to creating education markets, are often developed through reputation rather than public regulation and oversight; for example, the content of the baccalaureate degree has been developed by custom and is completely unregulated.[12] Industry- and employer-based credentials may be skewed toward industry interests rather than long-run student interests. Thus education markets in this country are created and regulated through credentials that are usually informal and imperfect, as we examine in Chapter 7.

In addition, prices in education markets are not like prices in markets for shoes or breakfast cereals. The student as consumer typically does not pay the cost of education, either because it is publicly subsidized or because parents subsidize the cost. Furthermore, institutions' decisions based on their costs and benefits are unlikely to be socially optimal. For example, community colleges are quite good at estimating the marginal costs of different programs; they are less likely to offer high-cost programs in nursing, engineering technologies, or computer numerically controlled machining, even though such programs may be among the most valuable for their individual benefits and social effects. Since there is no general relationship between institutional benefits and social benefits, or institutional costs and social costs, institutional decisions coincide with socially optimal decisions only by accident (Grubb and Associates, 1999, ch. 9).

The conditions for efficient markets are most likely to be met at the top of the occupational structure, in the market for post-baccalaureate professional education where consumers are relatively sophisticated. At that level institutions are more likely to have well-defined occupational missions and reputations, employers are sure that graduates are well-prepared for their jobs, and credentials are likely to be established through a licensing process involving many participants. At the lower end of the postsecondary market, consumers (including uninformed "experimenters") are likely to be less sophisticated; institutions are likely to be driven more by enrollments and "profit"—revenues in excess of costs—than educational quality; credentials are likely to be based on highly local reputations; and licensing mechanisms are rare. In job training programs, the market that links programs to jobs is almost nonexistent, leaving participants with few choices, large numbers of self-serving providers, and no credentials at all. Where sophisticated consumers face a choice among high-quality institutions with well-developed licensing mechanisms to regulate preparation, then we generally have fewer qualms about market mechanisms. Where unsophisticated consumers confront institutions of doubtful quality, with little oversight of a credential's content, markets do not work well.

These observations suggest a complex agenda for public policy—one that would move education and training markets at the middle and lower levels closer to the conditions at the upper levels. We will return to this agenda in Chapter 9, where we consider ways to create efficient and equitable markets in education. For the moment, we note that vocationalism has reinforced market-based ways of thinking about education, creating a new set of problems we must confront if we are to avoid the narrowest and emptiest forms of vocationalism.

Vocationalism and the American State

The conclusion that many quasi-markets in education and training are weak because of limited government intervention—including informal credentials and limited regulation of quality—leads to a broader observation: American education and vocationalism have developed within a laissez-faire state that does relatively little—compared with other developed countries—to ensure the well-being of the population as a whole.[13] The weakness of economic and social policies has in turn compromised the ability of educational institutions to carry out their roles—because conditions of poverty and family life prevent many students from completing high school, because there are few social policies that can help postsecondary students resolve the work-family-schooling dilemma, because the needs of individuals caught up in welfare are more complex than job search assistance and Work First can redress.

And yet, because Americans so consistently promote education to enhance economic opportunity and social well-being, they are caught in a labyrinth without an exit. The Education Gospel calls for greater commitments to education to resolve such social problems as poor schooling, continued poverty, racial and ethnic discrimination, and inequality of all kinds—even though education by itself cannot achieve these goals. Failure leads, in turn, to more criticism of education for ignoring the "demands of the twenty-first century" and for allowing the achievement gap to persist between rich and poor students, or among black, Latino, and white students. This has triggered yet more calls to improve schooling—or, in Bush's No Child Left Behind Act, the demand that schools eliminate the achievement gap—but without giving educators the financial and the human resources necessary to do this. Only by exiting the labyrinth—only by recognizing the need for policies outside education—will it be possible to meet the expectations of the Education Gospel.

We can quickly summarize many consequences of weak social and economic policies that undermine the Education Gospel's aspirations:

- The lack of an adequate health policy, and the incomplete coverage of health insurance, means that many low-income students are chronically sick, miss large amounts of school, and do poorly in the quest for educational credentials.

- The lack of adequate housing policies means that many low-income families and children move constantly because of unstable housing, contributing to unstable schooling and in turn undermining achievement and persistence.

- The lack of a serious urban redevelopment policy means that low-income children grow up in communities with the distractions of crime, gangs, deteriorating buildings, vacant lots, unsafe streets—threatening surroundings without much vision of hope.

- The lack of serious desegregation policies—for example, reinforcing integration through the location of public and mixed-use housing and by attacking redlining—has meant that schools are highly segregated by income and by race. Schools with high concentrations of low-income students are often of poor quality, both because fewer resources are spent on them and because unmotivated and low-performing students reinforce that behavior in others.

- A number of policy issues contribute to the family-work-schooling dilemma of many postsecondary students: the lack of comprehensive child care, low minimum wages, underuse of the Earned Income Tax Credit, weak employment leave provisions, insufficient student aid, and low levels of income support through welfare.

- The powerful hostility toward welfare, culminating in President Clinton's promise to "end welfare as we know it" and the welfare "reforms" of 1996, means that shamefully high levels of income inequality and poverty persist, much higher than in other developed countries.[14] Inequality and poverty influence virtually every aspect of formal schooling, from the access of parents to high-quality child care to the provision of reading-rich home environments to the ability to afford college. Inequality begets inequality—high levels of inequality in income contribute to the high levels of inequality in schooling and skills in this country.

- The weakness of policies designed to confront racist practices—particularly discrimination in employment and in housing—contributes to racial and ethnic gaps in earnings and employment. If these were seriously narrowed, it would be substantially easier for schools to eliminate the achievement gap.

Finally, few policies exist to improve the quality of work. While the rhetoric of the Education Gospel emphasizes how undereducated students are for the jobs of the twenty-first century, substantial numbers of workers have higher skill levels than the available jobs demand, as we will document in Chapter 7. There has been little experimentation with policies that might improve the quality of work, again because political conditions have made it difficult to intervene directly in labor markets.[15] As the Cardinal Principles of Secondary Education asserted in 1917, the worker "must adjust himself to complex economic order" rather than having economic practices (including employment conditions) adjust to the aspirations of workers.

These examples suffice to make an obvious but little-noticed point: among its other distinctive characteristics, the American approach to vocationalism is embedded in a weak welfare state, where noneducation policies are inadequate and efforts to intervene directly in labor markets are largely untested. Many of the rhetorical claims of the Education Gospel—mastery of the skills of the twenty-first century for all students, college for all, "saving inner-city children from academic failure"—also require substantial noneducation policies both to fulfill the promises of education *and* to improve the quality of life and work. Only then will we have an equitable form of vocationalism worthy of the claims of equal opportunity, and only then will we have a society committed to the well-being of all its citizens.

6

∼ The Public and Private Benefits of Schooling

*T*HE OCCUPATIONAL PURPOSE of schooling has implied a simple promise to students: those who stay in school will get well-paid jobs with prospects for the future, *careers* or *vocations* rather than mere work. This relationship has been asserted in many ways: in the human capital theory developed formally by economists and loosely restated by believers in education; in advice to young people to stay in school; in the image of the college graduate replacing the ideal of the self-made individual, and by college-going as the route to professions; in the goals of high school for all and now of college for all. Three-quarters of the public agree that a college education is more important than it was even ten years ago (Immerwahr and Foleno, 2000).

Often, however, the economic benefits of education and training have been *assumed* rather than *demonstrated*. This faith in education—what we might call a naive human-capital perspective—has been one of the dominant strands of the Education Gospel at least since the mid-nineteenth century. But the individual benefits of schooling have also been exaggerated, leading to disappointment and a suspicion of formal schooling when its promises are not realized—for example, when cyclical variation in demand leaves well-educated engineers or computer programmers unemployed, or when college students fail to find high-status employment after graduating and wind up driving taxis or working in restaurants, or when training does not increase earnings as promised. Higher levels of schooling cannot guarantee access to better employment and higher earnings; they may be necessary, but they are often not sufficient. Despite its popularity, the naive version of human-capital theory has never been quite right.

Vocationalism also promises the higher status that comes with having a professional career of increasing responsibility and stature. College and the baccalaureate degree have been especially important for the knowledge base associated with professionalism. But again, while more formal schooling certainly enhances the likelihood of professional status, it cannot guarantee that outcome. Furthermore, the constant escalation of education levels has outrun the supply of professional jobs even in the "knowledge economy"—and so here too formal schooling is often a disappointment, with increasing numbers of individuals earning a baccalaureate but failing to obtain a professional career (as we show later in this chapter). As always, the reality is more complex than the rhetoric.

Vocationalism has also promised public as well as private benefits—particularly economic growth and social order through employment, displacing the idleness that might otherwise generate instability and crime. Indeed, the economic role of schooling should create public and private benefits simultaneously: public funding generates individual incentives for higher levels of schooling, leading to individual income increases *and* the public benefits of growth and stability that in turn justify public resources. But while economists have worked hard to quantify the contribution of education to economic growth, it proves difficult to disentangle its influence from that of many other policies. Particularly toward the end of the twentieth century, after two decades of economic expansion, the reasons for that growth were more complex than simply increasing education levels. This particular public benefit of education is more elusive than its rhetoric implies.

The other major public benefit of schooling has always been its role in keeping the peace, or socializing the young for adult roles and moderating potential conflicts in a large, unruly country. Pre-vocationalized schooling in the United States played this role in obvious and didactic ways: "Foolishness is bound up in the heart of the child, but the rod of correction will drive it from him," stated a reader from the nineteenth century. Vocationalism provides different forms of discipline, predicated on the promise of employment for those who stay in school, work hard, and behave themselves. But as in the case of economic growth, the value of schooling proves to be exaggerated, since many factors in social unrest are beyond its capacity to address.

Both public and private benefits are thus contingent on multiple factors in addition to schooling, including a broad range of public policies and private actions. Inevitably the aspirations of the Education Gospel overpromise, leading to disappointments and yet another round of education reform. But what is most notable in the incantations of the Education Gospel is that private benefits outweigh public ones.[1] The result has been a fixation on schooling's vocational role in helping individuals get ahead.

The Individual Benefits of Schooling and Training

When Horace Mann claimed in the 1830s that the common schools would be "the most prolific parent of material riches" whereby "even the poorest may pass on to the realization of cherished hopes," he relied on simple faith in the power of schooling to enhance employment and income, not on evidence of the sort we would use today. Similarly, the proponents of vocational education at the turn of the century stressed "learning to earn," but without any real evidence about earnings.[2] Reliance on simple faith in education continues: Bill Clinton extolled the Hope and Lifelong Learning Tax Credits enacted in 1996, declaring (with so many others) that "the new economy is the knowledge economy" and asserting that "we want education in a community college like this, the 13th and 14th years of education, to be as universal when we start the new century as a high school diploma is today"— without recognizing the complexity of the economic returns to community colleges.[3]

When national data on education and earnings first became available, in the 1940 census, they revealed a now-familiar pattern. Median earnings for native white males with a high school education were about $1,029, and $1,955 for those with four years or more of college; comparable figures for native white women were $339 and $615.[4] Such findings have multiplied as data have become more sophisticated and as occupational purposes have transformed other levels of the educational system. Table 6.1 presents the average annual earnings for individuals at different levels of formal schooling, based on the most recent data

Table 6.1. Mean earnings of men and women by level of schooling, 2000

	< 9th grade	9th–12th grade	High school diploma	Some college, no degree	Associate degree	Baccalaureate degree	Master's degree	Professional degree	Doctorate
Men	$20,998	$21,940	$32,020	$35,704	$42,547	$63,216	$76,340	$110,517	$89,943
White	20,737	23,066	32,834	36,666	43,893	65,196	77,277	111,629	92,727
Black	22,367	17,352	27,776	30,345	33,081	51,980	52,127	56,887	56,333
Latino	19,806	19,898	26,328	28,669	34,313	51,658	51,422	94,081	91,965
Women	12,665	12,698	19,269	21,276	25,590	35,083	45,517	61,556	54,477
White	11,906	12,691	19,306	21,279	25,710	35,032	45,943	62,502	55,030
Black	16,237	12,811	19,340	21,719	25,013	35,862	42,872	63,793	47,851
Latina	11,033	11,704	17,138	19,865	22,959	33,283	45,153	57,259	35,876

Source: Current Population Survey, Annual Demographic Survey, March Supplement, 2000; ferrett.bis.census.gov/macro/032001/perina/new04-000.htm

available, for March 2000. High school dropouts earn much less than do high school completers, and so the pressure to complete high school certainly has a clear economic rationale. Individuals with baccalaureate degrees earn considerably more than those with high school diplomas, apparently justifying the goal of College for All. Those with two-year associate degrees also do substantially better than high school graduates, though not as well as those with baccalaureate degrees, which take twice as long to earn. Those with some college—a heterogeneous group ranging from individuals with a course or two, to those who have almost completed a baccalaureate—also do somewhat better, though a closer examination reveals that small amounts of college have trivial effects (Grubb, 2002a). Furthermore, in these and other results the benefits of education are slightly higher for women than for men, and slightly higher among blacks compared with whites—in some cases substantially so (Averettt and D'Allessandro, 2001). Even though there are familiar differences between men and women, and among racial and ethnic groups, all benefit substantially from completing high school and then subsequent postsecondary credentials. On the *average*, then, it is worth continuing in school as long as an individual can afford to do so.

These simple averages provide the empirical basis for the faith we place in formal schooling, but they conceal many other sources of variation. Individuals who continue to higher levels of education may be more able, or more motivated, or more diligent; they often come from families with higher incomes and higher levels of education, from whom they continue to receive both intellectual and financial support. Other factors affect wages and earnings: labor market experience, marital status, disabilities, union membership, location in certain regions of the country and in urban rather than rural areas. A host of personal characteristics affect employment and earnings; some—discipline, initiative, and teamwork—are widely praised, while others, like good looks and family ties, seem unfair. And so economists and sociologists have kept busy disentangling the *direct* effects of schooling from the effects of those characteristics that might simply be *associated* with schooling. On the whole, the simple differentials among education groups (the results in Table 6.1) are slightly lower when other variables are considered, but between 70 and 90 percent of the differences persist. The great majority of earnings differences among levels of school-

ing cannot be explained away by other factors. For those of us unwilling to go through a sex-change operation, cosmetic surgery, or a
personality makeover, formal schooling remains one of the best ways of
getting ahead in this country.[5]

Another way of demonstrating the economic value of education
draws on economists' allegiance to conceptions of capital. The figures
in Table 6.1 show whether more education leads to higher earnings,
but they say nothing about the costs of education. Internal rates of return—similar to the rates of return reported for financial instruments
like stocks and bonds—compare earnings with the costs of schooling,
both direct costs, such as tuition, and opportunity costs, such as the
earnings forgone when someone attends school. In a country where
much of education is publicly funded, the private costs of education are
significantly lower than the total or social costs, and so private rates of
return are higher than social rates of return. In the United States, the
private rates of return for secondary education have ranged from 13
percent in 1960 to 18.9 percent in 1970, considerably greater than rates
of return in capital markets. As Table 6.2 indicates, the private rates of
return for completing a baccalaureate degree have been between 11.6
percent and 16.5 percent; the social returns have been slightly lower.
The private returns for master's degrees tend to be in the range of 6 to
10 percent, and for PhD's around 9 percent. Even though rates of return may fall as the level of education increases, education at every level
is a good investment given the costs involved. Furthermore, the figures
in Table 6.2 suggest that both private and social rates of return have increased recently.[6]

In the last two decades of the twentieth century, another way of understanding the value of education became popular. Between 1979 and

Table 6.2. Internal rates of return for baccalaureate degrees, 1939–1980

	Private	Social
1939	15.0%	11.1%
1949	11.6	10.6
1959	12.3	11.5
1969	13.0	11.7
1973	11.7	11.6
1980	16.5	14.5*

*This figure is for 1976, not 1980.
Source: Leslie and Brinkman (1988), tables 4.2, 5.1.

1998, the real (inflation-adjusted) wages of high school dropouts fell 29.9 percent for men and 16 percent for women, while they fell only 16.8 percent for male high school graduates and 3.4 percent for females. At the same time, those with baccalaureate degrees have had real increases of about 18 percent for men and 21.1 percent for women, and those with graduate degrees have gained 14.2 percent and 22.5 percent, respectively (Mishel, Bernstein, and Schmitt, 2001). In the middle, men in the heterogeneous group with some college have lost while women in the group have gained slightly, though this pattern surely masks substantial differences *within* the group. The implication is that more education is one critical way for individuals to protect earnings from eroding over time, and to enjoy the increasing earnings that go with careers and middle-class status.

This evidence suggests that the promise of vocationalism has been delivered: formal schooling increases earnings, protects individuals from the effects of inflation, and increases earnings by more than the costs involved. However, these *average* effects become more complex when we examine the great variety of schooling and training, and at least four issues discredit a simple faith in education.

First, the figures in Table 6.1 ignore variations among occupations—that is, the specific occupational focus of schooling. At the high school level, with a few exceptions (like clerical programs for young women), vocational education has not made much difference to earnings relative to academic or general education.[7] At the postsecondary level, the economic benefits of one-year certificates are high for women in business and in health occupations, while fields like child care, engineering, and computer-related fields for women, and craft occupations for men, have low benefits or even no benefit. Among two-year associate degrees, only those in business, engineering- and computer-related fields, and health (dominated by nursing) are substantially more valuable than others, while those in education (largely child care), public service (like fire and police protection), and various craft occupations yield no greater benefits than a high school degree (Grubb, 1997b, 2002a). At the baccalaureate level, these differences become even clearer: graduates in engineering and health enjoy the highest benefits, followed by business and science/mathematics majors; those with degrees in the humanities, the social sciences, and education rank at the bottom (Rumberger and Daymont, 1993).

In graduate schools the differences continue to expand, in obvious ways: professional degrees in law, medicine, engineering, and business provide much greater advantages than degrees in semiprofessional areas like education, social welfare, journalism, forestry, or library science. The question of whether overtly occupational forms of schooling pay off therefore depends on the level of schooling involved. At the lowest level, in high school vocational programs, it is difficult to find any substantial effects of occupational specialization. At the baccalaureate and postgraduate level, these differences become increasingly substantial. In our system of vocationalism, the importance of a particular occupational focus matters the most at higher levels of schooling and the least at the lowest levels.

The differences among fields of study mean that the economic benefits of schooling overlap substantially. Men with an associate degree in math, science, or engineering earn more than those with a baccalaureate in education or the humanities; women with a certificate in health or business earn more than those with an associate degree in education or the humanities. The frequent complaint that schooling cannot *guarantee* higher earnings is therefore true: higher credentials lead to higher earnings *on the average*, but not for all individuals. The result is that some individuals with baccalaureate degrees (in the humanities, for example) work in modestly paid positions, as secretaries or waiters. Another consequence is "reverse transfer," where individuals with baccalaureate degrees in poorly paid occupations enroll in community college to train for well-paid fields, reversing the normal direction of the educational pipeline. The blanket recommendation of college for all may be right in general but wrong in detail, because college evidently does not benefit all those who attend.

Second, while the naive model of human capital implies that any additional schooling should lead to benefits—and while economists often blithely report average rates of return per year of schooling as if they applied to all kinds of schooling (see Heckman, 1999)—the effects of small amounts of college are both uncertain and controversial. Overall, the rates of noncompletion at both two- and four-year colleges have increased since the mid-1970s. Barton (2002) reported that the overall five-year completion rate at four-year colleges fell from 58 percent in 1983 to 51 percent in 2001, with a greater decline (from 52 percent to 42 percent) in public institutions. Rates of noncompletion are particularly high for community colleges and less-selective four-year colleges, a little-acknowledged complication of college for all.[8] While some college without a postsecondary credential may provide limited benefits, the effects of one year of college or less are uncertain. The benefits are often zero, and when they are positive they are quite small, in the range of 5 to 10 percent—substantially lower than those from associate degrees (Grubb 2002a, table 3). Again, the simple prescription of college for all is suspect: individuals who enter postsecondary education but don't complete may not benefit at all, and college *completion* rather than college-*going* is the real ticket to economic success.

Third, the transition from schooling into employment has been a continuing concern because under some circumstances the potential value of schooling may dissipate before individuals find "adult" employment. Early in the twentieth century, social commentators worried about the "wasted years" between leaving school at fourteen and finding an "adult" job at age sixteen or older; the intervening years provided opportunities for learning bad habits in the "school of the streets," and for losing the skills acquired in school. Youth unemployment rates in the United States have always been much higher than adult rates, and difficulties in transitioning into employment can create permanent employment problems (Ryan 2001, 46–50). Some youth— high school dropouts and minorities in particular—have much greater problems making the transition into adult employment. For example, Klerman and Karoly (1994) found that 25 percent of high school dropouts had not found a job lasting one full year until they were older than twenty-two, and still had not found a job lasting two years by age twenty-nine. Concern over this transition appeared most recently in the School-to-Work Opportunities Act of 1994, which tried unsuccessfully to imitate the German system by supporting more work-based learning and other links between schooling and employment.[9] The American inability to create a coherent system of education *and* employment, except perhaps in the highest-status professions, complicates the process of converting schooling into occupational advancement.

A fourth issue arises when students fail to find employment in the field for which they have been educated, a situation related to the criterion of *related employment*. High levels of related employment can be found in fields of postgraduate professional education, but even among those with baccalaureate degrees about 62 percent find related employment. The proportions are somewhat lower (averaging 55 percent) for those with certificates and associate degrees, and those with some college but no degree find employment associated with their studies at rates ranging between 33 percent and 50 percent. One little-noticed benefit of higher degrees, then, is an increased likelihood of finding related employment. And those in unrelated employment tend to earn less: among those with baccalaureate degrees, Rumberger and Daymont (1993) found an earnings penalty for an unrelated job of 22 percent for men and 13 percent for women. In our own work, the earnings penalty among those with baccalaureate degrees was 15 percent for men and a whopping 68 percent for women; among men with occupational associate degrees, the earnings penalty was 61 percent, and women did not benefit at all from occupational associate degrees and certificates unless they found related employment. Similar patterns apply to short-term job training, where finding related employment also leads to substantially higher earnings (Grubb, 1995c, tables 5–6, appendix). Therefore strong placement efforts are necessary since the real value of occupational education may not materialize, especially for women, unless individuals find related employment.

The naive human-capital perspective is overly simplistic. More formal schooling does increase earnings on the average, but not if individuals choose poorly paid occupations, or if they fail to complete substantial amounts of postsecondary education, or if the transition from schooling into employment is unsuccessful or just too slow, or if they fail to find jobs related to their occupational education. In the crannies of the education and training system, still other kinds of preparation have effects on employment that are close to zero. The general equivalency diploma, or GED, an alternative to the high school diploma, is not worth very much in employment and does not enhance rates of postsecondary enrollment.[10] As we clarified in Chapter 4, the vast array of job training programs created since the early 1960s have had relatively small or no effects on employment and earnings; in some cases they even *decrease* earnings by taking individuals out of the labor force while they are enrolled in training. Finally, publicly sponsored adult education has been almost completely ineffective in moving individuals up in employment. While the human capital narrative has generated political support for these programs, the employment benefits have been trivial.

We therefore confront a paradox. Overall, the relationship between formal schooling and earnings is quite powerful: more schooling is better than less, on the average; the standard advice to complete high school is correct; and the lure of the baccalaureate expressed in college for all is confirmed in more stable employment and higher earnings. But more schooling and additional training are not always beneficial. Credentials that are not widely known—the one-year certificate, for example, or the GED—may have little value. The variation in the benefits among occupations leads to substantial overlap among those with different levels of education. Small amounts of education and job training have substantial effects on employment and earnings only under special conditions, and occupational education and training disconnected from employment is unlikely to pay off. These conclusions are not surprising, but they mean that the standard assumptions of the Education Gospel are too simple.

Status Effects of Schooling

The inability of formal schooling to guarantee access to well-paid employment is perhaps most acute in considering a different advantage—access to occupations with professional status. Ever since the turn of the twentieth century, gaining access to professional positions has been part of schooling's appeal, particularly as graduate education became necessary for licensed professions and for most semiprofessions, and preferred for most managerial positions, especially in large corporations (Bledstein, 1978). These occupations have higher earnings and also higher status, greater autonomy in working conditions, greater security of employment (at least until recently), and much better prospects for advancement—they are *careers* or *vocations* rather than mere jobs.

Formal schooling does provide an advantage in access to professional and managerial occupations. In the results for 1990 shown in Table 6.3, only 12 percent of high school graduates had such positions, compared with 35 percent of those with associate degrees, 61 percent of those with baccalaureates, and about 85 percent of those with postgraduate degrees. Evidently, a near-guarantee of professional and managerial employment comes only with an advanced degree; about a quarter of those with baccalaureate degrees are in sales and clerical

Table 6.3. Occupations by levels of education, 1990

Occupation	Doctorate	Professional degree	Master's degree	Baccalaureate degree	Associate degree	Vocational certificate	Some college	High school	High school dropout
Managerial	15.2%	4.9%	19.3%	20.0%	16.0%	8.2%	12.9%	8.0%	2.8%
Professional	69.6	82.7	64.4	40.6	18.9	19.8	7.1	3.6	0.7
Technical	8.7	3.7	2.2	5.5	7.9	10.9	3.8	2.2	0.9
Sales/clerical	6.5	4.9	11.7	25.7	40.4	38.5	53.0	49.5	10.6
Service	0	3.7	1.9	5.9	12.0	16.7	16.3	20.9	40.5%
Mechanic/repairer/ precision production	0	0	0.3	0.7	1.2	1.4	1.4	3.0	3.5
Machine operator	0	0	0.2	0.6	1.9	3.1	2.8	8.3	20.4
Other*	0	0	0	1.0	1.7	1.4	2.3	4.3	7.3

*Includes laborers; farm, forestry, and fishery workers; construction workers; and transportation workers.
Totals do not sum to 100% because of rounding error and the omission of U.S. Armed Forces.
Source: Survey of Income and Program Participation, 1990, from Grubb (1996b), table 1.2.

jobs, with another 11 percent in technical and service work. But having some college—including the associate degree and vocational certificates—does at least provide access to middle-level technical and clerical positions, whereas high school graduates and especially high school dropouts disproportionately labor in production lines, service work, and other unskilled positions. More education has a defensive role, keeping individuals out of the worst work our society has to offer, even when it doesn't provide access to professional and managerial careers.

We can see the declining status effects of schooling by concentrating on professional and managerial occupations. Contrary to the trends in earnings, where the economic benefits of schooling have increased since the 1970s, the status effects of schooling have declined. In Table 6.4, the proportion of those with four or more years of college who found professional or managerial employment was about 85 percent in 1970, close to a guarantee of such a career. However, this percentage has fallen steadily since then for men, and fallen and then recovered somewhat for women; currently it is closer to 67 percent for men and 72 percent for women—and it has decreased both for those with baccalaureate degrees and for those with advanced degrees. The baccalaureate degree is no longer a near guarantee of professional or managerial status, which now requires post-baccalaureate credentials. The self-reinforcing effects of vocationalism we examined in Chapter 5 are clear: over time the only way to achieve professional or managerial status has been to increase levels of schooling, now to the postgraduate level.

The promises of the Education Gospel are therefore ambiguous.

Table 6.4. Individuals aged 25–64 with four years or more of college: Proportion professionals or managers

	1970	1975	1981	1985	1991	1995	2000
Men—all	84.1%	79.5%	76.3%	65.9%	65.7%	66.7%	66.7%
4 years	77.0	70.1	67.3	55.6	55.1	57.3	57.1
5 years +	92.7	90.2	86.9	81.8	79.8	83.2	83.9
Women—all	86.0	78.9	73.7	69.0	68.4	71.5	72.0
4 years	76.5	72.1	65.2	53.3	59.3	63.5	63.7
5 years +	93.4	89.8	86.5	80.8	82.6	88.2	89.5

Source: Current Population Survey, census.gov/population/www/socdemo/educ-attn.html, various years.

More schooling does result in many benefits, but not for everyone, especially not for those who choose low-paid occupations or fail to find related employment. And the effects on professional and managerial careers, while still substantial, are dwindling. In a society where college for all has become more and more the norm, there are simply not enough high-level occupations for everyone who aspires to them.

Economic Growth and the Role of Schooling

Vocationalism has always promised public benefits as well as private gain, ranging from economic growth to political coherence to social order to homeland security. This message supports almost every appeal for the expansion and improvement of education and suffuses every version of the Education Gospel, from Horace Mann's reference to schooling as "the most prolific parent of material riches" to the present versions.

Until quite recently, however, the contribution of education to economic growth has lacked any real evidence. When economists turned their attention in the 1960s to measuring the components of economic growth, they were not particularly successful. Their early efforts often attributed 50 percent or less of the growth in gross domestic product to increases in the stock of capital and the amount of labor. The residual presented a challenge, since it clarified that other factors—call them x-factors, unknown and potentially difficult to measure—were responsible for most growth. Two main candidates emerged: technological progress, or advances in the quality of capital; and human capital, the various forms of education and training that make workers more productive (Harberger, 1998).

Subsequent empirical efforts have incorporated measures of human capital to whittle away at the residual.[11] For example, Edward Denison (1967, 1985) measured human capital by differences in earnings among individuals with varying levels of education, the kinds of differences in Table 6.1. These results showed that education had contributed 14 percent of national income growth and 27 percent of growth in income per person between 1948 and 1972. Jorgenson and Fraumeni (1992) measured improvements in labor quality by *lifetime* earnings for different levels of education, and concluded that human capital accounted for about 26 percent of overall economic growth. Other empirical work is consistent with a contribution of education to economic growth of between 20 and 30 percent (Jones, 2000; Topel, 1999). Based on this evidence, it has become common to conclude that education has contributed substantially to U.S. economic growth since World War II.[12]

However, other evidence suggests that the contribution of education is more complex. Most efforts to explain the residual—the *x*-factors beyond the growth in capital and labor productivity—have concentrated on technology and education, but they have not calculated the contributions of government policies, business practices, shifts in cultural norms like the tendency to work harder, or anything else that is unmeasured or unmeasureable. In addition, measuring the contribution to growth by the earnings differences among well-educated and less-educated workers *assumes* that they reflect productivity differences rather than other factors—including the signaling of higher ability or some kind of irrational credentialism—and further assumes that these differences remain the same when the average level of education increases. Finally, these results calculate the increase in the *quantity* of education, assuming that *quality* has stayed the same, and they assume that education enhances growth, not that growth increases the amount (or quality) of education. Given these flaws, conventional estimates of education's contribution to growth may be too high.[13]

A different tactic for examining growth has been a microeconomic approach, examining a variety of factors (Harberger, 1998; Topel, 1999). For example, Landau, Taylor, and Wright (1996) explain the growth of industrialized societies in terms of national governance; sociopolitical climate, including stability; macroeconomic policies (fiscal, monetary, trade, and tax policies); institutional settings, including financial, legal, and corporate institutions; structural and supportive policies, including education, labor relations, science and technology policy; and regulatory and environmental policies. In addition, there may be factors specific to particular industries that help explain their growth or stagnation, as well as company-specific issues. In such a framework, education is only one of dozens of influences on growth, and its influence may be contingent on other policies. As one illustration, periods of instability or adverse fiscal policy may undermine the potential effects of education because employers are unwilling to hire better-educated workers or to invest in skill-using technologies. As the educational historian Lawrence Cremin (1989, 102) argued about growth and competitiveness, while excoriating the tendency to blame schools for economic woes:

> American economic competitiveness with Japan and other nations is to a considerable degree a function of monetary, trade, and industrial policy, and of decisions made by the President and Congress, the Federal Reserve Board, and the federal departments of the Treasury, Commerce, and Labor. Therefore to conclude that the problems of international competitiveness can be solved by educational reform, especially education reform defined solely as school reform, is not merely utopian and millenialist, it is at best a foolish and at worst a crass effort to direct attention away from those truly responsible for doing something about competitiveness and to lay the burden instead on the schools.

A kind of natural experiment over the past two decades provides a precise test of this multicausal approach. In 1983, the United States had endured a decade of relative stagnation, initiated by the oil crisis of 1973 and exacerbated by deliberate monetary policy that led to the recession of 1981 to 1983. Japan and the other "Asian Tigers" (Singapore, Korea, and Hong Kong) had much higher growth rates, and most European countries had higher growth, lower unemployment, and lower inflation than the United States. The familiar process of blaming education for economic and social ills ensued, as *A Nation at Risk* (1983) stated directly with its rhetoric about the country's "rising tide of mediocrity." The inevitable envy toward our more-successful competitors brought comparisons with Japanese, German, and other educational systems, and the conclusion that we lagged behind other advanced countries in our academic accomplishments (Cummings and Altbach, 1997; Stevenson, 1992) and in our vocational system (Hamilton, 1990).

By the end of the 1990s, however, Asian countries had gone through various crises of their own, including the financial collapse of 1997. Growth rates in Europe had slowed, many European countries suffered double-digit unemployment, and the Euro—symbol of a new, powerful, and integrated Europe—had fallen steadily against the dollar. Japan and Germany had declined, the Soviet Union had collapsed, and the

United States stood alone as the preeminent economic power. But the factors that explained the resurgence of the United States after 1983 had nothing at all to do with education. (They also had very little to do with the knowledge economy, we should point out.) Instead, a supportive mix of macroeconomic and microeconomic policies helped create growth during this period: deficit reduction; conservative monetary policy; reduced economic regulation of transportation, finance, and communications; trade liberalization; permissive antitrust enforcement; stronger intellectual property rights; federally supported research; and private-sector strategies in response to competition, including firm repositioning, product specialization, consolidation, internationalization of some operations, improvements in manufacturing processes, and cost reductions. Relative stability—the absence of major wars like the Vietnam debacle, or economic upheavals like the oil price increases of the 1970s—also played an important role (Board on Science, Technology, and Economic Policy, 1999). But there's absolutely no evidence that education contributed to the resurgence of growth; the problems in education that prompted *A Nation at Risk* had not been eliminated by 1999, and certainly not the problems of low-performing students in urban schools. Education did not cause the dismal economic times of the 1970s and early 1980s; by the same token, it did not trigger the economic resurgence of the '80s and '90s.

Furthermore, a series of industry-specific studies by the National Research Council revealed that education now plays only a small role in major sectors of the economy, ranging from grocery retailing to chemicals, computing, and biotechnology (Mowery, 1999). Many sectors had high levels of productivity growth during the 1980s and 1990s, even though they tended to hire low-skilled (or low-*schooled*) workers—among them grocery retailing, apparel, trucking, and retail banking. In the steel industry, new technologies required on-the-job training rather than formal schooling. The only bottlenecks due to education problems were in information technology, where frontline and relatively unskilled (or unschooled) workers in a number of sectors—retail banking, trucking, food distribution—lacked sufficient computer skills to keep up with changing technology. In these cases a policy of importing skilled labor—for example, information technology (IT) professionals from South Asia—has often substituted for a human capital strategy. The NRC studies expressed no alarm about the overall education level of the labor force and no sense that college for all would be necessary to sustain growth. Certain IT skills have become important, along with basic competencies in reading, writing, and mathematics, as well as flexibility in response to change, but otherwise economic growth at this point is not dependent on the expansion of schooling.

Only one factor promoting economic growth seems related to education. Many sectors reviewed by the National Research Council have benefited from technological innovation—new routing systems in trucking; inventory control mechanisms in grocery retailing; the development of biotechnology; new production processes in chemicals; innovations in semiconductors, disk drives, and computing generally. These innovations have often come not from industry itself but from close links between research universities and firms. The costs of developing new technologies have been socialized through public support for research and development in universities, and the results have been widely available rather than closely held by individual firms.[14] Therefore the research university, with its combination of research and education of high-level technical workers—engineers, chemists, biologists, computer scientists—has been an important component of both technological change and the preparation of skilled professionals necessary to sustain that change. In the American model of vocationalism, crucial contributions to economic growth now come primarily from a small number of elite research universities preparing a small elite of technical workers, rather than from the equitable extension of college for all to the mass of the population.

A further complication involves the *kind* of growth that has taken place in the United States, particularly in recent years. While the Education Gospel has unreservedly embraced economic growth, only a moment's thought clarifies that growth is not always desirable, or even a good measure of overall well-being. Growth with extensive pollution, for example, may lead to declines in health and aesthetic conditions; growth achieved through overly intensive work, like the long hours logged by many professionals, increases economic benefits at great personal and familial cost.[15] And unequal growth that fails to improve the well-being of the poor, or of immigrants, or of other groups outside the mainstream, is also an ambiguous benefit. While the Education Gospel seems to assume that growth is beneficial for all—reflected in the aphorism "a rising tide lifts all boats"—U.S. growth over the past quarter century has been associated with greater inequality, and advocates for the poor have countered with metaphors of their own: a rising tide fails to lift those with leaky boats, or those stranded on the shore.

Behind this war of metaphors is a complex relationship between growth and inequality. Many policies that fostered growth between 1983 and the late 1990s—conservative monetary policy, reduced economic regulation, trade liberalization, permissive antitrust enforcement, consolidation of firms, internationalization of manufacturing operations, cost reductions in production—increased unemployment, reduced spending on social programs, and encouraged firms to export employment to other countries, all policies that increase inequality. More generally, Barro (2000) has shown that while growth tends to decrease inequality for countries with low levels of output, it *increases* inequality in more developed countries. And when he examined the determinants of inequality, he found that countries emphasizing primary and secondary education ended up with lower inequality, while relatively higher enrollments in postsecondary education, as in the United States, increased inequality. So the policies our country has pursued, and the recent U.S. approach to vocationalism emphasizing postsecondary enrollments and the research benefits of elite universities, have contributed to higher inequality.

The social benefits of education through economic growth are therefore ambiguous in at least two ways. Most obviously, investing in education by itself does not automatically cause growth; other conditions are necessary for the *potential* productivity increases associated with more schooling to be realized. In addition, some ways in which formal schooling contributes to growth, as well as other policies that foster it, in fact exacerbate inequality. The policies that might stimulate high growth with greater equity are quite different from those we have followed.

New Ways of Socializing Youth

A different social goal, articulated for virtually every kind of schooling, has been the maintenance of social order. The forms of socialization have changed, not surprisingly, depending on the perceived threats that different periods have faced. In the Puritan colonies the Bible was the bulwark against sin, and so the Old Deluder law, the first effort to provide public funding for schooling, sought to promote Bible reading (Cubberly, 1934, 18–19): "It being the chief purpose of that Old De-luder, Satan, to keep men from the knowledge of the Scripture . . . It is therefore ordered that every township in this jurisdiction . . . shall then forthwith appoint one within their town to teach all such children as shall resort to him to read and write." Two centuries later, in the early nineteenth century, the chief threats were the vices of the city, and so urban schools were established for poor children who, "brought up in ignorance, and amidst the contagion of bad example, are in imminent danger of ruin" (Kaestle, 1973, 84). Apprenticeships also played a role in socializing youth, particularly through the paternal role of the mas-ter, but the frequency with which apprentices ran away from harsh masters was one sign of its decline and a cause for some alarm. The nineteenth-century common schools sought to instill a reverence for the laws created by the political process and a respect for figures of authority, ranging from parents and ministers to teachers, the police, and employers. The goals of the curriculum, with its emphasis on di-dactic moral readings, nationalistic history, and social studies to moti-vate good citizens, reinforced an ethic that combined political partici-pation with a patriotic acceptance of the American way. Schools have always tried to create orderly communities with their skeins of rules, their insistence on quiet in the service of learning, their creation of im-personal authority in teachers and administrators, and—recently—the use of security guards, metal detectors, and identity cards.

For most of their history, America's colleges have reflected similar expectations. The ideal of the nineteenth-century residential college has continued to shape public perceptions, and most undergraduate in-stitutions have continued the tradition of standing in loco parentis, re-sponsible for both the intellectual development and the moral charac-ter—or at least the good behavior—of their students. The collegiate rebellions of the 1960s and early 1970s over civil rights, the Vietnam War, and the regulations that controlled students' lives shocked most Americans because they overturned the role of colleges in enforcing re-sponsible behavior, and indicated the difficulty of standing in loco pa-rentis. Asserting parentlike control over college students on the cusp of adulthood—on such issues as alcohol, sex, and political participation as well as responsibility and initiative—has been especially difficult.

During the twentieth century, traditional forms of control in education have continued, including rules and regulations, suspensions and dismissals, the civics curriculum, codes of behavior, all updated to conform to changing fashions in psychology, child rearing, and perceived social threats. However, new forms of socialization and control emerged with vocationalism. One was simply the upward extension of education, starting around 1900, together with the enforcement of child labor laws and compulsory attendance statutes. These developments chased young people from the "school of the streets" and pulled them into real schools where they were subject to adult supervision—replacing the declining moral supervision of apprenticeships with the behavioral supervision of schoolmasters. Another has been the promise that good behavior in school will be rewarded by upward mobility, through schooling and then into the labor market. The old virtues of hard work, persistence, responsibility, obedience, and consistent attendance had in the nineteenth century promised their own rewards of moral character and ethical integrity, which would in turn lead to economic gain. As the twentieth century progressed, the rhetoric of moral progress gave way to the rewards related to improved learning, good grades, ascension to college and beyond, and employment. The work ethic in America is alive and well, except that it now stresses hard work and mastery of competencies in schooling rather than long hours working one's way up through the "school of experience." Conversely, the old evils that might lure students to Satan—sloth, carelessness, truancy, defiance—are now punished with a lack of progress in schooling and a future of low-status and stunted earnings.

American schools have continued to incorporate social and moral responsibilities by adding new initiatives to reduce delinquency and crime, early sexuality and pregnancy, drug abuse and drunk driving, and other social ills. Vocationalism has played an important role in these efforts too, since reducing socially irresponsible behavior is frequently promoted as a way to improve school success and continuation into employment. The effort against teenage pregnancy, for example, is no longer a moral crusade but rather an effort to prevent young girls from dropping out of school and perpetuating a cycle of poverty and dependence. The National Campaign to Prevent Teenage Pregnancy declared: "A basic tenet of the Campaign is that reducing the nation's rate of teen pregnancy is one of the most strategic and direct means available to improve overall child well-being and, in particular, to reduce persistent child poverty. Teen pregnancy is closely linked to a host of other critical social issues as well—welfare dependency, out-of-wedlock births, responsible fatherhood, and workforce development in particular." And dropping out of high school, for any number of reasons, is often presented first and foremost as a decision with economic consequences. The Advertising Council crafted this message:[16]

> More than 1,300 students drop out of school every day . . . Many of these kids don't think they have any options. The future seems bleak and hopeless, and quitting school can seem like the road to freedom and the opportunity to get a job and earn money. But that's not the case. The chances for success are automatically increased if you stay in school . . . Did you know that people who drop out of school earn 50 percent less than people who've finished high school? With job options limited, many high school dropouts depend on welfare for survival. Worse, some feel forced into lives of crime, either because of gang-involvement or because of low pay or lack of job options. If you are considering dropping out . . . Stop!

When schools have failed to keep students enrolled, nonschool training programs have been created as a second line of defense against disorder—the Youth Conservation Corps during the 1930s, dropout prevention programs and job training programs after 1960, summer youth programs to keep adolescents off the street, and other programs modeled on the Youth Conservation Corps and Job Corps, with their close discipline and practice of removing youth from their communities. New "youth development" programs are intended to develop teens' latent capacities rather than simply to regulate their behavior, as older programs based on deficiency models were. Some efforts—for example Youthbuild, which offers training in construction skills while rebuilding urban housing—operate by giving youths marketable skills and by embedding lessons about discipline, punctuality, and other behavior in work routines. But whether controlling or benevolent, these efforts reflect the notion that schooling or training can provide new incentives for good behavior by promising access to future employment.[17]

At the college and university level, incentives for appropriate conduct also exist, perhaps in even more powerful forms because the stakes are higher. College still is seen as a time to party, to "find yourself," to explore social and sexual identities as well as occupational alternatives—as in Erikson's (1959) notion of adolescence as a psychosocial moratorium. But students who are diligent and work hard reap the rewards of the baccalaureate degree, postgraduate education, and greater access to professional and managerial careers where the really big rewards lie. Those who do not fall back into the middle-level labor market, particularly into clerical and service work, with many fewer opportunities for professional success (as Table 6.3 clarifies).

However, the extrinsic incentives for good behavior embedded in vocationalism do not operate uniformly. As with everything else we have examined, they work better at the top of the system—in graduate schools and elite colleges, where the promises of *related employment* connected to an *occupational curriculum* are generally kept. But in high schools, in job training programs without much promise, sometimes in community colleges, hard work doesn't seem to be rewarded and the postponement of gratification doesn't seem to have much value. It is unrealistic to expect schooling to provide healthy and rewarding activities as substitutes for hanging out and the attractions of sex, drugs, and rock 'n' roll (or rap) unless those activities are indeed rewarded, and for too many adolescents the rewards seem implausible. The clearest examples of how the incentives of vocationalism can backfire involve African American youths who perceive, based on observations of the world around them, that discrimination and job ceilings will keep them out of the occupations for which education is supposed to prepare students; for them either dropping out of school or "mental withdrawal" is a rational response.[18] The job training and dropout programs for those who have left school, the most obvious efforts to keep youth busy and off the streets, have had almost no positive effects on noneconomic outcomes. Indeed, they often have made such behaviors worse: the Job Training Partnership programs *increased* arrest rates for young men who had not been previously arrested; the New Chance program for young mothers *increased* rates of pregnancy and abortion significantly; the JOBSTART program *increased* rates of pregnancy and birth, though it decreased arrest rates and drug use among men; the Summer Training and Employment Program (STEP) had only short-run effects on knowledge of contraception.[19] So the promise that vocationalism will help maintain social order—a promise that dates to the late nineteenth century—proves to be uncertain and unequal in its effects, powerful at levels of the education system where vocationalism is most complete, but weak at other levels.

Of course, educators themselves have been uncomfortable with the extrinsic incentives of vocationalism, preferring instead intrinsic motives—love of learning, dedication to a reasoned life—for their students. When intrinsic and extrinsic motives complement each other rather than replace each other, the power of formal schooling to engage adolescents *and* keep them out of trouble is especially clear. For middle-class students, the pressure from parents and peers to complete high school and proceed to college may be sufficient, but their high schools are also more likely to be pleasant places where social life, extracurricular activities, and classroom learning are consistent with one another and with familial incentives. But where high schools are uninviting, demoralizing, infantilizing places, where the messages from schools conflict with information from families and communities, then the extrinsic motivation of vocationalism may not be powerful enough to overcome the dismal aspects of continued attendance. Under these conditions it becomes necessary to transform schools as well as to make good on the promises of vocationalism, and therefore reformers have tried to create small schools, schools within schools, and other learning communities where teachers can get to know students well. Feeling connected to school can increase student motivation and engagement in academic tasks, which in turn reduces drug and alcohol abuse, violent or deviant behavior, pregnancy, and emotional distress (Blum, McNeely, and Rinehart, 2002; Manlove, 1998; Ladner, 1995, ch. 5). Where schools simultaneously create personalized environments and enhance academic progress, *and* where future rewards through graduation or postsecondary enrollment seem realistic, then students can be educationally engaged *and* social problems can be reduced.

Every society needs some way to socialize its young people, and all educational institutions are in the business of helping students develop socially acceptable norms of behavior. A vocationalized education system is not exceptional in that regard, though it has changed the basis of controlling behavior by bringing extrinsic incentives into schools and colleges that depend on the economic value of doing well in education.

There's no longer any need to appeal to moral arguments or community coherence or nation building to explain the value of good behavior. Instead, vocationalism relies purely on self-interest and individual advancement to secure social order, a much easier sell in a country where moral codes have fragmented and where individual incentives have become so powerful. But here the incompleteness and unequal power of vocationalism becomes a curse, since it cannot work well when economic rationales are weak, or when students don't believe the entreaties to "stay in school to get a job," or when schooling itself is so grim that the utilitarian calculations of present pain against future benefits lead to dropping out. And so the vocational incentives embedded in schooling cannot be a complete approach to socializing youth.

Facing the Current Century

By and large, schooling in the twentieth century made good on the private promises of vocationalism. More education does *on average* lead to higher earnings, more stable employment, greater choices of working conditions, and a higher probability of entering the professional and managerial positions that define middle-class careers. However, exaggerated forms of this promise are untrue, including the notion that all forms of education and training are beneficial, or that more schooling can guarantee higher earnings or access to professional work. There is still plenty of room for disappointment among people who have enrolled in further education and short-term training but failed to advance much, and therefore the "case against college" and arguments for the school of experience remain prevalent. But on the whole, the employment effects and the status effects of formal schooling are substantial; the promise of schooling is as close to a sure thing as there is for Americans without inherited wealth.

However, the public benefits of schooling are considerably less certain. While the rhetoric of economic growth has motivated public support for schooling and training, education is only one of a large constellation of factors responsible for growth. Schooling may contribute to the American form of unequal growth—particularly through research and the associated high-level technical preparation that contributes to technology. But schools and colleges cannot create growth by themselves, and many other factors have been responsible for the rise and fall of growth rates in the last century, particularly over the past three decades.

Similarly, the effects of schooling and job training programs in controlling unruly youths are uncertain. Most schools and training programs preach the value of good behavior with only checkered success. Broader cultural norms for adolescence and sexuality, the perception that opportunities are limited, and the attractiveness of some juvenile crime make rhetorical appeals to youth—"Just say no," or "Stay in school to get a job"—meaningless to many. The specific efforts in job training and other programs for high school dropouts to curb drug abuse, crime, and pregnancy have often backfired, neither curbing these behaviors nor increasing job opportunities. So long as economic opportunities through schooling are so unequal and the messages of the larger culture are so powerful, schooling alone is unlikely to solve the social problems of American youth.

The ambiguous public benefits of education and training stand in sharp contrast to the clarity of individual gain. The differences between genuine private benefits and rhetorical public benefits are likely to persist, especially if the occupational changes associated with the Knowledge Revolution continue to generate individual benefits for schooling while the public benefits depend on a constellation of influences not under the control of formal schooling. If the private benefits of schooling continue to outrun the public effects, several consequences will increasingly shape this dimension of American vocationalism. One is a continued escalation in education levels as individuals try to outdo one another for credentials in order to get ahead. Another consequence of an essentially private system of schooling is likely to be a more privatized form of public funding, in the form of vouchers and other marketlike mechanisms in K–12 education, to match the marketlike mechanisms that have always existed in postsecondary education—a shift that can only reinforce the tendency to think of education in terms of individual goals rather than public purposes (Levin, 1980). A continued emphasis on the private elements of vocationalism and voucherlike funding can only further undermine those public and collective values associated with older conceptions of education, including the moral, civic, and intellectual elements and the promotion of equity that seem to count only for educators and intellectuals. Our greatest fear is that public education will cease to be a sphere in which to debate and define and promote the common good (Cuban and Schipps, 2000), leading over time to the narrow and privatized form of vocationalism that we call HyperVoc (see Chapter 9).

If our analysis of the imbalance between the private and public forms of vocationalism is right, then it is crucial to develop a more publicly responsible form that acknowledges the power of schooling in giving individuals access to employment, but that avoids the excesses of the current American version. Indeed, we think that it should be liberating to recognize that education is only one of many factors influencing growth, and only one of many social forces affecting the behavior of the young, because formal schooling no longer has to bear the burden of doing everything imposed on it by the Education Gospel. It simply isn't necessary to emphasize job-ready skills and "the skills employers want" to the exclusion of other competencies, because narrowly defined skills are not the most crucial elements contributing to growth. The critical roles of schooling are to teach a *broad* base of fundamental competencies—including, at this stage of technological development, widespread (though low-level) computer competencies—as well as to provide sufficient flexibility to respond to changing job conditions and enough advanced programs to build the technological base for some components of growth. To calm the more extreme rhetoric of the Education Gospel, then, it is necessary to have a more complex understanding of the contribution of education, and to emphasize once again the importance of nonschool policies.

A related goal should certainly be to moderate the rhetoric of the Education Gospel and its simpleton twin, the naive form of human capital. Our rhetoric should acknowledge that some forms of education and training have no payoff, including short-term job training, small amounts of postsecondary education, education for poorly paid occupations, short-term adult education programs, GED programs, education and training in low-quality programs wherever they exist. With more moderate rhetoric, we hope that the education and training system will become more transparent, so that prospective students will understand which programs have promise and which do not, so that providers will be more honest about their programs' effects, and so that employers can rely on the quality of graduates. The private version of vocationalism tends to be opaque because there are few incentives for transparency. One way to get ahead within the American system is to be an insider who knows how the system works. Making such knowledge widely available—for example, through sophisticated and continuous guidance and counseling that teach all children the secrets of mobility—has so far been impossible.

Recognizing the limitations of schooling and training would allow us to view more clearly the relationships among inequality, education, and social policies. The form of economic growth that we have promoted, particularly in the past twenty-five years, follows a particularly inegalitarian pattern, emphasizing growth at the expense of full employment, greater equity in the distribution of earnings, consumer and environmental protection, and other elements of the common good. And education's role as a protector of social stability, with vocationalism providing new approaches to an old issue, has disintegrated over the issue of inequality, since the incentives for good behavior vanish among students whose schooling doesn't deliver on the promises of the Education Gospel. The need to look for nonschool policies becomes obvious once we are honest about what schools can and cannot do.

This honesty would then allow us to restore our sense of public purpose in education. In the history of both K–12 and higher education there is much to build on—in past debates over our common culture and values in a nation of immigrants, over the meaning of democratic participation and its purposes, over the multiple goals of education, including its humanistic and aesthetic components as well as the moral and civic elements we have often stressed. The best side of American democracy has wrestled hard with questions of the common good and the good society, even if the dominant form of democracy at the moment—like the dominant form of vocationalism—stresses individual gain (and sometimes simple-minded entertainment) to the exclusion of common purpose. We can build on the commitments to the public purposes of education once we acknowledge that public goals do not require us to develop narrow forms of schooling.

Overall, then, the future of schooling requires that we develop a more modest and more public-minded version of the Education Gospel—at least if we are to avoid an unbridled, narrow, and inegalitarian form of vocationalism. A more transparent schooling system that replaces naive human capital conceptions with a more sophisticated understanding of when school pays off and when it does not would be one way to moderate extremist rhetoric. Moderating the rhetoric about growth would free up schools to pay attention to those broader forms of schooling that turn out to be in the best interests of students as well as closer to the competencies necessary for growth. The more that educational institutions improve so that students are connected to them through the academic challenges and the *believable* occupational promises they provide, the greater the chances that some of the social problems young people face can be moderated. Perhaps a more modest vision of the Education Gospel could help vocationalism keep its promises.

7

∼ The Ambiguities of Separating Schooling and Work

A VOCATIONALIZED education system promises to prepare people for occupational roles by teaching the competencies necessary for employment, not merely by certifying ability or providing a credential without content. The language of the Education Gospel—preoccupied by New Basics, skills for the twenty-first century, higher-order skills for high-performance workplaces, SCANS skills—reflects this assumption about the transferability of school-based learning into employment. The longer a student stays in school, the more competencies or skills he or she can learn, presumably to prepare for more complex occupations. At the same time, the school-based approach assumes that formal schooling is superior to alternative forms of preparation, including apprenticeships, the "school of experience," and (in debased form) Work First.

The shift of work preparation into educational institutions over the twentieth century effectively separated work preparation from work itself. Individuals progress from education to employment sequentially, or more precisely—when large numbers of teenagers and students in their early twenties have unskilled transient jobs—schooling becomes a prerequisite for finding "real" or "adult" employment. This separation has caused many difficulties in the school-to-work transition, problems that *necessarily* arise once schooling is separated from employment (Ryan, 2001). The problem has come to public attention repeatedly since the identification in the early twentieth century of the "wasted

184

years" between leaving school and finding permanent employment. During the 1970s, the problematic transition between school and work reared its head as part of charges that high schools had become too distant from adult life, especially work life (Panel on Youth, 1974; National Commission on Youth, 1980). The School-to-Work Opportunities Act of 1994 tried unsuccessfully to address the same issues by developing work-based learning and linkage mechanisms connecting schools and work opportunities.[1]

Of course, several mechanisms linking schooling and work exist. These range from attempts to make vocational and career guidance more effective to cooperative arrangements between workplaces and schools to credentials and licensing that connect what students learn to work competencies, often indirectly. But these linking mechanisms often falter, particularly in a laissez-faire system of education and employment in which individuals look for work on their own, employers hire whom they want, and education and training institutions decide what they will teach. The competencies necessary for success in school —"school skills"—often differ from the competencies necessary for success on the job, or "work skills." This disjunction is endemic to a vocationalized education system, and it has been criticized repeatedly ever since debates over the Morrill Act, by the opponents of "fancy farmers" and "fancy mechanics," by the proponents of the "school of hard knocks," by the critics of credentialism. The underlying challenge is how to overcome this disjunction.

At the macro level of the economic system, the separation between school and work has stimulated debates about the extent of undereducation versus overeducation. The Education Gospel has maintained that undereducation is a serious problem, with individuals too poorly educated for existing and future jobs, leading in turn to support for the doctrine of college for all. In these discussions the persistent problem of overeducation (or over*schooling*) has gotten less attention. Often linked to the view that Americans are overcredentialed, overeducation is a problem when individuals are forced for defensive reasons to continue in school to the point where they have more schooling than the available jobs require. The American form of vocationalism exaggerates both undereducation and overschooling, an inefficient and inequitable result that has been the price of laissez-faire policies in an inegalitarian society.

Even though there are effective mechanisms for linking school and work—like the incorporation of more work-based learning into schools, and the extension of professional credentials established by tripartite groups—certain inconsistencies are inevitable, given the history of our schools, the nature of current employment patterns, and the laissez-faire nature of our education and labor-market institutions. Indeed certain inconsistencies are *desirable*, since a system that ties schooling too tightly to employment necessarily limits the moral, intellectual, and civic purposes that elevate education over mere job training. But the tendency to define education and work issues in either-or terms has seriously hampered our institutions' ability to play different and complementary roles. The conflict between believers in the Education Gospel, who want to force schools to prepare students more specifically for the skills employers want, and the dissenters who promote experience rather than schooling, has not been particularly fruitful. We need to ask how occupational preparation might be distributed throughout the institutions of our society, with different institutions playing different roles, given the inevitable and often desirable disjunction between schooling and employment.

Linking Schooling and Employment

Since the inception of vocationalized schooling, various links between the educational system and employment have been created, both informal and formal, private and government sanctioned, institutional and market driven. One link has been the attempt to prepare rational individuals who are able to make their own decisions in a complex society, including decisions about schooling and employment. A second effort has linked schools and employers directly, where employers influence what schools and colleges do or, less often, where the workplace is explicitly connected to schools through cooperative education or internships. A third link involves credentials and licenses, which have value in the labor market because they provide information to employers about the competencies of students, at the same time that they inform students and educational providers about the requirements of employment. These linkage mechanisms vary substantially, but they all acknowledge (usually implicitly) that school-based occupational preparation needs to establish closer connections to employment if it is to work well.

Preparing Rational Choosers

In a world without occupational choices, where sons succeed their fathers and daughters become mothers and homemakers, there are few occupational decisions for young people to make. But as occupational possibilities expand, some mechanism must facilitate the choice among them. As occupational preparation moved into schools and colleges, occupational choices began to take place within educational institutions, and *occupational* decisions turned into *educational* decisions.

Schools prepare students to make choices in many different ways. The very idea of a formal institution like schooling standing between the intimate world of the family and the impersonal world of adult responsibilities implies a transition between the two. Schools have developed in ways that ease this transition. The early grades introduce young children to the differences between familial roles and social roles (like that of teacher); to the differences between enduring relationships in families and episodic relationships in the larger society; to the subtle combination in social behavior of cooperation interlaced with individualism and competition (Dreeben, 1968). Schools then allow greater choice over time, moving from prescribed coursework from a single teacher in the elementary grades, to limited choices with more teachers in middle schools, to still more choice and many more teachers in the "shopping mall high school" (Powell, Farrar, and Cohen, 1985), and finally to the enormous array of alternatives available to prospective college students.

If expanding options and practice in making choices created rational choosers, then students would emerge from schooling as knowledgeable individuals capable of making their way in a market society. Since this does not always occur, schools and colleges have turned to more explicit efforts to prepare students for decision making, particularly through vocational guidance and student counseling. Unfortunately, however, career-oriented counseling has now virtually disappeared from high schools. Because it is a service that is not a core academic function, it has been chronically underfunded, with too many students for each counselor. Over time, career advice has evolved into a combination of academic advising—what courses to take to get to the next level of schooling—and personal or psychological counseling, and counselors have also been burdened with many administrative duties.

When counselors (and some teachers) do get around to career counseling, the dominant advice is simply college for all. The principal approach is so-called trait-and-factor counseling, in which counselors assess the interests and personality traits of students and then provide information on the most "appropriate" occupations. This process is sometimes derided as "test 'em and tell 'em," and it often amounts to little more than dumping information on unprepared students.

In community colleges, many students—especially those coming from high schools without much counseling—are experimenters who have enrolled to figure out which occupations might fit their interests and abilities. Most colleges provide standard counseling services, available at the initiative of students; a few have devised semester-long courses designed to help students reflect on their interests and the employment options available, or learning communities that incorporate counselors, or cooperative education programs that allow students to experience a variety of occupations. But many students are on their own: academic counseling trumps career counseling, and the conventional information dump provides no active way for students to learn how to make decisions for themselves.[2]

Only in affluent high schools and elite colleges is the situation better. For the middle-class students in these institutions, there is a surfeit of information to help them make decisions—manuals about colleges, private counselors to supplement meager public resources, the direct experience of parents. Some colleges have adopted the concept of *student development*, viewing students as individuals who face a variety of decisions and developmental tasks, and encompassing activities like dorm life, seminars, counseling, intramural sports, other extracurricular activities, and smaller groups like houses or honors colleges (Ratcliff, 1995; Knock, 1985). But outside of elite colleges, this developmental approach to helping students choose among life's many options rarely occurs.

The most obvious characteristic of career-oriented guidance and counseling is how unequal it is. Sophisticated students in elite colleges receive the best-developed services, while others—non-college-bound high school students, experimenters in community colleges, and clients in short-term training—receive almost nothing. A second characteristic is that locating guidance and counseling within educational institutions has allowed school-related agendas to take over, displacing career counseling with academic counseling, and often with personal counseling and administrative paperwork. A third characteristic is that resources are inadequate. Even when resources exist they are not used well, since they tend to focus on conventional trait-and-factor counseling or different versions of the information dump. As a result, students are often badly misinformed, numerous high school students are unaware of the requirements for college, and many enter community colleges by accident or as ill-informed experimenters. Excessive numbers of individuals have "misaligned ambitions," with high educational and occupational goals but without the educational plans necessary to realize those goals (Schneider and Stevenson, 1999).

In effect, we have created a society in which cultural norms, including the stereotypes on television and in movies, create unlimited ambitions, while another system—the education system, without the glitz and power of Hollywood, with overworked counselors and teachers of shrinking authority—must explain the harsh realities of labor market competition and help students make "realistic" choices. In the process, the role of guidance and counseling in bridging the gap between school and employment has been undermined by the institutional realities of poor funding, peripheral status, and academic agendas.

Institutional Connections

A different linkage mechanism relies on direct connections between schools and workplaces. Examples include school-business partnerships, advisory committees, cooperative education programs in which schools and employers jointly prepare workers, and customized training in which colleges provide training for specific firms. Implicitly, such connections acknowledge that an educational system aspiring to prepare people for occupations should be more directly linked to the workplace. But schools and colleges are often at odds with employers, who are primarily concerned with immediate productivity and short-run profit.

To take one example, during the 1980s a movement developed to promote school-employer partnerships. The rhetoric stressed benefits to schools, which received additional resources (like computers); benefits to students, who developed closer connections to employment; and benefits to employers, who could play a more active role in shaping their local schools—a win-win-win situation. The partnerships that sprang up were quite varied, of course, as befits the diversity of American education. However, many of these partnerships were short-term and opportunistic. The schools hoped to find additional resources and the firms sought publicity, but they lacked common goals and accomplished relatively little (ERIC Clearinghouse, 1990; Clark, 1988). In another example, providers of occupational education sometimes develop close working relationships with individual employers, particularly when community college and professional programs establish regular contact with a few large firms. However, the quality of these advisory committees and institutional connections varies enormously (Grubb, 1996b, ch. 6). Most public institutions do not commit themselves to job placement; they often declare, "We're educators, not employment agencies"—an approach that can give private "occupational colleges" with better ties to employers a distinct advantage (Deil-Amen and Rosenbaum, 2001).

Another long-standing practice linking schools and employment opportunities has been manpower forecasting to identify local labor market trends. Such efforts have worked well when local education and training programs have been able to target fast-growing and well-paid occupations (King et al., 2000; Osterman and Lautsch, 1996). However, predicting occupational trends is exceedingly difficult, particularly at the local level where high schools and community colleges operate, and manpower forecasting has fallen into disrepute as a way of linking schooling and employment. Furthermore, many public education providers (especially community colleges) are forced politically to offer a broad range of programs to serve a wide public, and thus cannot concentrate on a few fast-growing occupations as proprietary schools can.

Potentially the most promising institutional links are cooperative education and internship programs. Such programs allow high schools, colleges, and post-baccalaureate institutions to develop close contacts with workplaces, particularly in coordinating the school-based and work-based components. Where co-op education has been widely adopted, as in the Cincinnati area, many employers are knowledgeable about local schools and colleges, and they participate in designing programs. Each side in the co-op relationship works to maintain the quality of its own offerings and to make sure the other side does the same, creating a high-quality equilibrium (Villeneuve and Grubb, 1996). However, aside from a few institutions (like Northeastern University in Boston and Drexel University in Philadelphia) and a few occupations (like engineering and nursing), co-op programs are comparatively rare, despite our periodic efforts to emulate the German system.[3]

Few would describe these varied efforts to link schools and work-places as successful. Rarely have they changed educational practices, except in a few cases of co-op education or specific placement relations with local employers. The most effective links probably exist at elite graduate professional schools, which often have strong placement pro-grams, active advisory committees, and constant interaction with the corporations and law firms that hire their graduates. Less selective uni-versities and community colleges have considerably weaker links, and high schools have almost none.[4]

The underlying problem is that schools and firms have conflicting cultures and imperatives. Schools and colleges are dominated by their academic core; most are ambivalent about closer connections between schooling and employment, since links to workplaces might challenge academic goals by putting education in the service of occupations. And while employers claim to favor such linkages, they rarely do much to support them; they often evaluate them on whether students contrib-ute immediately to productivity, rather than on how much students learn—a problem since the early days of apprenticeship.[5] Even when resources become available, such as through the School-to-Work Op-portunities Act of 1994 or through tax incentives to employers, the ten-dency is to use the money for conventional activities. It has also been difficult to institutionalize cooperation: business-school partnerships come and go without leaving any lasting relationships, many co-op programs don't last, and the STWOA ended without having many per-manent effects. Without sustained interaction between educators and employers, linking mechanisms are exceedingly hard to maintain.

Credentials and Licenses

Credentials and licenses are yet another linkage mechanism. They in-clude diplomas from educational institutions, occupational licenses granted by state governments, certificates awarded by employers and professional associations, and informal awards reproduced on Xerox machines. When an educational credential works as intended, it creates a set of uniform expectations for all participants. Employers can specify the competencies they need; education and training programs can use credential requirements to shape their curriculum and motivate students with the promise of employment; and students know what competencies they must master to become marketable. This is the positive sense of credentials: they are market-making devices that coordinate the activities of employers, education providers, and students, giving consistent incentives to all participants.

However, unlike prices in conventional markets, credentials are not set by the invisible hand of the market. They require considerable institutional effort to create and to enforce. In theory, credentials require three distinct elements: (1) competencies or standards, (2) a method of assessing competencies, and (3) a mechanism for policing the process. Each of these elements is complex and potentially controversial, and each can be implemented in many different ways ranging from informal to formal, laissez-faire to highly bureaucratic. If any of the three elements is inconsistent with the others, then the value of a credential becomes uncertain and "credentialism" takes on the negative connotation of educational requirements not rationally related to employment requirements (Collins, 1979). If, for example, employers hire on the basis of experience or other qualities and ignore the credential in hiring, then the credential may seem superfluous. If for any reason (including the pace of change or the distance between educators and the workplace) the competencies taught are not those required on the job, then both students and employers are disappointed with the results. When jobs require skills (such as highly specific skills) that schools cannot or should not teach, and that are not included in credential programs, then the mismatch generates employer complaints that students lack necessary training. If a credential requires certain courses or prerequisites but students are not aware of them—as is true for many uninformed students with "misaligned ambitions"—then the expectations of students and those of educators are inconsistent. And when credentials appear to be unrelated to job requirements, and seem to be used simply to reduce the pool of eligible applicants or to discriminate against women, minorities, or some other group, then they are subject to legal challenges as well as public critique. While developing a coherent system of credentials can alleviate these inconsistencies, such a project requires substantial institutional energy and considerable government intervention.

In our country, credentials are most coherent in the case of state-required licenses. These are common in the high professions and many semiprofessions, but they are also required in subprofessional occupations where health and safety are important, like aviation mechanics, some construction trades, cosmetology and barbering. Licensing exams are usually established by boards made up of practicing professionals, employers, and training providers—the closest system we have to European tripartite planning. Licensing can also be used to regulate supply and increase earnings, and some of the highest and most stable returns to education exist in programs subject to licensing, like health occupations. But licensing also imposes substantial costs—including the time and collaboration necessary to create licensing procedures—and additional effort from students. A complex licensing system may become rigid and outdated, reinforcing rather than diminishing the differences between school skills and work skills. And licensing often limits entry to occupations by low-income or minority students, immigrants without English skills, or welfare recipients lacking prerequisites.[6]

Despite these difficulties, the power of credentials and licenses is evident from the recent expansion of private and voluntary credentials. Many of these have been created by industry associations or professional groups, such as the National Automotive Technicians Education Foundation for automotive technicians, the American Welding Society, the National Board for Professional Teaching Standards for teachers. Individual firms have also created their own credentials; for example, Microsoft has established the Microsoft Certified Systems Engineer (MCSE) and the Microsoft Office User Specialist (MOUS) credentials; Cisco has developed the Cisco Certified Networking Associate (CCNA) specifically for those working with Cisco software. In contrast to these private efforts, the federal government's efforts to create new skill standards and credentials through the National Skills Standards Board have largely failed—illustrating once again the bias of the American political economy, where public participation in areas seen as the prerogative of private employers is often ineffective.[7]

The apparent explosion of credentials comes in part from the Education Gospel: keeping the workforce up to date requires new skills and new mechanisms of certification. Many recent efforts to develop new credentials depend explicitly on the language of the Education Gospel. For example, a recent proposal for a three-year, three-level certification process for the "profession" of manufacturing representative—arguably an occupation where specific knowledge is more critical than general knowledge—rested on rapid change, globalization, and the need for a highly trained labor force (Weinrauch, Stevens, and Carlson, 1997). In addition, the members of the Education Coalition benefit from credentials: employers benefit from increased certainty in hiring; students benefit from a greater likelihood of finding related employment; education and training providers benefit from the help received in devising occupationally relevant curricula. Against this coalition, the dissenters who worry about the long-run escalation of meaningless credentials or the additional costs and rigidity of credentialing are relatively unorganized and powerless.

But even as credentials are expanding, Americans remain ambivalent about them. One reason is the negative view of credentialism, that educational requirements are not closely related to employment requirements. Another is that employment-oriented credentials often seem at odds with the academic goals of schools and colleges, since they undermine the independence of educational institutions to determine what knowledge and competencies are most valuable. From the perspective of the student who sees in a credential only its employment value, the incentive is to get the credential without learning much—an emphasis on quantity over quality that further empties schooling of its content (Bishop, 1989). Americans are also ambivalent about the regulation necessary for a real system of credentials; the German system, with its complex of 900-plus credentials, would strike most American as overly bureaucratized and rigid. So most of our publicly recognized credentials—at least 90 percent—are what we might call laissez-faire credentials, established by educational institutions with little input from employers, government regulators, or even other educators.[8] Laissez-faire credentials are certainly consistent with the autonomy of educational institutions and with weak government intervention in labor markets, but not with the requirements of a coherent credential system linking schooling and employment. In the absence of a carefully developed and well-policed system, employers are forced to rely on such laissez-faire credentials, but it shouldn't be surprising that the competencies certified are not necessarily those required in employment.

Overall, there are substantial weaknesses in each of the mechanisms linking schooling with employment. Guidance and counseling are inadequate, except perhaps at the highest levels of the education system. Institutional links vary and the most effective—cooperative education —are comparatively rare. The majority of credentials are still school-generated, despite the interest in industry-based credentials. The links between schooling and employment work best at the upper levels of the occupational structure, in the professions and professional schools; they work substantially less well in nonelite universities and community colleges, and they are virtually nonexistent in high schools, which are almost completely out of touch with the world of employment. The shift of preparation into schools and colleges has separated schooling from employment, yet efforts to overcome that separation by creating links between schooling and employment have been largely impotent.

Skills and Competencies

The efforts to link schools and workplaces have recognized, often implicitly, the differences between the competencies readily learned at school—school skills—and the work skills necessary on the job. The distinction is crucial to understanding the limits of American vocationalism. Even the vocabulary with which we describe competence has been affected. Usually, the abilities acquired in formal schooling are described as "skills," or sometimes as "competencies" (as in competency-based education). These descriptions connote abilities that individuals possess, that they can transfer from setting to setting—now in one job, now in another, in a political activity like voting, or in a familial activity like helping children with homework. Literacy is such a "skill," as are numeracy, the ability to identify chemical solutions, the knowledge of demand-supply analyses, and "higher-order skills" such as problem solving, judgment, and communications. In the widespread metaphor of human capital, individuals accumulate stocks of these skills over time and then benefit individually from their consequences in employment. We may worry about the transferability of skills—the ability of individuals to apply them in different situations, particularly as they move from job to job (Perkins and Salomon, 1988)—but there is little doubt that the skills are theirs.

The contrary view is that the abilities necessary in employment are not necessarily the property of individuals but instead are dependent on the work setting itself and on the interaction of individuals in particular settings.[9] Many believers in the "school of experience" have assumed that competence can be learned only on the job, under real conditions, in the fellowship of other workers. Those studying the nature of work have articulated many ways in which necessary "skills" depend on the work setting. For example, Darrah (1996) examined several high-tech workplaces, showing that their idiosyncratic features affect both workers' performance and their abilities to learn new tasks. Drawing on idealized conceptions of apprenticeship, Lave and Wenger's (1991) work argues that preparation for work is a process of socialization into a community of practice, starting with the "peripheral participation" of the novice and expanding over time with competence acquired within the community. From these perspectives, the concept of *individual* skills is radically incomplete, since it disregards the setting in which such abilities are both developed and used.

However, in the American approach to vocationalism, where occupational preparation usually takes place before employment and away from the job, a decontextualized notion of skill is the logical extension of the separation of schooling from work. Instructors can't easily know what the specific demands on their students will be; they can only guess at the nature of the jobs students will enter. Their guesses are better informed when they know more about the occupations their students enter (as occupational instructors often do), or when there are skill standards and credentials to guide them, or when programs are tied to specific employers through institutional linkages. But in most cases, and certainly in academic programs that don't prepare students for specific occupations, the competencies required in particular contexts cannot be known, and so individual and decontextualized conceptions of skills dominate. This in turn leads to occupational programs and professional schools that stress individual technical ability over context-dependent competencies—leading to critiques in virtually all professional areas (as we reviewed in Chapter 2). Most people talk about individual skills because the separation of schooling from employment in the American approach to vocationalism imposes this conception on educators and students alike.

The distinction between school skills and work skills also shows up in the endless battles over general versus specific skills. In one formulation, general skills are those (like literacy, or perhaps computer competency) required by all employers, while specific skills are those required by a particular employer (Becker, 1993). Individual firms often prefer to hire individuals who have specific skills—knowledge of how to run a particular machine or use a certain software package—because they can begin production with little additional training. However, students have little incentive to pay to acquire such skills, because they are not useful in the broader job market or easily transferable to other firms. Conversely, since general skills are useful in most employment situations, individuals are more likely to pay to learn them, giving schools a substantial advantage over work-based preparation. Individual firms have little incentive to provide general education because other firms may hire the trained individuals away—the problem of poaching. The distinction between specific and general skills has led to a conventional division of labor in which firms provide specific (and contextualized) training, while schools teach general (and decontextualized) skills that are widely applicable in the job market. Some employers sometimes acknowledge that educational institutions cannot provide specific training; as a manager for a cable manufacturing firm admitted, "This plant needs a specific type of worker. To train [in a school] for this specific type of worker—I don't know if you can actually do that" (Grubb, 1996b, 22). Yet other employers complain when schools fail to provide them with job-ready, or "turnkey," graduates (Devenport and Hebel, 2001). Particularly at the local level, many pressure high schools and community colleges to teach specific skills, and they have advocated customized training programs where public funds are used for employer-specific skill development.

A variation in the tension between general and specific training involves *job*-specific versus general skills. This conception focuses on the conflict between the short-term interests of employers seeking turnkey workers with complete job-specific skills versus the long-term interests of students in learning broader competencies for career mobility. Unfortunately, the conflict places educational institutions in a jam. When programs teach more job-specific skills, becoming more attractive to local employers and students seeking immediate employment, they are criticized for offering narrow "trade training" rather than an education that will serve students over the long term. When they strive to impart more general competencies—the "industrial intelligence" of 1900, or the higher-order skills of the current Education Gospel—they are invariably criticized for teaching "abstract" knowledge of limited utility in the workplace. One resolution is again the division of labor, with schooling teaching general competencies and employers imparting specific skills on the job. But this resolution only further separates school skills and work skills.

The distinction between school skills and work skills reflects genuine differences between schools and workplaces as sites for learning. These differences can be further understood by examining the pedagogy of schools, the nature of academic instruction, and the distinctions among types of competencies.

Pedagogy

Despite the advent of vocationalism, schools have retained their traditional ways of teaching. In Resnick's (1987) influential formulation, students in schools usually work individually and are individually judged, graded, and promoted—reflecting the individual concept of skills—while employees in the modern corporation usually work in groups, sharing complementary competencies to perform tasks that are much larger than any one worker could carry out. Indeed, the high-skill workplace that has fewer layers of hierarchy places increased responsibility on individuals to cooperate with many others. To be sure, some educators have recognized that collective learning is powerful, and have introduced cooperative learning and group projects that build on conceptions of "distributed cognition"—that the knowledge necessary for most tasks is distributed among members of a group. Such approaches are also more consistent with many nonschool activities and with learning in the workplace. But pedagogical practices and the individualistic conception of skills are hard to change.

A second pedagogical feature of formal schooling is its emphasis on conveying facts and procedures to students, breaking complex competencies—reading, writing, and mathematics, for example—into subskills, and then teaching those subskills through drill and repetition. This occurs across the curriculum, in both academic classes and vocational teaching, in professional education's emphasis on facts and procedures, and even in firms, when they mimic the "skills and drills" approach in their in-house training. But such teaching makes little sense in preparing individuals for the flexible jobs of the twenty-first century, so different from the assembly-line work spawned by the Industrial Revolution. As work becomes less routine, requires greater judgment, and depends on interaction with a wider variety of coworkers and customers, then routinized and decontextualized learning is even less appropriate (Berryman and Bailey, 1992; SCANS, 1991; Gott, 1988, 1995). Of course, schools and colleges can adopt different pedagogies, moving toward practices variously described as constructivist, or meaning-centered, or problem-based. But changing teaching methods has proved difficult, especially at the high school and postsecondary levels (Cuban, 1993; Grubb and Associates, 1999), and so traditional pedagogy continues to have powerful influence.

The Nature of Academic Competencies

The academic content of schooling is also different from the requirements of the workplace. When schools teach academic subjects, they are usually "school subjects" rather than competencies used in the external worlds of work, politics, or community. For example, reading and writing as taught in school tends to take a single form involving literature, the interpretation of fiction, and the exploration of literary genres and authorial voice. In contrast, literacy varies in nonschool settings. Texts at work are very different from texts in school; they include instruction manuals, parts manuals, diagrams and charts, and other ways of displaying information. The ability to "read" these different texts is not usually taught in schools, except when occupational instructors take care to introduce students to the special genres used on the job. School approaches often stress individual interpretation—of literature, historical events, or economic and political developments—whereas the texts read for work, and writing undertaken on the job, must be unambiguous; novel or creative interpretations play little or no role at work, and may even be dangerous. Similarly, the standard school approach to mathematics marches through a menu of subjects including arithmetic, algebra, geometry, and calculus, a series of separate procedures and contrived problems often taught without regard to applications. In contrast, math on the job tends to require a set of interrelated procedures, none of which is very complex, but where the sequence of steps is crucial and the problem itself is likely to be ill defined, especially when compared with the formulaic problems in math textbooks.[10]

Again, there are ways for educational institutions to bridge the divide between school-based forms of academic subjects and work-based forms. Some colleges have developed applied academic courses—math for health occupations, business English, technical math for engineering applications, and the like—that combine academic competence with occupational applications. In other cases, learning communities integrate several courses of study, including both academic and occupational courses.[11] Academic institutions need not treat academic subjects as distant from the requirements of production—although most of them do.

Cognitive and Noncognitive Abilities

Schools and colleges invariably give substantially greater weight to cognitive competencies over other, noncognitive competencies important at work (Cook-Gumperz, 1986). These noncognitive abilities may include visual competencies, crucial for activities ranging from high art to engineering to midlevel occupations like drafting and carpentry; kinesthetic or manual skills, necessary for craft work as well as for medical fields and engineering; aural skills, necessary for music and languages, for perceptual feedback in production processes, in medicine for understanding what organs should sound like, in automobile repair for knowing how a well-tuned engine hums; and interpersonal skills, necessary in a wide variety of service occupations as well as for cooperative production, and often included among the "soft skills" necessary in employment. Sometimes these other abilities or "intelligences" (Gardner, 1983) are explicitly taught in the labs and workshops of occupational programs, or in role-playing activities in professional programs; they are often learned in internships, co-op education programs, and other forms of work-based learning. But even in the occupational or professional classroom they are often ignored. Little time is spent on manual skills or visual abilities, even in fields where they seem essential; for example, many engineers report that they have never been instructed in the spatial dimensions of their work (Bell and Linn, 1993). While the ability to extract information from diagrams and charts is crucial to various kinds of work, the pedagogy of teaching this is rarely explored.[12]

Other competencies necessary at work include the shortcuts, tacit knowledge, and unwritten conventions or "lore" that develop in virtually every workplace. Ethnographers of work have described a range of these abilities. Expert technicians, for example, combine school-like analytic competencies with the lore of craft workers (Barley and Orr, 1997). Software designers often fall back on pragmatic strategies and "what works," even though they also hold analytic views of why software may fail (Pentland, 1997). Emergency medical technicians use knowledge picked up on the job and circumvent standard protocols if they think it is in the best interests of patients (Nelsen, 1997). Lab technicians develop the skills necessary to avoid errors on the job by consulting one another about anomalies instead of following established procedures (Scarselletta, 1997). Tacit knowledge and lore involve highly context-specific competencies that arise from the "school of experience" specific to particular jobs. They often reflect social norms governing work and the sharing of knowledge, rather than the individual abilities we think of as skills. Occasionally instructors in occupational and professional programs teach this lore through personal stories, or create role-playing activities to illustrate the interpersonal dilemmas that arise in work; work-based placements offer other ways to learn these competencies. But teaching tacit knowledge and job lore in a school setting is usually impossible, since such abilities by their nature arise in specific work contexts not replicable in schools and colleges designed to provide general preparation.

The most powerful consequence of the separation of school skills from work skills is that individuals are not fully prepared to start work when they finish their education. Unless they are in overly specific training programs, they are unlikely to be turnkey graduates. Many complaints about schooling in the Education Gospel bemoan this particular disjunction, which exists at the high school level all the way up to professional education. Of course, many occupations have structured some kind of induction period to compensate for the impossibility of finding job-ready graduates: residencies and internships for doctors, the grunt work assigned to new lawyers, professional development for new teachers, and probationary periods built into many jobs. The necessity for such transitions comes directly from the fact that schooling cannot by itself produce graduates who are fully ready for work.

A more subtle consequence involves the idea of who is and is not skilled. Once schooling has become the locus of work preparation, then an individual who is considered *skilled* is virtually always *schooled;* those who are considered unskilled are those who have little or no schooling. Yet many jobs defined as relatively unskilled require quite sophisticated competencies. For example, Fearfull (1996) examined clerical workers in the credit sector who used a variety of interpersonal and technical abilities to calm angry customers, negotiate with customers and fellow employees, make appropriate judgments, and advise management. While essential to their success on the job, these skills were not recognized in their job descriptions, and management regarded these competencies as "innate abilities" rather than developed skills. Similarly, Harper (1987) describes an old-fashioned rural mechanic whose mechanical ability, picked up over time from his father in the school of experience, was quite different from the methods of auto repair "by the book," though much more effective in his context. After observing and interviewing a variety of workers to examine know-how on the job, Kusterer (1978) rejected the notion that any job is unskilled, since all workers learn many technical and interpersonal skills to cope with recurring problems. More generally, Attewell (1990) has argued that when skills have been learned so well on the job as to become automatic, it is unfair to view those workers as unskilled since their substantial competencies are invisible.

However, while "unskilled" jobs may require substantial competence, the belief that school-based knowledge is more powerful than knowledge learned on the job is part of vocationalism. Harper's rural mechanic would not get hired in a garage using complex electronics and computer diagnostics. Other workers who have picked up skills on the job would have difficulty if their job changed even in small ways. For example, Crandall (1981) described clerks who perceived themselves as poor readers but who had learned to find crucial information on patent applications without much reading—a tactic that works only in highly stable and specific work conditions. In another example of competing conceptions of skill, an older worker described the change in the paper pulp industry, which has been transformed by computerized continuous-process technology: "The new people are not going to understand, see, or feel as well as the old guys . . . The computer can't feel what is going on out there. The new operators will need to have more written down, because they will not know it in their gut." In contrast, a process engineer schooled in computer-based techniques had little patience for "gut" knowledge: "Computer analysis lets us see the effects of many variables and their interactions. This is a picture of truth that we could not have achieved before. It is superior to the experience-based knowledge of an operator. You might say that truth replaces knowledge" (Zuboff, 1988, 65, 67). Even as Americans argue about how to connect school-based and work-based skills, there is little doubt that the process engineer has won the debate.

The Mismatch of Overschooling and Undereducation

In a vocationalized system, appropriate levels of schooling are defined by the schooling required for jobs—not by the requirements of political participation, nor by conceptions of liberal education, nor by vague notions of "educating all children to the limit of their abilities." If individuals care about schooling only for its economic value, then the quasi-markets in formal education created by vocationalism should establish an equilibrium between the supply and demand for skills. As occupations become more complex, young people and schools should receive clear information about the requirements for more skilled occupations; students should stay in school long enough to gain the competencies necessary to be successful at these jobs, and no one should complain about undereducation or the failure to learn the skills of the twenty-first century. Similarly, employers should have no incentive to hire workers with more schooling than they need, and the problem of overeducation should be avoided. When markets work as they are supposed to, there ought to be a perfect match between the amounts of schooling and skill individuals attain and the amounts that employers require.

However, in practice markets don't work perfectly and mismatches occur, especially in education, and especially in a country like the United States, where antipathy toward government intervention allows

market failures to occur. The dominant fear of the Education Gospel
has focused on *under*education, with the claims that school-based skills
are inadequate for the jobs of the Knowledge Revolution, that the
higher-order skills are poorly taught in school, that we need college for
all. This element of the Education Gospel has focused on the low skill
levels evident in the workforce—the complaint of manifestos such as
America's Choice: High Skills or Low Wages!—and about the "skills gap"
relative to other countries and relative to what we need for high-
performance workplaces. Although we may be skeptical about these
claims, as is evident when we look at the slow changes in schooling requirements like those shown in Table I.1, the rhetoric about novel
technologies and new skills is still powerful enough to create fears of
undereducation.

A more dangerous form of undereducation involves the large proportion of students, most of them low-income, minority, or recent immigrant students, who leave high school unprepared to work in the
high-performance economy—a manifestation of *inequality* in skill levels rather than low overall or average skill levels. Like the Education
Gospel itself, these worries have a long history, from the early twentieth century debates about "laggards" in high school who eventually
dropped out, to the mid-twentieth-century fears about "social dyna-
mite" among dropouts, to current "youth development" and other
dropout-prevention programs. Even after a century of efforts to reduce
dropouts, about 25 percent of every cohort fails to graduate from high
school. These individuals have very little chance at well-paid jobs, as
Tables 6.1. and 6.3 clarify, and their earnings in real terms have been
declining over the past two decades. Their prospects through second-
chance programs—GED preparation programs, short-term job training, adult education—are not particularly good, as we documented in
Chapter 4. Many of those who do graduate and go on to community
and four-year colleges find themselves in remedial programs and often
drop out before they complete any credential. The dilemma for those
at the low end of the educational hierarchy is especially acute: they are
simultaneously undereducated for jobs of decent status and earnings,
including the jobs of the knowledge economy, but they are overeducated for the unskilled jobs they hold, as we will see in Table 7.1.

At the same time, there has been a persistent concern with individuals completing more formal schooling than their jobs require—usually

termed overeducation, but more precisely called *overschooling*. (Note that the concept of overeducation makes little sense in a nonvocational system designed to prepare individuals for political participation and intellectual life: the idea of having too much education is absurd.) In the 1970s, for example, Freeman (1976) wrote about *The Over-Educated American* based on evidence that economic returns were declining, and Bird (1975) exposed *The Case against College* by describing the large number of worthy jobs that required no postsecondary education. Another way to document overschooling has been to compare the schooling *requirements* of occupations with the average *attainments* of people holding those jobs. This exercise reveals an increase in overschooling during the 1960s and 1970s. For example, in 1960 the two highest levels of schooling were required by 15.3 percent of jobs, while about 20 percent of those employed held such levels of education. By 1976, 19.7 percent of jobs required the highest levels while almost 33 percent of the population had corresponding credentials—implying that perhaps 40 percent of those with the highest credentials were overeducated for the work they did.[13] More recent results confirm that about 35 to 40 percent of those in the labor force in the United States may have too much schooling for their jobs, and that overschooling here is substantially higher than in Germany with its highly regulated education and labor markets.[14]

The figures in Table 7.1 measure overschooling by asking individuals about the requirements of their work. In 1991 only 65 percent of college graduates indicated that their job required a four-year college education, suggesting that about 35 percent were overeducated. Nearly 66 percent of those with some college and 85 percent of those with a high school diploma indicated that the level of schooling they had attained was unnecessary, suggesting that overeducation is greatest at the lowest levels of schooling, where individuals find only unskilled work. Where formal schooling becomes the dominant route into occupations, individuals competing with one another tend to accumulate more formal schooling than their jobs require as a way of beating out the competition or of attaining professional status. In addition, where the information about the qualifications of individuals seeking employment is imperfect, as it is with "informal" credentials, then individuals obtain more schooling to signal their greater ability—a *socially* irrational escalation of schooling that is still *individually* rational.[15] Politically,

Table 7.1. Education and training required for employment, 1991

	% of labor force	No training	Formal schooling only	Other training	Formal schooling required				Training required				
					High school vocational training	Post-high school vocational training	Community college/technical institute	Four years of college	Formal company training	Informal on-the-job training	Armed Forces training	Correspondence course	Training from friends, others
All workers, 16 and older	100.0	43.3%	32.1%	24.6%	3.9%	2.7%	7.7%	18.8%	12.1%	27.2%	2.1%	1.1%	7.4%
High school dropouts	13.5	72.2	4.1	23.7	1.6	1.1	1.1	0.2	4.6	18.1	0.4	0.4	5.9
High school graduates	39.5	53.8	15.0	31.2	6.0	3.2	5.3	1.1	11.6	26.4	2.1	1.0	7.2
Some college	22.1	36.9	35.7	27.4	4.5	4.1	19.5	10.8	15.9	32.1	3.1	1.5	8.0
College graduate	24.7	16.2	71.7	12.1	1.2	1.5	4.6	64.7	13.7	29.0	2.1	1.2	7.9

Proportions may not sum to 100% because of multiple sources of training.
Source: A. Eck, Job-related education and training: Their impact on earnings. *Monthly Labor Review* 116, no. 10 (1993): 21–38, table 6.

the pressure from virtually all members of the Education Coalition has been to escalate years of schooling, most recently in the move toward college for all. But when individuals are overeducated, the economic benefits of schooling are lower, amounting to about half to three-quarters of the returns for required schooling (Groot and Van den Brink, 2000). Berg (1970) labeled overschooling "the great training robbery," because it requires individuals to invest more in schooling than is strictly necessary. Overschooling has powerful effects on equity as well, since low-income and minority Americans who have striven to increase their schooling still find that they lack the education required for middle-level positions.

A different mechanism also leads to overschooling, one rooted in the workplace rather than in the expansion of schooling—the de-skilling of work. One way for employers to minimize costs is to substitute cheaper unskilled workers for more skilled workers (Braverman, 1974). De-skilling often takes place as occupations are divided into components— for example, as medical practice became divided into a hierarchy of doctors, physicians' assistants, nurses, licensed vocational nurses, and practical nurses, or as the field of computer operations was divided into systems design, routine programming, and the use of low-level applications (like word processing) that require no programming skill. The legal profession has added paralegal assistants, while accountants are now using para-accountants for the most routine aspects of their jobs. De-skilling can undermine experience-based skills—"gut" knowledge—as well as school-based skills. But when it creates low-skill work with lower educational requirements, then it contributes to the social problem of overschooling because those individuals whose jobs are de-skilled will have more schooling than they need.

The reliance on formal schooling to prepare for employment, together with trends in de-skilling work, thus leads simultaneously to overschooling and undereducation. These different and apparently contradictory mismatches then fuel complaints about the occupational relevance of formal education. Unfortunately, there is no simple way to resolve these mismatches. The Education Gospel's fear of undereducation comes in part from the unresponsiveness of educational institutions to changes in the economy, and in part from individuals' ignorance of the skills they need. While these factors might be corrected with a greater responsiveness of educational institutions to labor markets and better transmission of information to students, the problems are deeply rooted in the nature of academic institutions. The other sources of undereducation—low income, poverty, immigration, racial discrimination, the neglect of urban communities, the dismal state of housing and health policies—are not readily fixed, since they require broader economic and social policies (the subject of Chapters 8 and 9). The only politically attractive and cheap remedy, it seems, is the rhetorical effort of the Education Gospel to make educational institutions more flexible and urge higher levels of schooling, even in the face of slow growth in the demand for educated workers (Table I.1 and Hecker, 2001). And it is difficult to turn off the pressures leading to overschooling: The search for individual advancement through schooling is one of the fundamental processes unleashed by vocationalism, and it cannot readily be constrained in a liberal society. The process of de-skilling, or of simultaneous de-skilling and re-skilling that creates greater inequality in skill levels, is difficult to control in a laissez-faire economy where employers fight furiously against any government intervention. The result is the odd American combination of overschooling and undereducation, in which individual decisions to stay in school or to drop out lead to socially irrational outcomes.

Taking New Paths

Since the American version of vocationalism has created a division between school skills and work skills, we might conclude that the vocationalizing impulse was the wrong one, and that we should return to a world of apprenticeship preparation, firm-based training (like McDonald's Hamburger U), and narrowly firm-specific credentials, such as Microsoft's MOUS certificate. But whatever its attractions, the fantasy of de-vocationalizing schools and replacing them with work-based preparation is badly flawed. Returning to work-based learning would ignore the extraordinary benefits of a vocationalized educational system: the extension of educational opportunities for many Americans; the expansiveness of an educational system with some commitment to democratic goals; the introduction of broader conceptions of academic and occupational competence in place of narrow technical skills; and an abatement of the tension between production and education that plagues work-based preparation. In addition, most employers in the

United States abandoned work-based learning (except for a few well-placed employees) at the end of the nineteenth century, and it would take an extensive cultural and economic shift to get them to support it now. And the consensus that schools ought to prepare individuals for the workplace is so powerfully supported by the Education Coalition that any effort to de-vocationalize schools would be politically inconceivable.

We therefore need to have a vision other than de-vocationalizing schools. Our goal instead should be to have schools and colleges fulfill their broad intellectual, political, and moral purposes while simultaneously carrying out vocational goals more effectively. One way to accomplish this would be to strengthen the more promising mechanisms linking schooling and work. The most effective, it seems to us, are professional collaboratives in which groups of educators, professional associations, and employers, with the support of government, devise licensing standards and curricula for broad forms of professional and occupational preparation. In addition to aligning the expectations of students, the offerings of educational providers, and the desires of employers, they also introduce greater transparency into all forms of occupational preparation. The fact that debates over academic and vocational standards are public, with participation by employers as well as professional associations representing practitioners and students, has the potential for avoiding *both* the narrow preparation typical of employer-based training *and* the overly distant "academic" preparation that educators often devise.

Another promising mechanism for linking schooling and employment is cooperative education. This linkage occurs in at least two ways: when employers and educators collaborate to devise complementary curricula, one work-based and one school-based; and when programs integrate general and specific competencies, normally the separate responsibilities of schools and employers. To be sure, the recommendation to improve work-based learning comes up against a century of failed efforts to do so, most recently in the 1970s and again in the 1990s with the School-to-Work Opportunities Act. It requires overcoming the withdrawal of employers from training responsibilities that began around 1900. It also depends on devising work placements with learning in mind, and providing opportunities to integrate school skills and work skills, and both general and specific competencies.[16] Distinctive change won't happen overnight or on the cheap: the failure of the STWOA is partly attributable to the ludicrously short timetable (five years) and the piddling sums of money involved. But we can learn from these failed efforts, particularly about the need for more sustained efforts to change both schools and workplaces, for substantial resources to link the two, and for greater responsibility among employers. Without such changes, the American form of vocationalism will continue to be hounded by the critique that formal schooling is inadequate to preparing a labor force.

A third important linkage mechanism would be a serious system of preparing students for decisions about their occupational future. The current efforts at guidance and counseling are relatively ineffective because they are underfunded, driven by academic agendas, and burdened with ineffective methods. But there are many promising practices that embed career-oriented information and guidance into the curriculum, rather than leaving it on the margins. Efforts to integrate academic and broadly occupational education in "education through occupations" programs often include five- to ten-week "exploratories" in which students learn about the technology and the nature of work in several broad occupational areas. The Puente program in some California high schools and community colleges creates small learning communities incorporating classes in math, English, and Latino literature, and counselors participate alongside instructors to provide information to students and parents about future options. Similarly, the School Development Program developed by James Comer (1996) creates Student Support Teams—composed of an administrator, a school psychologist, a school social worker, a counselor, the school nurse, and other support staff—that both diagnose the situations of individual students and develop preventive strategies focusing on in-class support rather than "pull-out" counseling. Many community colleges have created learning communities—groups of courses that students take simultaneously—that include counselors who provide career and academic counseling in the context of broad occupational or academic areas. Valencia Community College in Florida has devised a comprehensive program, called LifeMap ("Life's a trip. You'll need directions."), that integrates classes and many other services to help students move from the stage of "Postsecondary Transition," when they first approach the college, through three stages of increasing independence and finally to "Lifelong Learning," when students are successfully employed and recognize "the need for continued learning, the retooling of skills/knowledge and the need to create new skills." All these efforts integrate counselors more fully into the instructional life of the school, and embed planning for the future in the curriculum.[17]

Two other changes would help eliminate mismatches between school skills and work skills, though bringing them about would be daunting within the U.S. political system. The first would be to stop the continuing incidence of undereducation in the United States—particularly the undereducation of low-income and minority students, which makes a mockery of the Education Gospel and its stress on expanding educational opportunities. Of course, correcting the economic and social inequalities causing undereducation is politically difficult in a country with a weak welfare state, and with fiscal, monetary, and tax policies that favor the wealthy over the poor. Nevertheless, as we will argue in Chapters 8 and 9, fulfilling the claims of the Education Gospel will require reconstituting the nonschool policies that affect undereducation.

The second reform, perhaps the hardest of all to achieve, would require changes in the nature of work. Many school skills are simply not used in the routinized, unreflective employment that dominates labor markets. While public rhetoric stresses the undereducation of workers, there is powerful evidence that work often underutilizes the competencies of workers. (Indeed, one could argue that the oft-discussed "dumbing down" of American education has been a partial response to the dumbing down or de-skilling of work.) One solution to the disjunction between school skills and work skills, then, would be to change the nature of work—rather than having workers "adjust to a more complex economic order," as the Cardinal Principles of 1917 asserted and as practices since then have institutionalized. There are many ways of reorganizing work so that it is more educative and more fully utilizes the competencies of individual workers, as we examine in Chapter 9—even though it will be politically Herculean to do so in a country that views government intervention as a form of socialism. But difficult as these changes may be, the mismatches of undereducation and overschooling will persist unless we address them as a nation.

At the same time, we must be prepared to live with a certain inconsistency between schooling and employment. Most of us want our educational institutions to incorporate political, moral, and intellectual learning, even if these purposes have been weakened by vocationalism. Specialized vocationalized institutions—including private "occupational colleges," the technical institutes that forgo any general education, the short-term *training* that eliminates any broader forms of *education*, the narrow form of vocationalism that we ridicule as HyperVoc —are less conflicted about their goals than comprehensive institutions, but they also give up on our highest hopes for education. Work certainly could be improved in many ways, if we as a society were serious about improving it, but it would still focus on productivity, efficiency, and output—and not always on its educative power. And so while distinct improvements are possible, we must be willing to suffer some disjunction between what schools do and what employment requires, since most of us want the two to be different.

8

∽ The Evolution of Inequality

$\mathcal{T}$HE TRIUMPH of vocationalism provided the basis for a mass system of secondary and then postsecondary education, creating an enterprise central to every economic and social goal in American life. Its implications have extended well beyond preparation for work life. Vocationalism has changed our conceptions of what knowledge is most valued, of how we might achieve growth and stability, of what we as a society might do about troublesome adolescents, of how individuals find a place and an identity for themselves in a mass society—issues both intensely personal and unavoidably social.

Vocationalism has also changed the mechanisms generating inequality, and American conceptions of equity. Vocationalism did not, of course, create inequality, and it certainly did not create the extremely high levels of economic inequality that distinguish the United States from other developed countries.[1] The nineteenth century was a period of relatively high and increasing inequality, especially as the population moved into cities and as occupations became more differentiated (Williamson and Lindert, 1980). Then as now, parents varied substantially in their ability and desire to keep their children in school, and the familiar differences associated with class (or income), between native-born and immigrant families, and between white and black families were all too obvious. But vocationalism changed many of the mechanisms underlying inequality, particularly by shifting Americans from a world in which parents directly fostered the success of their children—through apprenticeships or the inheritance of a farm or a family business—to more indirect sponsorship of success through formal schooling. As schools and colleges developed clearer connections to occupations, struggles over access to formal schooling became more critical because the consequences for earnings, class standing, and upward mobility became so enormous. Vocationalism has made equity in education worth fighting over, in battles raging around access, desegregation, affirmative action, school financing, other resource disparities, the costs of college, curriculum tracking, and now academic standards.

Vocationalism has had contradictory effects on the equity of schooling. While the expansion of schooling led to greater equity, as different students—the "children of the plain people," "nontraditional students"—gained greater access, the forms of schooling that students entered became more highly differentiated, to match varying occupations. Expansion in access and vocational differentiation went together, pushed along by the choices that students (and their parents) made about further education. And so vocationalism fostered greater equity through enhanced access and led simultaneously to greater inequity through the endless differentiation of schooling. The balance of these two outcomes has shifted from decade to decade and has involved intense struggles precisely because the stakes are so high.

Along the way, vocationalism changed our principal conception of equity, equality of educational opportunity. The common-school conception of equity was relatively simple: all students should have access to a common curriculum and should complete the undifferentiated grammar school (up to grade eight). Schooling after that was voluntary, comparatively rare, and inconsequential except for a small elite. As the high school became more explicitly vocational around 1900, older conceptions of equity gave way to a differentiated idea of equality of educational opportunity, one that emphasized curricular variation and choice instead of uniformity.

In most countries, especially those that the United States has considered its peers, equity has been the responsibility not simply of education but also of the welfare state, a term encompassing the various actions a government takes to ensure the well-being of all its citizens. The U.S. version of the welfare state developed in bursts, in particular after 1900, in the 1930s, and again in the 1960s. But as many observers have noted, the American welfare state is particularly weak, constrained from intervening in markets, and limited in its power to move people out of poverty (save for its success in supporting the elderly). Moreover, the relentless attack on social policies of the past thirty years, as well as on the broader post–World War II social compact that includes union benefits as well as the welfare state, has effectively reversed its meaning. "Welfare" now connotes policies that benefit irresponsible and shiftless individuals, rather than policies committed to a common prosperity—a tragic shift away from any notion of public responsibility (Esping-Anderson, 1990; Katz, 2001; Piven and Cloward, 1997).

Americans now have a nearly impotent welfare state that asks educational institutions to redress social problems that they cannot possibly solve on their own. This creates an impossible dilemma for schooling, particularly in a country with such high levels of inequality. Our country needs a different concept of public responsibility—one that we call the Foundational State—that would provide the preconditions or foundations for a richer, more equitable version of the Education Gospel. The Foundational State would encompass a range of policies and goals: overcoming barriers to opportunity within schools; strengthening quasi-markets in education (especially higher education); investing in areas like health, housing, and urban development that are complementary to education; and intervening more directly in labor markets. These comprise a substantial and open-ended agenda for reform, but without such changes we will have to remain content with a pallid and inequitable version of the Education Gospel.

Changing Mechanisms of Inequality

Vocationalism has substantially altered the mechanisms of advancement. In the eighteenth and nineteenth centuries, parents were more directly responsible for the success of their children, either by continuing their sons in a family business or trade, or by finding appropriate apprenticeships or marriages. Middle- and upper-class children stayed in school longer than working-class children, but the occupational relevance of schooling—both in the sense of *occupational curricula*, and in the sense of finding *related employment*—was distinctly limited. Today, after the transformations of vocationalism, parents sponsor their chil-

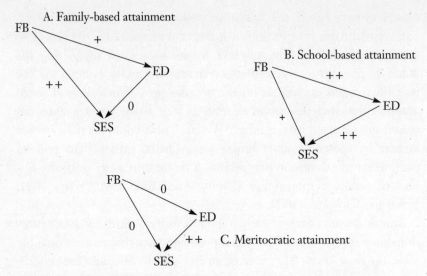

Figure 8.1. Differing effects of family background (FB) and education (ED) on socioeconomic status (SES).

dren's success largely by gaining them access to the levels and types of schooling that lead to well-paid occupations, especially the professions.

We can represent these changes with simple diagrams of the type sociologists have used to model the transmission of socioeconomic status. In Figure 8.1, *A* is a schematic representation of pre-vocational patterns, when family background (FB) influenced the socioeconomic status (SES)—the occupation and earnings—of children directly, while schooling (ED) was largely irrelevant to status, even though wealthier or higher-status families might obtain more education for their offspring. (The pluses and zeros reflect the strength and direction of causal mechanisms.) *B* represents school-based mechanisms of attainment, where the direct effects of family on children's socioeconomic status are less important but the effects of schooling become more powerful. *C* represents a meritocratic world in which the purest forms of equality of educational opportunity have been achieved: individual effort and ability in schooling explain variations in education and socioeconomic status, and family-background effects are eliminated because the same opportunities are provided to all children.

The shift to status attainment through schooling has had potentially ambiguous effects on equity. On the one hand, the successive expansion of high schools, universities, and community colleges has promised new opportunities to the "children of the plain people," to working-class and immigrant students—as in Figure 8.1C. On the other hand, in practice we live in a world much closer to Figure 8.1B than 8.1C. Every analysis of schooling practice has found powerful effects of family background on educational outcomes, much more powerful than the influence of schooling resources.[2] Family background operates in many different ways: through the ability of high-status parents (especially professionals) to teach their children the cognitive abilities and noncognitive behaviors necessary in schools; through the role models and values parents (and their communities) provide children; through the income differences that allow some parents to provide more books and computers, travel and recreation, private tutoring and college tuition; through the greater ability of some parents to negotiate the formal education system on behalf of their children, partly because of the cultural compatibility between middle-class families and educational institutions.

These processes may seem biased and unfair, at least to those who believe in meritocracy and the American dream, but it's hard to imagine a vocationalized schooling system in which powerful effects of family background do not exist. When the high-status tracks of schools and universities prepare students for high-status occupations—particularly professional and managerial positions—then they inevitably favor (or "privilege") those cognitive abilities, values, and behaviors associated with such occupations. Inevitably, these are learned earliest by the children of professionals and managers, and reinforced most powerfully by their parents. If educational practices developed abilities and norms that favored children from working-class backgrounds, this could occur only in programs or tracks preparing for working-class jobs. Inevitably these would become second-class alternatives like the dumping ground of traditional voc ed or the occupational programs in community colleges criticized for cooling out nontraditional students. So the high levels of economic inequality among families in the United States in turn generate large inequalities in schooling. Inequality begets inequality in many ways, now through the mechanisms of vocationalized schooling rather than the direct transmission of wealth.

Every examination of adult status has found powerful effects of schooling on adult status, another obvious consequence of vocationalism. So both of the powerful causal mechanisms in Figure 8.1B, the connections from family background to schooling and from schooling to socioeconomic status, have been strengthened—and to some extent created—by vocationalism. The central role of schooling in attaining adult status has meant that no one—no parent, no student, no advocate for the poor or displaced, no policy maker—can be indifferent to the inequality of schooling, since it influences so powerfully the distribution of earnings, status, and other social goods.

Expansion and Access

The growth of vocationalism after 1890 prepared the way for steady expansion in enrollments. Most of this expansion extended access to groups who had previously not had much chance at schooling. The expansion of high school after 1890 meant that more working-class students, immigrants, and African Americans gained access to secondary education, and over the twentieth century Americans moved toward high school for all. Similarly, the expansion of higher education in the 1920s came partly through the growth of city colleges, which made night classes available for working immigrants, and of all-purpose colleges, which had lower tuitions and more flexible attendance patterns than the elite residential colleges. After World War II, the GI Bill funded higher education for former soldiers, middle-class and working-class alike, largely in public institutions. Starting in the early 1970s, student grants and loans expanded federal funding for low- and moderate-income students. The expansion of community colleges and second-tier universities that started in the 1960s promoted access for individuals who would not earlier have gone on to college, the "nontraditional" students or "forgotten Americans" who were so different—in academic preparation and family support—from earlier generations of college students. So the greater access possible with vocationalism has created one dimension of greater equity in schooling.

But *greater* access has not meant *equitable* access. The promise to make the high school a universal institution has fallen short, because 25 percent of students fail to graduate, and the dropouts tend to be lower-income, black, and Latino students who are then more likely to become poor. Despite the expansion of subsidies for postsecondary education in many forms, family income remains a substantial barrier to college-going, even when other factors (like grades and test scores) are con-

nority and low-income students. But these ideas have collided with earlier conceptions of an elite education and the supposedly meritocratic approach to college admission that developed in the 1920s. Without the kind of high-minded civic rationale for equity that the common school ideal developed for K–12 education, postsecondary education has had no counter to the process of occupational differentiation.

With our differentiated conception of equal opportunity, one major impulse in American education has been to create yet more forms of differentiation whenever evidence of unequal outcomes emerges.[3] For example, vocational differentiation in the high school around 1900 was followed by ability grouping, special classes for the "feeble minded" and then special education, the fragmentation of special education, special classes for English-language learners, and continuation schools for those leaving for employment. Similarly, the creation of multipurpose colleges, of public city colleges aimed at working immigrants, of community colleges and the less-selective comprehensive universities, and of endlessly differentiated professional majors represent other forms of differentiation, each leading to a separate segment of the labor market. *If* differentiated forms of education were in some sense equal, then differentiation might be equitable. But that would require maintaining alternative forms of schooling that are "separate but equal," for example by providing as many resources to lower tracks as to upper tracks, or by creating small schools within high schools that all have similar graduation rates and postsecondary outcomes, or by allocating equivalent funding to community colleges and research universities and assuring that their occupational consequences are roughly equivalent. But with the exception of special education, differentiation has always led to unequal resources, both in secondary education and in the vast postsecondary "structure of inequality," and vocationally differentiated programs have led inescapably to wildly differing occupations. The combination of expanded access and differentiation has invariably led to more inequality.

Student Choice

Another crucial transformation under vocationalism is the expansion of choice—largely student choice, though influenced by parents and sometimes teachers and counselors. Choice is a quintessential element

sidered. Students whose parents did not attend college—the first-generation students celebrated by community colleges—are less likely to attend, and family background affects college aspirations and expectations in many other ways as well. The inclusiveness of the common school movement and the ambition of college for all may remain admirable, but their implementation is still incomplete.

Differentiation in Practice

Another consequence of vocationalism is that the "new students" have consistently gained access to educational institutions that have been differentiated along occupational lines. In high schools, manual training programs in the 1880s accommodated African Americans. Slightly later, educators recognized the value of vocational education in coping with the increasing numbers of working-class and immigrant students, and of sorting students by their "evident and probable destinies." Clerical programs and home economics were created after 1900 especially to give young women an education appropriate to their future vocations, just as industrial education prepared working-class boys for factory work. The division of the high school into an academic track for the college bound, "terminal" vocational education for those going into employment, and a general track leading nowhere—epitomized by the Life Adjustment movement of the 1940s and 1950s—meant that working-class and immigrant students gained greater access to an institution with internal tracks leading to very different types of opportunities. Ability grouping joined occupational differentiation after 1920, and even after de-tracking became popular in the 1990s, informal tracks led students in very different directions (Lucas, 1999).

Similarly, nontraditional students in postsecondary education have gained access to a highly differentiated system. For the most part they have enrolled in community colleges and second-tier universities with lower levels of resources and lower rates of completion, aiming at the middle level of the labor market rather than the upper level of professional and managerial occupations. In the great "structure of inequality" we described in Chapter 2, college for all has promised greater *access* to college, but not to the same kind of college, the same levels of resources, or the same kinds of occupational outcomes.

The differentiation of every educational institution along roughly occupational lines has been both *horizontal* in differences among tracks and majors—the college track distinct from ag ed or business ed, engineering majors distinct from education majors—and *vertical* in differences among institutions preparing students for different levels of the occupational system—the high school preparing modestly skilled workers, community colleges preparing middle-level employees, universities preparing professionals and managers. Indeed, it's hard to imagine a vocationalized system of schooling that is not differentiated in this way: so long as doctors and lawyers require different amounts of schooling and different forms of preparation than do accountants and teachers, clerks and auto mechanics, then the schooling system preparing individuals for these positions must be internally differentiated along the lines of *occupational curricula*. What is not inevitable is differentiation in the resources available at different levels of occupational preparation, nor the different rates of *related employment* and *required schooling*. Community colleges, where the needs of students are greater, receive less resources than the second-tier universities, whose resources are slim compared with the elite colleges and universities. And then the familiar differences of income and class, of race and ethnicity, of foreign birth and language status, and of gender show up once again, now through the mechanisms of vocationalism.

Differentiation in Theory

In pre-vocational schooling, equity was relatively straightforward. The common school ideal provided access to a similar schooling for all students, at least through grade eight, so that they could learn the academic competencies and moral responsibilities necessary for citizenship. As high schools became more widespread, they were initially dominated by a unitary curriculum that emphasized mental discipline and moral values. As late as 1894, when the movement for high school vocational education was gathering steam, the Committee of Ten, in attempting to create a coherent curriculum, argued that "every subject which is taught at all in a secondary school should be taught in the same way and to the same extent to every pupil so long as he pursues it, no matter what the probable destination of the pupil may be" (Lazerson and Grubb, 1974).

As vocationalism developed, it made older ideals of equity seem

dated. It no longer made sense to pretend that the schools were preparing all boys to become president, as the school board chair in Muncie, Indiana, acknowledged during the 1920s. Once it became clear that schools were preparing students to become professionals and businessmen, metalworkers and electricians, or (for girls) schoolteachers and secretaries, then a presidential education was largely irrelevant, inefficient, and unproductive. A uniform curriculum now seemed *in*egalitarian, and equity changed from providing the *same* education to providing *different* educations appropriate to students' different futures (Elson and Bachman, 1910, 361): "Instead of affording equality of educational opportunity to all, the elementary school by offering but one course of instruction, and this of a literary character, serves the interests of but one type of children and neglects in a measure the taste, capacity, and educational destination of all others, and of those, too, whose needs are imperative and to whom the future holds no further advantage. In a word, what was intended to be a school for the masses and afford equality of educational opportunity to all . . . serves well the interests of but the few." The new conception provided different opportunities for students based on their "evident and probable destinies": the academic track for middle-class students "whose needs are imperative," bound for college and professional and managerial work; industrial education for working-class boys heading for factories, "to whom the future holds no further advantage"; commercial education for working-class girls likely to take clerical positions; and home economics for future homemakers (Lynd and Lynd, 1929).

Postsecondary education, increasingly the most relevant level of schooling as educational expansion has taken place, was never burdened by a conception of equity like the common school ideal. In its origin as the preparer of leaders, college in this country was fundamentally elitist. The conditions of enrollment—supported almost entirely by tuition paid by parents, with colleges situated in rural locations so that students had to live away from home—ensured that few from the working class could attend. Only in the past thirty years has there been any effort to overcome the income barriers to attendance and to apply conceptions of equitable access from common school ideals to higher education. This in turn has generated demands for subsidized universities, for grants and loans to moderate the effects of income differences, for bridge programs and affirmative action to prepare and enroll

sidered. Students whose parents did not attend college—the first-generation students celebrated by community colleges—are less likely to attend, and family background affects college aspirations and expectations in many other ways as well. The inclusiveness of the common school movement and the ambition of college for all may remain admirable, but their implementation is still incomplete.

Differentiation in Practice

Another consequence of vocationalism is that the "new students" have consistently gained access to educational institutions that have been differentiated along occupational lines. In high schools, manual training programs in the 1880s accommodated African Americans. Slightly later, educators recognized the value of vocational education in coping with the increasing numbers of working-class and immigrant students, and of sorting students by their "evident and probable destinies." Clerical programs and home economics were created after 1900 especially to give young women an education appropriate to their future vocations, just as industrial education prepared working-class boys for factory work. The division of the high school into an academic track for the college bound, "terminal" vocational education for those going into employment, and a general track leading nowhere—epitomized by the Life Adjustment movement of the 1940s and 1950s—meant that working-class and immigrant students gained greater access to an institution with internal tracks leading to very different types of opportunities. Ability grouping joined occupational differentiation after 1920, and even after de-tracking became popular in the 1990s, informal tracks led students in very different directions (Lucas, 1999).

Similarly, nontraditional students in postsecondary education have gained access to a highly differentiated system. For the most part they have enrolled in community colleges and second-tier universities with lower levels of resources and lower rates of completion, aiming at the middle level of the labor market rather than the upper level of professional and managerial occupations. In the great "structure of inequality" we described in Chapter 2, college for all has promised greater *access* to college, but not to the same kind of college, the same levels of resources, or the same kinds of occupational outcomes.

The differentiation of every educational institution along roughly occupational lines has been both *horizontal* in differences among tracks and majors—the college track distinct from ag ed or business ed, engineering majors distinct from education majors—and *vertical* in differences among institutions preparing students for different levels of the occupational system—the high school preparing modestly skilled workers, community colleges preparing middle-level employees, universities preparing professionals and managers. Indeed, it's hard to imagine a vocationalized system of schooling that is not differentiated in this way: so long as doctors and lawyers require different amounts of schooling and different forms of preparation than do accountants and teachers, clerks and auto mechanics, then the schooling system preparing individuals for these positions must be internally differentiated along the lines of *occupational curricula*. What is not inevitable is differentiation in the resources available at different levels of occupational preparation, nor the different rates of *related employment* and *required schooling*. Community colleges, where the needs of students are greater, receive less resources than the second-tier universities, whose resources are slim compared with the elite colleges and universities. And then the familiar differences of income and class, of race and ethnicity, of foreign birth and language status, and of gender show up once again, now through the mechanisms of vocationalism.

Differentiation in Theory

In pre-vocational schooling, equity was relatively straightforward. The common school ideal provided access to a similar schooling for all students, at least through grade eight, so that they could learn the academic competencies and moral responsibilities necessary for citizenship. As high schools became more widespread, they were initially dominated by a unitary curriculum that emphasized mental discipline and moral values. As late as 1894, when the movement for high school vocational education was gathering steam, the Committee of Ten, in attempting to create a coherent curriculum, argued that "every subject which is taught at all in a secondary school should be taught in the same way and to the same extent to every pupil so long as he pursues it, no matter what the probable destination of the pupil may be" (Lazerson and Grubb, 1974).

As vocationalism developed, it made older ideals of equity seem dated. It no longer made sense to pretend that the schools were preparing all boys to become president, as the school board chair in Muncie, Indiana, acknowledged during the 1920s. Once it became clear that schools were preparing students to become professionals and businessmen, metalworkers and electricians, or (for girls) schoolteachers and secretaries, then a presidential education was largely irrelevant, inefficient, and unproductive. A uniform curriculum now seemed *in*egalitarian, and equity changed from providing the *same* education to providing *different* educations appropriate to students' different futures (Elson and Bachman, 1910, 361): "Instead of affording equality of educational opportunity to all, the elementary school by offering but one course of instruction, and this of a literary character, serves the interests of but one type of children and neglects in a measure the taste, capacity, and educational destination of all others, and of those, too, whose needs are imperative and to whom the future holds no further advantage. In a word, what was intended to be a school for the masses and afford equality of educational opportunity to all . . . serves well the interests of but the few." The new conception provided different opportunities for students based on their "evident and probable destinies": the academic track for middle-class students "whose needs are imperative," bound for college and professional and managerial work; industrial education for working-class boys heading for factories, "to whom the future holds no further advantage"; commercial education for working-class girls likely to take clerical positions; and home economics for future homemakers (Lynd and Lynd, 1929).

Postsecondary education, increasingly the most relevant level of schooling as educational expansion has taken place, was never burdened by a conception of equity like the common school ideal. In its origin as the preparer of leaders, college in this country was fundamentally elitist. The conditions of enrollment—supported almost entirely by tuition paid by parents, with colleges situated in rural locations so that students had to live away from home—ensured that few from the working class could attend. Only in the past thirty years has there been any effort to overcome the income barriers to attendance and to apply conceptions of equitable access from common school ideals to higher education. This in turn has generated demands for subsidized universities, for grants and loans to moderate the effects of income differences, for bridge programs and affirmative action to prepare and enroll mi-

nority and low-income students. But these ideas have collided with earlier conceptions of an elite education and the supposedly meritocratic
approach to college admission that developed in the 1920s. Without
the kind of high-minded civic rationale for equity that the common
school ideal developed for K–12 education, postsecondary education
has had no counter to the process of occupational differentiation.

With our differentiated conception of equal opportunity, one major
impulse in American education has been to create yet more forms of
differentiation whenever evidence of unequal outcomes emerges.[3] For
example, vocational differentiation in the high school around 1900 was
followed by ability grouping, special classes for the "feeble minded"
and then special education, the fragmentation of special education,
special classes for English-language learners, and continuation schools
for those leaving for employment. Similarly, the creation of multipurpose colleges, of public city colleges aimed at working immigrants, of
community colleges and the less-selective comprehensive universities,
and of endlessly differentiated professional majors represent other
forms of differentiation, each leading to a separate segment of the labor
market. *If* differentiated forms of education were in some sense equal,
then differentiation might be equitable. But that would require maintaining alternative forms of schooling that are "separate but equal," for
example by providing as many resources to lower tracks as to upper
tracks, or by creating small schools within high schools that all have
similar graduation rates and postsecondary outcomes, or by allocating
equivalent funding to community colleges and research universities
and assuring that their occupational consequences are roughly equivalent. But with the exception of special education, differentiation has always led to unequal resources, both in secondary education and in the
vast postsecondary "structure of inequality," and vocationally differentiated programs have led inescapably to wildly differing occupations.
The combination of expanded access and differentiation has invariably
led to more inequality.

Student Choice

Another crucial transformation under vocationalism is the expansion
of choice—largely student choice, though influenced by parents and
sometimes teachers and counselors. Choice is a quintessential element